THE ENGLISH ELIOT

THE ENGLISH ELIOT

Design, language and landscape in
Four Quartets

Steve Ellis

London and New York

First published 1991
by Routledge
11 New Fetter Lane, London EC4P 4EE

Simultaneously published in the USA and Canada
by Routledge
a division of Routledge, Chapman and Hall, Inc.
29 West 35th Street, New York, NY 10001

Set in 10/12pt Palatino by Witwell Ltd, Southport
Printed and bound in Great Britain by T J Press (Padstow) Ltd,
Padstow, Cornwall

British Library Cataloguing in Publication Data
Ellis, Steve
The English Eliot: design, language and landscape in
Four Quartets
I. Title
821.912

Library of Congress Cataloging in Publication Data
Ellis, Steve.
The English Eliot: design, language and landscape in
Four Quartets/Steve Ellis.
p.   cm.
Includes bibliographical references.
1. Eliot, T. S. (Thomas Stearns), 1888–1965. *Four Quartets.*
2. Landscape in literature.   3. England in literature.   I. Title.
PS3509.L43F6445   1991
821'.912—dc20   91–9517

ISBN 0-415-06688-3

CONTENTS

PLATES

ACKNOWLEDGEMENTS

The author and publishers would like to thank the following copyright holders for permission to reprint material:

POETRY

Collected Poems of 1954 by C. Day Lewis: 'The Magnetic Mountain', reprinted by permission of The Estate of C. Day Lewis, Random Century Group, Jonathan Cape & The Hogarth Press, and the Peters Fraser & Dunlop Group Ltd.

Faber & Faber Ltd. and Harcourt Brace Jovanovich (US):

Collected Poems 1909–1962 by T. S. Eliot: 'The Love Song of J. Alfred Prufrock', 'The Hollow Men', 'Mr Apollinax', 'The Journey of the Magi', 'Whispers of Immortality', 'Ash-Wednesday', 'Sweeney Erect', 'The Rock', 'A Note on War Poetry', 'The Waste Land'.
Four Quartets, by T. S. Eliot: 'Burnt Norton', 'East Coker', 'The Dry Salvages' and 'Little Gidding'.
Murder in the Cathedral, by T. S. Eliot.
The Family Reunion, by T. S. Eliot.

Faber & Faber Ltd. and Random House (US):
(Some of the following poems appear in the text under their original titles.)

Collected Longer Poems by W. H. Auden: 'Letter to Lord Byron'.
Nones by W. H. Auden: 'In Praise of Limestone'.
The Orators by W. H. Auden.
The Ascent of F6 by W. H. Auden and Christopher Isherwood.

ACKNOWLEDGEMENTS

Another Time by W. H. Auden: 'Spain 1937'.
The Dog Beneath the Skin by W. H. Auden and Christopher Isherwood.
Poems 1930 by W. H. Auden: 'Sir, no man's enemy', 'Paid on Both Sides'.
Collected Shorter Poems 1927-57 by W. H. Auden: '1929', 'Death's Echo', 'Easy Knowledge', 'As I Walked . . .', 'Five Songs no III', 'Sonnets from China', 'A Bride in the '30s', 'Twelve Songs: III'.
Look, Stranger! by W. H. Auden: 'I. Prologue', 'XIV. Brothers . . .', 'V. Look, Stranger . . .', the Epigraph.
Collected Poems, by Louis MacNeice: 'Eclogue from Iceland' and 'The Hebrides'.

PLATES

1 Courtauld Institute; **2a** Courtauld Institute; **2b** John Sinclair; **3** Birmingham University Library; **4** Courtauld Institute; **5** Faber & Faber Ltd. and Birmingham Library Services; **6** Aberdeen City Arts Department, Art Gallery & Museums; **7** Towner Art Gallery and Local History Museum, Eastbourne; **8** Birmingham University Library; **9** Architectural Press and Birmingham University Library; **10** B. T. Batsford Ltd.; **11** Birmingham Library Services; **12** Shell UK Ltd; **13** Aberdeen City Arts Department, Art Gallery & Museums; **14** Towner Art Gallery and Local History Museum, Eastbourne; **15** Albright-Knox Art Gallery, Buffalo, New York, Room of Contemporary Art Fund, 1948.

For support and advice of various kinds in the writing of this book I should particularly like to thank Anne Buckley, A. S. Byatt, David Lodge, Chris Lord, Joanna Porter, Jane Redfearn, Steve Regan, John Sinclair, Michael Spender, Mark Storey, and the staffs of the University of Birmingham Library, the Barber Institute Library, the City of Birmingham Reference Library and the British Library. I dedicate the book to my colleagues in the School of English, University of Birmingham; they have stretched me and tested me, and made me feel at home.

I would also like to thank Jane Armstrong, Rebecca Barden, Jill Rawnsley and Sarah Yorke from Routledge, and Jenny Overton, for their work on the manuscript.

ACKNOWLEDGEMENTS

Every effort has been made to obtain permission to reproduce copyright material. If any proper acknowledgement has not been made, or permission not received, we would invite the copyright holder to inform us of the oversight.

ABBREVIATIONS AND EDITIONS USED IN THE TEXT

.

Works by Eliot

CPP   *The Complete Poems and Plays* (Faber, 1969)
ICS   *The Idea of a Christian Society and Other Writings*, introd. David L. Edwards, 2nd edn (Faber, 1982)
NDC   *Notes Towards the Definition of Culture* (1948; rpt. Faber, 1962)
OPAP *On Poetry and Poets* (Faber, 1957)
SE   *Selected Essays*, 3rd edn (Faber, 1951)
TCTC *To Criticize the Critic and Other Writings* (1965; rpt. Faber, 1978)

Works by Auden

EA   *The English Auden: Poems, Essays and Dramatic Writings 1927–1939*, ed. Edward Mendelson (1977; rpt. Faber, 1986)

INTRODUCTION

'He had become more English than the English in dress and manner.' The words are those of a recent British Council touring exhibition on Eliot's life and work, held to mark the centenary of his birth, and found under the section headed 'More English than the English, 1925–1945'. In this book I am discussing a rather more problematic conception of Eliot's Englishness than is allowed for by the above commonly received idea of him; indeed the cliché 'more English than the English' totally obscures the qualifications attaching to nationalism and patriotism that are foregrounded in much of his later work, poetry and prose. The fact is that the years of Eliot's greatest concern with English institutions and contexts in his writing – which we can agree are 1925–45 – coincide with his keenest interest in a Latin tradition that, in writers like Virgil and Dante, represents a universality that all national concerns must be related to. This study is indeed rather more about Eliot's being less English than the English.

It is also, as may already be apparent, very much about Eliot's 'classicism', an affiliation constantly stressed in his own later criticism. 'The idea behind the modern movement in the arts is a return to the architectural or classical idea', R. H. Wilenski wrote in 1927, in opening his *The Modern Movement in Art*, and in what follows I attempt to relate this 'classical idea' in European and English art and architecture during the 1930s to Eliot's classicism as it developed over the same period.[1] The so-called 'International Style' in architecture and the abstract and constructivist movements in painting offered the possibility of a 'universal language' in design that might overcome national separatism, and offer suggestive parallels with Eliot's emphasis in *Four Quartets*, which are my major focus, on the work's

1

formal and structural properties. In chapter 3 of this book I continue exploring literature-art relationships by offering a commentary on the landscape of the *Quartets* that features the work of several contemporary landscape painters.

One ambition here is to put Eliot's work of the 1930s and early 1940s rather more firmly in its cultural context, given the tendency of critics to displace it, doubtless because the 'agèd eagle' is seen as sitting in reactionary and isolated splendour on one side of the fence while Auden and company pursue revolution and communism on the other. Standard accounts of the 1930s – like that by Bernard Bergonzi[2] – tend either to ignore Eliot or to write his concerns off as outmoded or peripheral;[3] Valentine Cunningham's admirable and encyclopaedic *British Writers of the 1930s* similarly gives little sustained attention to Eliot.[4] Where his influence is admitted in the 1930s scene it is held to derive solely from the 'radical' early poetry, as in the dubious suggestion in Hynes's excellent *The Auden Generation* that *The Waste Land* is the 'principal literary ancestor' of Auden's *The Orators*.[5] D. E. S. Maxwell in his *Poets of the Thirties* rightly stresses that writers like Spender, Day Lewis and Grigson openly proclaimed their preference for early Eliot, on which basis he too seems to proceed to discount the later Eliot as a true '30s poet'.[6] And yet Eliot's classicism, and the new note of stylistic austerity in the post-*Waste Land* poetry that signals it, certainly had some influence on the younger poets, as I argue below, and the 'respect for 18th-Century ideals' that Michael Roberts sees in many of his 1932 *New Signatures* poets owes much to Eliot's critical revaluations.[7] One major feature of this book is indeed the relation between Eliot and another writer respectful of eighteenth-century poetry, W. H. Auden, with the congruence and oppositions between them; in giving the book its title I am deliberately gesturing to Mendelson's collection *The English Auden*, in exploring the relationship between two fundamentally and consciously opposed approaches to Englishness.

I should stress here that Eliot's concept of 'classicism' is a rather unusual one, though one shared by several of his contemporaries, in both literature and the visual arts as we shall see: when the term is met with in these pages then it will generally have silent (where not overt) inverted commas round it. Eliot himself understood the term differently at different stages of his career, and to the question 'What is a classic?' he was returning constantly more refined and subtle answers. It is essentially with the work from the late 1920s onwards that I am concerned, the period during which he evolves a theory and practice of classic poetic diction and formal design that is absent from his early work. It is true that as early as 1916 he is aware of living at a 'classical' moment:

> The beginning of the twentieth century has witnessed a return to the ideals of classicism. These may roughly be characterized as *form* and *restraint* in art, *discipline* and *authority* in religion, *centralization* in government (either as socialism or monarchy). The classicist point of view has been defined as essentially a belief in Original Sin – the necessity for austere discipline.[8]

The full embracing of these various implications of classicism came, however, slowly to him; as far as 'restraint in art' goes, for example, his youthful delight in what he later called the 'extravagances' of Elizabethan, Jacobean and Caroline writers leads to an early poetry differing greatly from the 'Dantesque' economy of the post-*Waste Land* output, though as I shall argue such extravagances seem often to be ironically scrutinized even in the process of being practised.[9] The comment equating classicism with original sin above indicates that Eliot probably knew something of T. E. Hulme's writing from very early in his career,[10] but again it is not until a good deal later that Hulme's understanding of classicism, which is crucial for Eliot, becomes a fundamental part of his outlook.

Critics have it is true often spoken of the classicism of Eliot's early poetry; a chapter entitled 'The new classicism' in Maxwell's 1952 book on Eliot finds plentiful examples of 'Augustan wit' there combined with that impersonality that comes from subservience to the tradition, both features being reactions to the heady emotionalism of much nineteenth-century poetry.[11] Obviously valid points like these throw into relief the somewhat problematic later 'classicism', where the poetry forsakes both wit and, on the face of it, impersonality (*vide* the confessional nature of *Four Quartets*) yet coexists with the highest point of Eliot's commitment to the classical tradition in his prose essays. Classicism for Eliot indeed becomes something increasingly dour and ascetic, interlocked with 'original sin', and its great exemplars Virgil and Dante (not of course the English Augustans) are themselves seen as thoroughly ascetic. If Hulme is clearly at the back of this then so are developments in the field of the visual arts which Hulme himself had taken a keen interest in.

Eliot's later classicism is largely devoid of much in the way of humanism, and again it is Hulme's quarrel with humanism that is pursued in his work. Although critics like David J. De Laura can talk of Eliot's 'Christian humanism', De Laura's long, searching essay expounding Eliot's 'exaggerated thesis of the virtual identity of Christian and classical values within the synthesis of western culture' itself shows not a balance between those values in Eliot's work but a complete absorption of the classical tradition within an austere Christianity, with Virgil becoming a spokesman for a kind of proto-monasticism.[12] Eliot held that humanism was a necessary part of religion, but not because of any belief in the dignity or value of the individual which it might underline; rather he saw one aspect of the classical tradition as representing a severe, intellectual scepticism that would have its uses in preventing the Church sliding into liberalism and sentimentality.[13] When humanism offers itself autonomously, or as anything but a handmaid to religion, he is scathing about it.

It is perhaps because Eliot's classicism has such a strange look to eyes accustomed to traditional responses to the antique that many critics reject it completely, though usually with the intention of claiming Eliot, despite all his protestation, for the 'Romantic' camp. The argument is as old as Middleton Murry's essays in the *Adelphi* of 1926, where the highly personal 'disorder' of Eliot's work to date is seen as exemplifying that individualistic quest for truth that characterizes romanticism.[14] Murry is writing at a time that predates Eliot's thoroughgoing commitment to classicism, though there is no shortage of recent critics to continue his argument even with the full range of Eliot's work available. Thus Edward Lobb judiciously selects from Eliot's career in order to place him within the 'romantic critical tradition', focusing almost entirely on his 'great period as a critic (roughly 1918 to 1936)'.[15] This arbitrary but cautiously broad periodization dismisses the essays from the late 1930s and early 1940s completely; by hardly considering any work that postdates *The Use of Poetry and the Use of Criticism*

(1933), by taking no notice whatsoever of Eliot's writing on
Virgil and in particular of the key essay 'What is a classic?'
(1944), and by leaning selectively on Frank Kermode – *Romantic
Image* adduced constantly, *The Classic* never mentioned – Lobb
proceeds on the basis of an unhelpful and misleading Romantic-
classic antithesis in claiming Eliot for the former camp. A
constant element in romanticism, he tells us, is 'nostalgia . . .
Eliot looks back in various essays and lectures to the Greeks, to
Dante, and to the metaphysicals – but most often, and most
consistently, to Dante'. In this 'use of medieval art and thought
as a standard by which to judge the modern (cf. Ruskin, Hulme,
Yeats, Pound)', Eliot necessarily declares his hand against
classicism (pp. 136–7). By this account, however, any traditionalism would be *per se* 'Romantic' and any looking back to earlier
writers as models of style or diction merely 'nostalgic'; neo-
classicism would become by definition impossible. As for
Dante, I have tried to show elsewhere how Eliot's reading of
him is a rescue attempt from much that was formulated in the
nineteenth century.[16] Another misleading claim repeated by
Lobb is the idea of a pervasive Wordsworthian element in
Eliot's 'landscape' poems, including the *Quartets* (pp. 70–4); the
second half of this book attempts an answer to the number of
critics who have espoused this view.

By concentrating on the earlier work it seems in any case that
Lobb tacitly admits that Eliot's later classicism is less easily
stood on its head; the *Quartets* in particular seem to me to raise
enormous problems for those in search of the 'Romantic' Eliot.
More questioning of the classic Eliot is found in C. K. Stead's
well-known and still influential *The New Poetic*, where Eliot's
constant insistence on the mysterious sources of poetry deep
within the individual is documented, which Stead sees as
upholding an essentially Romantic idea of 'inspiration'.[17] Eliot's
'classicism' is held to pertain only to more superficial matters of
poetic technique. Certainly Eliot himself gives support to this
dichotomy, as in his *Dial* review of *Ulysses*, where classicism is

> a goal toward which all good literature strives, so far as it
> is good. . . . One can be 'classical', in a sense, by turning
> away from nine-tenths of the material which lies at hand
> and selecting only mummified stuff from a museum. . . .
> Or one can be classical in tendency by doing the best one

can with the material at hand. . . . And in this material I include the emotions and feelings of the writer himself, which, for that writer, are simply material which he must accept.[18]

This emphasis on being 'classical in tendency' is one that rises repeatedly in Eliot, where classicism represents among other things the attempt to impose form on an acutely sensed chaos; the inter-war years were certainly not a classic age in Eliot's eyes, one defined by him in 'What is a classic?' as a time 'when men have a critical sense of the past, a confidence in the present, and no conscious doubt of the future' (*OPAP*, p. 57). One might grant to Stead that all modern classicism, not simply Eliot's, is a kind of holding operation against deeper forces within the self, or in history; or in Eliot's own much-quoted statement, 'It must not be forgotten that a poet in a romantic age cannot be a "classical" poet except in tendency'.[19] This hardly means, however, that we can ignore or write off these tendencies, especially when, as in Eliot, they are so strenuously theorized, and when the attempt to ignore them, in Stead and others, is part of a wholesale dismissal of the poetic value of the *Quartets*.[20]

Eliot's comment about mummification from the *Dial* quoted above reveals his belief that a modern classicism is to be other than an approved copying of Greek or Latin models or a revival of the English eighteenth century. If in what follows I make the case that *Four Quartets* is an exercise in classicism within Eliot's own understanding of the term, it is important to realize that the poem can also be seen as a criticism of many other classicizing conventions. I too therefore make reservations about the 'orthodoxy' of Eliot's classicism, though not with the intention of thereby turning him into a crypto-Romantic; Eliot himself was sceptical about such an ossified polarization, and it is used as little as possible in the following pages.[21] In chapters 3 and 4, however, where landscape is under discussion, it is more difficult to avoid, especially since polemic over the English landscape in the 1930s and 1940s resorts readily to writers like Wordsworth and Ruskin, either approvingly or not. A good deal of work has recently been done on the extraordinary enthusiasm for the English countryside in this period, and the 'search for England' exhibited in the vast number of travel books, rural novels, paintings, railway posters and so forth, the best-known survey being that incorporated in Martin J. Wiener's study.[22] There is a tendency, however, for all such research to see this type of interest in 'England' as essentially pastoralist and celebratory in its flight from industrialization; the infra-rural debate, which is extremely active, is more or less ignored, and it is within the terms of this forgotten debate that I try to place Eliot's construction of England in this book, attempting some classification, however preliminary, of the vast mass of rural writing in the period leading up to the completion of *Four Quartets*.[23]

1

CLASSIC DESIGN

In a lecture on 'Modern art and its philosophy' delivered in 1914, T. E. Hulme adduced cubism as evidence in art of a 'change of sensibility at the present moment':

> Expressed generally, there seems to be a desire for austerity and bareness, a striving towards structure and away from the messiness and confusion of nature and natural things.[1]

Such 'austerity and bareness' was a key feature of what Hulme and Eliot after him understood as 'classic' art, but it was not until 'The hollow men' of 1925 that Eliot began to reject the 'Elizabethan' ornateness of his early work, as discussed in the following chapter, and conduct that 'gradual purging out of poetical ornament' that he describes in the Yeats lecture of 1940 (*OPAP*, p. 259). This development takes place primarily under the banner of Dante, whose poetry is held to exemplify 'the greatest economy of words' and 'the greatest austerity in the use of metaphor, simile, verbal beauty and elegance' ('Dante', *SE*, p. 252). Although one can sympathize with Eliot's insistence on these basic qualities in Dante, it still seems remarkable that the polyphony of the *Commedia*, with all its different voices and modes of speech, its command of a varied conversational idiom, should become honed down to represent the austerely homogeneous classic; we need only compare the stately 'Dantesque' exercise in 'Little Gidding' with the briskly colloquial quality of its supposed forebear in the *Inferno* to realize inadequacies in Eliot's reading of Dante.[2] This suppression of the plurality of Dante's voices is, however, exactly paralleled by the gradual elimination of voices in Eliot's own work, as we shall see.

8

After referring to the 'gradual purging out of poetical ornament' in Yeats's verse plays, Eliot continued:

> This, perhaps, is the most painful part of the labour. . . .
> The course of improvement is towards a greater and
> greater starkness. The beautiful line for its own sake is a
> luxury. . . . What is necessary is a beauty which shall not
> be in the line or isolable passage, but woven into the
> dramatic texture itself.
>
> (*OPAP*, pp. 259-60)

Although he is discussing drama here, Eliot is manifestly
striving for such a programme in the *Quartets* too, with their
deliberate discounting, as 'Little Gidding' has it, of the
'ostentatious' word or phrase in the interests of an overall
structural emphasis, 'The complete consort dancing together'
(*CPP*, p. 197). Several of Eliot's critics have complained of what
they see as the cold formality, or 'abstraction', of his later style;
thus Orwell, reviewing the *Quartets* in 1942, lamented the
absence of the 'memorable' lines and passages that characterized Eliot's early work, quoting sections from poems like
'Whispers of immortality' as examples of a past 'vitality and
power' that exposed by contrast Eliot's present failure.[3] There
is no sympathy with, indeed no understanding of, Eliot's desire
to communicate via the formal totality of the *Quartets* rather
than through the felicities of 'isolable passages' or lines, and no
recognition that some suppression of local decoration is necessary to do this; little notice is taken, we might say, of 'Burnt
Norton's stressing that the poem succeeds 'only by the form,
the pattern' (*CPP*, p. 175). Looking back on the Dantesque
episode in 'Little Gidding' in 'What Dante means to me' (1950),
Eliot speaks to a large degree of the *Quartets* as a whole in
describing his aspiration towards a 'very bare and austere style,
in which every word has to be "functional" . . . the language
has to be very direct; the line and the single word, must be
completely disciplined to the purpose of the whole' (*TCTC*, p.
129).

'Burnt Norton' indeed might be said to be the most discipli-
narian of the *Quartets*, lamenting the mobility and plurality of
language in ways I shall discuss in the following chapter, and
stressing the difficulties of the formal government of words
that will not 'stay still'. By 'Little Gidding' the sequence shows a

measure of self-congratulation and greater relaxation in having achieved a conformism of the part to the whole:

> And every phrase
> And sentence that is right (where every word is at home,
> Taking its place to support the others,
> The word neither diffident nor ostentatious,
> An easy commerce of the old and the new,
> The common word exact without vulgarity,
> The formal word precise but not pedantic,
> The complete consort dancing together)
> Every phrase and every sentence is an end and a beginning,
> Every poem an epitaph.

(*CPP*, p. 197)

This passage, in positing an integrated mean between various types of extreme, exemplifies what Eliot is calling for in a good number of essays and lectures contemporary with the *Quartets*, namely that poets should be working in what he terms the 'common' or 'classic' style, a style that 'makes us exclaim, not "this is a man of genius using the language", but "this realizes the genius of the language" ' ('What is a classic?', p. 63). During the late 1920s and 1930s he castigates those writers like Milton and Donne whose individualistic style refuses to conform to this hypothetical norm; indeed, the idea that there is something inherently nonconformist in the English tradition – a too ready surrendering to the intractability and copiousness of the English language itself – means that his classic models have to come from abroad: 'the language of each great English poet is his own language; the language of Dante is the perfection of a common language', in a sense 'more pedestrian than that of Dryden or Pope' ('Dante', p. 252).

Certainly Eliot's approach to this common language is extremely complex. For all his enthusiasm he is aware of the dangers of ossification, as we shall see (below, pp. 52–3); moreover he can be found both bemoaning its disappearance from present-day writing and acknowledging its emergence. Lecturing on Johnson in 1944 Eliot casts himself as a voice in the wilderness: 'I think that the absence of any common standard of poetic diction is a weakness both of modern verse and of our criticism of it' ('Johnson as critic and poet', *OPAP*, pp. 186–7). He concludes that 'amongst the varieties of chaos in which we find ourselves immersed to-day, one is a chaos of language, in which there are discoverable no standards of writing, and an increasing indifference to etymology and the history of the use of words' (p. 192). Although he is careful to qualify his praise for the eighteenth century's 'common standard of poetic diction' (as he is when discussing Pope in 'What is a classic?'), he retains that respect for the discipline and anti-individualism of English neo-classicism which he has expressed much earlier in his writing (and rather more immoderately); thus Dryden had been seen as the man who 'put the English language straight again' after Milton,[4] and to whom, 'as much as to any individual, we owe our civilisation'; who 'for the first time, and so far as we are concerned, for all time, established a *normal* English speech, a speech valid for both verse and prose'.[5]

And yet, for reasons which will become plain, Eliot's fundamental and durable classic models were foreign, as remarked above; Dante, and, in Eliot's major essay on classicism, the *Aeneid*, the achievement by which Roman literature signals its willingness to sacrifice 'the opulence and variety of later tongues' to provide posterity with the common style in its perfection, just as its hero Aeneas exemplifies the sacrifice of personal love and pleasure to duty and destiny ('What is a classic?', p. 70). The extraordinary Latinity of the *Quartets'* diction is immediately apparent from the nouns of 'Burnt Norton': abstraction, speculation, deception, circulation, compulsion, concentration, and so on. If classic style 'realizes the genius of the language' it is crucial to Eliot's purpose that that genius should be seen as synonymous with the language's roots in another tongue, and that 'true' or essential English in fact gestures across national boundaries in evoking the common parent of other European languages and literature. The *Quartets* again exemplify Eliot's insistence in 'What is a classic?' that 'the blood-stream of European literature is Latin and Greek – not as two systems of circulation, but one, for it is through Rome that our parentage in Greece must be traced' (p. 70); as 'European literature is a whole', so 'Europe is a whole (and still . . . the organism out of which any greater world harmony must develop)' (p. 69). In 'Ash-Wednesday' Eliot had attempted to transcend national boundaries on a more iconographic level, attempting, that is, a kind of revival of allegory; 'speech varies, but our eyes are all the same', as he put it in the Dante essay

11

(*SE*, p. 243). In the *Quartets* the medievalizing icons are replaced with a strategy of 'classic' form and diction that acknowledges but overcomes national constraints in ways the rest of this book will discuss. Only an English nourished by the European 'blood-stream' is safe from the decline that is evident in the isolation that besets English music and English cuisine;[6] it is a fact that the major English poets, with their tradition of individualistic and 'uncommon' diction, have not in a sense been writing genuine English at all. This can be found only in a correct balance between English and Latinity, what one might call an Anglo-Catholic poetic, though of course Latin is there to regulate English rather than swamp it, as Eliot's attack on Milton in his essay of 1936 indicates (*OPAP*, pp. 138–45).

How do the *Quartets* display, in Hulme's phrase, a 'striving towards structure' and a foregrounding of form rather than of local elaboration? The very title of the poem, *Four Quartets*, is a kind of tautology, imparting at the outset a sense of the primacy of the poem's overall design and logical coherence. This structural emphasis is aided by the regularity and conspicuous homogeneity of diction, tone and, to an extent, metre: the almost total exclusion of different languages, texts and 'voices' which makes this poem a complete reversal of the methods adopted in *The Waste Land*. Even though the work incorporates different poetic forms, the lyric of 'East Coker' iv, the sestina of 'The Dry Salvages', the 'imitation' of Dante's *terza rima* in 'Little Gidding', the formality of tone and Latinity of diction remain constant; there is very little utilization of the different discourses – spoken, regional, racial – that go to make up the plurality of contemporary English. That the movement away from *The Waste Land*'s stylistic variety is an entirely self-conscious and volitional one is a fact amply evidenced by numerous comments in Eliot's later prose writing, as in those at the opening of this chapter. In the next chapter I shall discuss this assessment of the *Quartets* in detail; here I simply wish to establish Eliot's emphasis on subordinating homogeneous parts to the shape of the whole. He had declared his ambition in 1933 'to write poetry which should be essentially poetry, with nothing poetic about it, poetry standing naked in its bare bones, or poetry so transparent that we should not see the poetry, but that which we are meant to see through the poetry'; in the *Quartets* this preference for a 'very bare and austere style' (above, p. 9) continues so to speak under the rubric from 'East Coker', 'the poetry does not matter' (*CPP*, p. 179).[7]

What is referred to above as the foregrounding of form rather than of local elaboration in the *Quartets* leads here to what I see as the most useful and illuminating parallel with Eliot's classicism in the 1930s and 1940s, and one adduced throughout this book, namely developments in the field of the visual arts, and in particular in modernist architecture. Here the emphasis on severely dominant form and structure, and on the suppression of local decoration, is axiomatic; as one of the foremost pioneers of modern design, Adolf Loos, put it,

> the lower the cultural level of a people, the more extravagant it is with its ornament, its decoration. . . . To seek beauty only in form and not in ornament is the goal toward which all humanity is striving.[8]

This was written in 1898, and it may seem far-fetched to relate it to Eliot's formalist ambitions and quest for the 'purging out of poetical ornament' forty years later. But it was not until the 1930s that the theory and practice of modernist architecture became established in England, as illustrated, for example, by the publication by Faber of Walter Gropius's *The New Architecture and the Bauhaus* in 1935. Where Eliot spoke of poetry being purged, Gropius refers to architecture being 'purified' and characterizes Bauhaus aims as including 'the liberation of architecture from a welter of ornament, the emphasis on its structural functions, and the concentration on concise and economical solutions'.[9] Gropius also blasts the architecture of 'the last two or three generations' for its 'meticulous concealment of the verities of structure under a welter of heterogeneous ornament' (pp. 55–6). Le Corbusier's *Towards a New Architecture*, translated into English in 1927, takes much of its inspiration from the buildings of ancient Greece and Rome, the latter being characterized by 'absence of verbosity, good arrangement, a single idea, daring and unity in construction, the use of elementary shapes', the whole amounting to 'a sane morality'.[10] Le Corbusier's major exemplar is the Parthenon, prototype of the new classicism: 'We shall be able to talk "Doric" when man, in nobility of aim and complete sacrifice of all that is accidental in Art, has reached the higher levels of the mind: austerity' (p. 204). In 1936 Faber published Nikolaus

Pevsner's enthusiastic manifesto on behalf of the new architecture, *Pioneers of the Modern Movement from William Morris to Walter Gropius*.

I do not think one can get very far with any direct comparison between the *Quartets* and, say, Gropius's own Bauhaus building of 1925 at Dessau (Plate 1), though the 'clear and crisply simplified' forms he recommends to architects in his book (p. 32) might find a poetic equivalent in the unity and clarity of the *Quartets'* four-part design. The modernist emphasis on the use of glass in building, resulting in work that is 'true to itself, logically transparent and virginal of lies or trivialities', in Gropius's words (p. 56), can be equated with Eliot's desired 'transparency' referred to above, a quality exemplified for him again by Dante: 'the thought may be obscure, but the word is lucid, or rather translucent. In English poetry words have a kind of opacity which is part of their beauty' ('Dante', *SE*, p. 239). 'The great poet's craft may sometimes fail him', he notes in the Kipling essay of 1941, 'but at his greatest moments he is . . . writing transparently, so that our attention is directed to the object and not to the medium. Such a result is not simply attained by absence of decoration – for even the absence of decoration may err in calling attention to itself – but by never using decoration for its own sake' (*OPAP*, p. 235). The traditional opacity of English poetry, its tendency towards decorative 'overloading', is discussed by Eliot with reference to Tennyson's 'Ulysses' in the Dante essay (pp. 248–9), and in the *Quartets'* striving after austerity and 'transparency' Eliot is conscious of working against a powerful but insular tradition. Of course, Eliot's noting above that 'the absence of decoration may err in calling attention to itself' alerts us to the unlikeliness of his having had any direct sympathy with Bauhaus aims; the brave new world of glass, steel and chrome whose secular and de-mystificatory significance is rapturously saluted in Pevsner's writing on Gropius (*Pioneers*, p. 206) is after all hardly calculated to appeal to someone of Eliot's political and religious temperament.[11] Probably a better architectural parallel with the *Quartets* is offered by the widespread movement in the twentieth century towards a more traditional neo-classicism which yet shows the influence of modernist emphases on austerity, simplification and monumentality, a style variously termed 'stripped' or 'abstract' classicism (Plate 2).[12] Such a style was popular all over Europe in the first forty years of the century, though of course it could be varied greatly in the hands of architects like Gropius's teacher Peter Behrens, Albert Speer and Loos himself.[13] Buildings in the 'stripped classical' style moreover generally retained the 'axial symmetry' which Gropius and his followers were keen to abandon but which the *Quartets* can certainly be said to embody (see *The New Architecture*, p. 56).

How far Eliot in the 1930s was aware of developments in modern design, and in the thinking behind them, is arguable, though he could hardly help having a general knowledge of the widespread and intense controversy the uncompromising nature of the new formalism aroused, controversy which is amply documented in, for example, Roger Hinks's *Criterion* 'Art Chronicle' during the period. We may note that Eliot uses the modernist architectural watchword 'functional' in his comment quoted above (p. 9) to describe the austere disciplining of part to whole, and his enthusiasm for and knowledge of Hulme's writing, which I shall have many occasions to bring forward, obviously involves taking on board Hulme's correlation between the new dominance of structure in the visual arts and the imposition of order in religion and ethics; between, that is, classicism and original sin. Eliot's interests overlap with issues much debated by contemporary artists and designers in three main areas: first, the shared idea that the abstraction from detail and from Hulme's 'messiness and confusion of nature' towards simplified form can have some transcendental signification, can 'reach / The stillness', in 'Burnt Norton's words; second, the claim that the new movements in design continue the traditions of classicism, though updating it in particular ways for the twentieth century; and third, touched on in Eliot's own case above, the reassessment of the notion and the desirability of a national art, given the possibility of a 'universal language' the new formalism offers.

The first point, though it concerns the architectonics of the *Quartets* as a whole, has a particular relevance to 'Burnt Norton', originally an independent poem appearing in the mid-1930s and partaking rather more than the other quartets (a point developed in the following chapter) of the then prevailing aesthetic of abstraction in England; a work in other words

15

contemporary with Ben Nicholson's first white reliefs, with the *Unit One* group, with the appearance of the magazine *Axis* and with the publication in English of Gropius's account of the Bauhaus. In discussing his work in *Unit One* Nicholson maintains that

> painting and religious experience are the same thing, and what we are all searching for is the understanding and realisation of infinity. . . . Painting and carving is one means of searching after this reality, and at this moment has reached what is so far its most profound point.[14]

When he reviewed *Unit One* in the *Criterion*, Roger Hinks quoted from this part of Nicholson's statement and saw it as typical of the entire movement: 'Both the sculptors and the majority of painters stated that they were most attracted to the study of abstract form, and this for spiritual reasons. . . . This neo-Pythagorean attitude to form is extremely interesting and ought to be examined at some length.'[15]

Eliot's version of this 'attitude to form' is found in 'Burnt Norton' v:

> Words move, music moves
> Only in time; but that which is only living
> Can only die. Words, after speech, reach
> Into the silence. Only by the form, the pattern,
> Can words or music reach
> The stillness, as a Chinese jar still
> Moves perpetually in its stillness.
>
> (CPP, p. 175)

This 'stillness' is represented throughout the poem as the axial centre of the 'turning world', and is invested with a more explicit Christian significance as the *Quartets* progress. The play throughout 'Burnt Norton' with symbolic forms and axial geometry, and with the idea that the artwork's formal emphasis in some way reflects or represents cosmic design, and the designer behind it, had as Hinks says a good deal of currency at the time. Consider, for example, the caption accompanying the photograph of the Parthenon in Le Corbusier:

> The Greeks on the Acropolis set up temples which are

16

animated by a single thought, drawing around them the
desolate landscape and gathering it into the composition.
Thus, on every point of the horizon, the thought is single.
(*Towards a New Architecture*, p. 204)

Le Corbusier sees this unifying character of Greek art, its
creation of a centralizing axis, as an attempt to manifest
universal 'harmony':

This is indeed the axis on which man is organized in
perfect accord with nature and probably with the
universe, this axis of organization which must indeed be
that on which all phenomena and all objects of nature are
based; this axis leads us to assume a unity of conduct in
the universe and to admit a single will behind it.[16]
(pp. 208–9)

Classic art sits on and signals the universal axis then, as does
'Burnt Norton's Chinese jar, and as mentioned above the
foremost magazine of the English abstract movement,
published between 1935 and 1937, bore the simple title *Axis*.
Another example of this mystical appropriation of the abstraction from detail towards form occurs in a work Eliot doubtless
knew, Paul Valéry's dialogue *Eupalinos: or the Architect*:

Music and Architecture . . . seem dedicated to reminding
us directly – one, of the formation of the universe, the
other, of its order and stability; they invoke the constructions of the mind . . . they therefore neglect the particular
appearances with which the world and the mind are
ordinarily preoccupied. . . . I have even observed sometimes, when listening to music . . . that I was as it were no
longer perceiving the sounds of the instruments as sensa-
tions of the ear. The symphony itself made me forget the
sense of hearing.[17]

I quote this at length because it reminds us of the frequency in
this type of argument of the association between visual and
musical harmony (so that the *Quartets'* emphasis on musical
form is entirely consistent with the visual arts correlations I am
claiming for the poem – see also John Bigge's essay in *Unit One*
(pp. 49–51)) and also because it may provide some kind of
source, as Barbara Everett has recognized, for one of the

descriptions in 'The Dry Salvages' of moments when the universal order is apprehended; when 'music [is] heard so deeply / That it is not heard at all, but you are the music / While the music lasts'.[18]

In the next chapter I shall substantiate the above discussion with a detailed look at Eliot's language, and shall also suggest how another mid-1930s artistic fashion, the geometrical austerity of so-called kinetic sculpture, offers a further parallel with Eliot's presentation of the reconciliation between motion and stasis in 'Burnt Norton'. The correlation between abstraction and universality is spelt out by him in the ending of his 'A note on war poetry' (1942):

> But the abstract conception
> Of private experience at its greatest intensity
> Becoming universal, which we call 'poetry',
> May be affirmed in verse.
>
> (CPP, p. 202)

When the term 'abstraction' appears a mere six lines into 'Burnt Norton' itself we should not then underestimate its significance:

> What might have been is an abstraction
> Remaining a perpetual possibility
> Only in a world of speculation.
>
> (CPP, p. 171)

The 'what might have been' here is not a vague or merely theoretical realm of being (i.e. in the common understanding of 'abstraction') but precisely the reverse, as the poem goes on to show; it is the visionary world of the garden which the protagonist later has access to but from which the exile into temporality has to be re-enacted, with the injunction 'Go, go, go, said the bird: human kind / Cannot bear very much reality'. As Roger Hinks put it in his *Criterion* review of *Circle*, published by Faber in 1937 and presenting artists belonging to that development of the abstract movement known as constructivism, 'to identify the abstract with the real has been the mark of all intellectualist doctrines from the time of Parmenides to the present day'.[19] It is something of an irony that critics who object to the relative sparseness of sensuous imagery in the *Quartets* compared with Eliot's early work will use the term 'abstract' in a condemnatory way, but with little thought for its historical relevance;[20] although there are obvious limits to the useful comparison between verbal and visual texts, I would suggest that the relation between the *Quartets* and the arts movements discussed thus far has in fact more substance than the more frequently treated *Waste Land*-cubism parallel. Critics who posit, on a purely technical and stylistic level, an increasingly reactionary and outdated Eliot in the *Quartets* might do well to reflect that few poems of the period show an equal contemporaneity in terms of design.

Passing on to the second point listed above, we might ask in what ways such design can be called 'classical' – how does the new formalism, be it in Eliot's 'purging out of poetical orna-ment', or in the austerity of Le Corbusier's new 'Doric' (above, p. 13), establish itself within such a tradition? It was largely T. E. Hulme who was responsible in England for redefining classic art as the expression of a belief that man 'is judged to be essentially limited and imperfect', and 'endowed with Original Sin' and hence in need of discipline and authority; in his writing he thus wrestles the term 'classical' away from any idealization of human or natural beauty as in, say, the Parthenon sculptures.[21] As Michael Roberts noted in his 1938 book on Hulme, classicism for him was represented by Egyptian, Indian and Byzantine art, whereas 'he regard[ed] Greek architecture and sculpture as humanist, not classical';[22] no less than in Eliot's later work, as we shall see, the pretensions of humanism and of humanist art are subject to severe examination throughout *Speculations*. Classicism becomes for Hulme synonymous with the 'striving towards structure' and austerity (above, p. 8), a movement indeed towards 'abstract forms' which is *not* manifested in the most celebrated periods of antique art (see 'Humanism and the religious attitude', p. 57), but rather in

> Egyptian, Indian and Byzantine [art], where everything tends to be angular, where curves tend to be hard and geometrical, where the representation of the human body, for example, is often entirely non-vital, and dis-torted to fit into stiff lines and cubical shapes of various kinds.
>
> ('Modern art and its philosophy', p. 82)

This last extract shows Hulme repeating the ideas of his

great mentor, Wilhelm Worringer, whose *Abstraction and Empathy* (1908) saw historical styles in art manifesting two opposing tendencies. Periods of 'empathy', as in the great Athenian period of the fifth and fourth centuries BC, were ones in which 'Man was at home in the world and felt himself its centre', experiencing a secure and happy pantheistic relationship with natural phenomena.[23] The art he produces tends to be naturalistic, a loving transcription of the world he empathizes with. In periods of abstraction, however, 'Naive sensuous oneness with nature is replaced by a disunion, a relationship of fear between man and world, a scepticism toward the surface and appearance of things above and beyond which the ultimate cause of things, an ultimate truth was sought' (p. 102). In such periods (like the Egyptian and Byzantine) the non-naturalistic stylization of art is an attempt to take 'the individual thing of the external world out of its arbitrariness and seeming fortuitousness, of eternalising it by approximation to abstract forms, and, in this manner, of finding a point of tranquillity and a refuge from appearances' (p. 16). This search for 'redemption from the anguish of the relative' leads Worringer to postulate the following equation: 'It is evident that transcendental notions in a religious respect, and the urge to abstraction in an artistic respect, are expressions of the same psychic disposition *vis-à-vis* the cosmos' (p. 103). Worringer wrote this account before the modern period had clearly shown itself to be an age of 'abstraction' too, so it was left to Hulme and to Herbert Read, in books like *Art Now* (1933), to explain much contemporary art as a manifestation of twentieth-century anxiety and alienation along Worringer's lines.

Worringer's equation between transcendentalism and abstraction seems to me a very suggestive one in considering 'Burnt Norton's 'urge to abstraction', discussed above, especially when in Worringer's *Form in Gothic* (1912; English translation 1927), we find Oriental art allocated to the abstract, rather than empathetic, pole; it exhibits 'an absolute redemptive character', a 'sharply outlined, transcendentally abstract complexion', a formulation illuminating Eliot's choice of a 'Chinese jar' (rather than, say, a Greek vase) as transcendental emblem. For Worringer Oriental art shows 'no joyful affirmation of sensuous vitality' but belongs rather entirely to the other domain, which through all the transitoriness and chance of life strives for a higher world, freed from all illusions of the senses, from all false impressions, a domain in which inevitableness and permanency reign.[24]

The equation between classicism and austerity, formal severity and abstraction does not, however, mean a wholesale jettisoning of the western 'classical' tradition as overly humanist, though it does mean in Eliot and others a revaluation of the different parts that make up that tradition. There is a tendency to search out and stress those aspects of Greek and Roman art which might be seen as prefiguring the new dominance and disciplinarianism of structure, or which express a prototypical austerity or 'streamlining'. Thus Le Corbusier posits the correlation between Doric architecture and modern machine design in setting a photograph of the Parthenon alongside that of a sports car of 1921 (*Towards a New Architecture*, p. 135) (Plate 3), whereas Loos opines that the Greek vase is 'as beautiful as a bicycle'.[25] Loos in fact had a preference for the more imposingly authoritarian Roman art over the Greek, and he castigates the latter's phases of excessive ornamentation.[26] In the writing of Hulme's associate Anthony Ludovici the claim is made that the great period of Greek art is not the Periclean age, with its works like the Elgin Marbles, but the period before the fifth century BC, when a monumental stylization much indebted to Egyptian influence had not yet surrendered to the striving for realism.[27] Ludovici's diagnosis is indeed an unashamed apologetic for the 'Symmetry', 'Sobriety' and 'Simplicity' of what he calls 'Ruler-Art' (pp. 217, 232), and the anti-individualist, anti-democratic implications of his aesthetic are shared by many writers for whom a rigorous subordination of part to whole is both an artistic and a political necessity. One of the major influences on Gropius, and on modern design generally, Hermann Muthesius, for whom in Banham's words 'Form' was 'a kind of geometrical essence distilled from neo-Classical design' (*Theory and Design*, p. 74), equated an 'architectonic culture' with 'that order and discipline of which good Form is the outward manifestation'.[28] The equation between Form and conformism is a ready one in the hands of English commentators in the 1930s who, as we shall see, attack the new

movements in architecture and in related fields like con-
structivism as the noxious wind of totalitarianism blowing in
from the continent. This is thus the prehistory behind Winston
Smith's confrontation with the Ministry of Truth, that
'enormous pyramidal structure of glittering white concrete'
based on London University's Senate House (Plate 4), in *Nineteen
Eighty-Four*.[29] Although in the following two chapters I shall
discuss the authoritarian strategies of the *Quartets* in some
detail, I should stress here that Eliot's classicism is not bent on
promoting the pretensions of secular power; indeed the *Quartets*
have levels of sophistication that question their own formalist
practice in ways undreamt of in the crude triumphalism of, say,
Nazi stripped neo-classicism. The idea of unitary forms being a
means of instilling a measure of unity into a populace, and the
equation between aesthetic discipline and political or religious
ordering, these are concepts that surface in writers like Le
Corbusier and even Gropius, and have a currency that goes far
beyond their assimilation into fascism.

Eliot's quarrying of the classical tradition might be claimed as
a similar search for a prototypical austerity to that pursued by
modern designers. Greece tends to be subsumed within Rome
(above, p. 11), and in 'What is a classic?' the tradition centres on
the great axial monolith of the *Aeneid*, itself a study in linguistic
and ethical self-denial (see below, p. 74). Certainly there seems
little place in twentieth-century classicism generally for the
sweetness and light of Victorian Hellenism, and already in
Eliot's early poems like 'Sweeney erect' or 'Sweeney among the
nightingales' we have a kind of exposé of the rhetoric of
classical myth and legend, a constant dwelling on the facts of
murder, treachery and rape in the stories of Agamemnon,
Ariadne, Philomel and so forth, together with the suggestion of
the powers of art to gloss over those 'Sweeneyesque' constants
in human life, to misrepresent them as epic: 'Display me Aeolus
above / Reviewing the insurgent gales' ('Sweeney erect', *CPP*,
p. 42). The later poetry, rather than ironizing scenic display as
here, tends to dispense with it altogether. It is impossible to
imagine Eliot or Hulme sharing those ideals of natural or
athletic perfection traditionally seen as embodied in the
sculptures of the Periclean age, or saluting that vision of a
perfection 'quite conceivably attainable by man' often traced
there.[30] On the contrary, the context I am attempting to

establish for Eliot's classicism would underline its severity, both formal and ethical, and its non-humanism. These features I return to below, in looking at the *Quartets* in detail; here I might simply remind readers of Eliot's tendency to discount the pronounced humanist-classical element in Dante (see my *Dante and English Poetry*, pp. 222–3).

In his second article on 'Views and valuations of ancient art since Winckelmann', published in the *Criterion* in 1926, Paul Jacobstal provided what turns out to be a kind of summary of the points I have been making. Tracing the contemporary preference for the pre-naturalistic phase of ancient art, he notes how its development is at present widely regarded as 'a gradual decline from the height of original monumentality and crystalline severity', that is, from Babylonian-Sumerian, through Egyptian to Greek. He suggests that this new under-standing of the antique reflects a modern *taedium vitae*, and that there are consequences for Greek literature too: 'At the present day the Parthenon sculptures and Sophocles, to say nothing of Euripides, have a smaller circle of appreciative admirers than Olympia, Pindar and Aeschylus.' [31] Eliot himself was a member of the 'larger' circle of admirers, as *The Family Reunion* suggests; a mixture of Aeschylus with original sin (as if in deliberate endorsement of Hulme's redefinition of classicism throughout *Speculations*), the play provides nothing of that reassuring establishment of order we have at the end of the *Oresteia*, with the Eumenides now agents of social and political justice work-ing within the city-state; rather Harry goes off in the Furies' company to some unspecified, endless and essentially solitary expiation of inherited guilt. In the following chapter I shall discuss the relation in Eliot's work between the 'purging out of poetical ornament' and the issue of religious purgation; here, in using Aeschylus as a vehicle for his own asceticism, Eliot reminds us of the tendency under discussion to subsume the classical tradition within the new austerity. 'Good poetry is classic and austere', says Auden in 'Letter to Lord Byron', referring to his early acquiescence in the *Criterion*'s judgements rather than in Matthew Arnold's, and indeed it is only in the period under examination that the two adjectives have been so emphatically synonymous (*EA*, p. 195). As I have said, archi-tectural historians have a term for the widespread mani-festation of such an outlook in the buildings of the first four decades of the century, in particular, the term 'stripped' classicism, and I can think of no better term to describe the aesthetic principles governing *Four Quartets*.

My third point above concerned the relation between the new formalism and nationalism, and the debate between the two is fundamental to this present study as a whole. The classical tradition in architecture, with its imperialistic past and its relatively unvarying pattern-book of styles and devices, had long been regarded as a 'universal language', and the movement towards a simplified and severer form of the tradition in the 1930s intensified such a claim.[32] The new purities of abstraction in painting too gestured towards a crossing of national frontiers; Paul Nash in his contribution to *Unit One* dwelt much on the 'international character' of contemporary art, which,

> by destroying the false values of nationalism, opens the way for a purely academic approach to the question of national idiosyncrasy, and, in proportion as art becomes more abstract, so the nuances of national or racial distinction become more subtle and, consequently, more interesting to trace.
>
> (p. 80)

One critic has suggested that the internationalist endeavours of *Unit One* should be seen against the background of a revival of 'militant cultural nationalism' in England in the early 1930s,[33] and a similar anti-chauvinism seems to me a major impetus behind Eliot's writing during the same period, culminating in the *Quartets*. I noted above how the simplification and Latinity of the poem, posited as synonymous with the 'genius of the language', look to escape a narrowly individualistic 'Englishness'; such qualities moreover make the poem available for export via translation in a way Dante's language is, according to Eliot, but Shakespeare's is not ('Dante', p. 241). It is true that Nash within this internationalist perspective wishes to retain something that is distinctively and romantically English, a nuance of 'national distinction' that he cautiously defines as a spirit 'of the land', or the 'lyrical' expression of the *genius loci*, and that he traces in the work of artists like Blake and Turner. His stressing the subtlety, almost ineffability, of the English spirit, as well as its actual incarnation in his mysticist, depopulated landscapes, might be seen as an attempt to preserve a notion of England that will elude any jingoistic appropriation in the 1930s and 1940s. Though Eliot's 'land-scapes' in the *Quartets* are very different from Nash's, the rather bleak and spartan settings in the poem might serve a similar function, and in chapter 3 below I return to these landscapes in the context of a vigorous contemporary debate over the representation of England in literature and art, where the severity of the new classicism has its scenic consequences also.

A universal language of classic or abstract style had received its imprimatur in 1932 with the coining of the term 'International Style' to describe the spread of a homogeneous modernist architecture inspired by men like Gropius and Le Corbusier.[34] The idea of a kind of world unification in aesthetic terms that the movement suggested had its political corollary too in much writing of the 1930s. We find editorials in *Axis* suggesting that 'pure abstract work' is an index of a new communal ideal, of 'a passionate belief in the power for good';[35] we find the constructivists rehearsing throughout *Circle* 'their touching belief in the perfectibility of man, their milleniarist optimism', as Hinks puts it in his review (*Criterion* 17, p. 88). Such beliefs were treated with a good deal of suspicion by writers for whom the new style could mean only political tyranny, as remarked above; another reviewer of *Circle*, for example, suggested that in the movement's 'geometrical inventions' the 'rigidity and conformism cherished by the Totalitarian States would find a perfect expression'.[36] It is important to realize that Eliot's harnessing of the new formalism shares a political stance with neither the extreme left nor extreme right. Certainly his desire to escape as far as possible national constraints, and to write in a more 'universal' language, harbours no belief in international brotherhood in any positive sense and certainly not in human 'perfectibility'; structure and form are seen rather along Hulmean lines as a kind of holding operation against humanity's ineluctable sin and alienation. And this postlapsarian perspective on 'universality' also distances him from any totalitarian deployment of form and discipline; in the *Quartets*, as noted above, form gestures to a complete transcendence of secular ambition and the poem in fact ironizes, as we shall see, ideals of imperial power. The desolation of the *Quartets*, the poem's suppression of human subjects and speakers, its curious air of depopulation and evacuation, its strenuous 'purging out' of poetical diction and ornament, its formal discipline and austerity, all this might be cold water flung in the face of those who see new political hopes in a 'universal language' of form. And these features are no less apparent in the quartet published in 1936, 'Burnt Norton', than they are in those written during the war when such hopes might seem a mockery indeed.

In his 'Commentary' in the *Criterion* for January 1934, Eliot stresses the importance of V. A. Demant's observation that 'consciousness of "the nation" as *the* social unit is a very recent and contingent experience' and compares such an attitude of reservation favourably with the fervent rhetorical nationalism of recent works like Winston Churchill's *Marlborough* and Sir George Macaulay Trevelyan's *British History in the Nineteenth Century*.[37] That the English race is something historically very much wider than modern England is a point Eliot is fond of emphasizing, as when in *Murder in the Cathedral* he has the assassins William de Traci, Reginald Fitz Urse, Hugh de Morville and Richard Brito declare themselves as 'four plain Englishmen who put our country first' (*CPP*, p. 277). In featuring his own English ancestor Sir Thomas Elyot in the *Quartets*, and the village of East Coker, he also reminds us of a common root behind the modern divergence of nations; not only are the 'English' very much an admixture of the foreign, but 'foreigners' themselves can once have been English. Certainly in declaring that 'the last three of my quartets are primarily patriotic poems' Eliot seems to feel that the American setting of 'The Dry Salvages' in no way disrupts his concept of the *patria*.[38] Both linguistically and thematically, Eliot is concerned to show the inseparability of English and Englishness from a wider context; to show a necessary universality inherent within these modes.

'History is now and England', as 'Little Gidding' has it. Before nationalists get too excited about such an identification, however, they might note that to a great degree the entire realm of 'history' is marginalized in the *Quartets*, in ways I shall discuss in future chapters. In any case, the perception of 'the intersection of the timeless movement' reveals the provisionality of earthly nations and is enacted in 'Little Gidding' in the rather more ambiguous location of 'England and nowhere'. Eliot's 'patriotism' in the *Quartets* has therefore to be approached in a very circumspect way; certainly his construction of England in the poem has a decidedly odd air compared with the enthusiastic home-front, neo-Georgian or Churchillian modes with which we generally associate wartime England. In a *Criterion* 'Commentary' of 1937, Eliot is concerned to distinguish universality from internationalism, and perhaps has the architectural 'International Style' specifically in mind in stating 'I cannot think of art as either national or international – these, after all, are modern terms – but as racial and local.' [39] The example of Dante is again paramount:

> Some of the character of this univeral language [i.e., medieval Latin] seems to me to inhere in Dante's Florentine speech; and the localization ('Florentine' speech) seems if anything to emphasise the universality, because it cuts across the modern division of nationality.
>
> ('Dante', *SE*, p. 239)

The concept of race is therefore catholic in a sense that 'the nation' is not, and moreover it makes nonsense of any narrowly held ideals of nationhood.

And yet Eliot is aware of the dangers of 'rootlessness' in both a linguistic and a geographical sense. Just as the *Quartets* are largely set in a specific, though provisional, English time and place, so their language cannot be the universal one of medieval Latin but one in which some of that language's character can merely 'inhere' (as with Dante's Florentine). In the *Criterion* 'Commentary' mentioned above Eliot notes how 'an art which is not representative of a particular people, but "international", or an art which does not represent a particular civilisation, but only an abstract civilisation-in-general, may lose its sources of vitality' (p. 82). To write in English is to be representative of a 'particular people', or, as Eliot puts it in the same piece, 'the limitation of a particular language is the condition of a writer doing anything at all' (p. 83), though the frustrations arising from the limitation of the language he is writing in are a prominent feature of the *Quartets*. Eliot's preferential use of terms like 'universal', 'racial' and 'local' to 'international' or 'national' leads us into problems, however, in considering the idea of locality in the *Quartets*. In an essay of 1953 Eliot suggests that it is doubtful whether 'a poet or novelist can be universal without being local too', [40] and in 'The music of poetry' (1942),

27

he stresses that such music must be 'a music latent in the common speech of its time. And that means also that it must be latent in the common speech of the poet's *place* . . . it is the poet's business to use the speech which he finds about him, that with which he is most familiar' (*OPAP*, p. 31). As a rider, he adds: 'Of course, we do not want the poet merely to reproduce exactly the conversational idiom of himself, his family, his friends and his particular district: but what he finds there is the material out of which he must make his poetry' (p. 32). It is difficult to believe, however, that the 'speech' of the *Quartets* is founded on any particular 'locality', and though localities are visited in the poem there is no sense of any integration with them; rather notes of exclusion, almost of trespass, feature throughout: 'Go, go, go, said the bird' ('Burnt Norton'), 'If you do not come too close, if you do not come too close' ('East Coker'). Bearing in mind Eliot's original title for the poem we can perhaps best understand the *Quartets'* 'locality' as middle-class Kensington, despite their rural settings.[41]

This, however, involves a good deal of stretching of the concept of 'local' speech, and indeed *Four Quartets* remains a resolutely anti-local poem, for Eliot's search for a 'classic' English, the realization of 'the genius of the language', hypothesizes some placeless linguistic essence along the lines of Dante's *volgare illustre* in the *De vulgari eloquentia*, rather than of the specifically Florentine character of the *Commedia* itself (though even with 'Dante's Florentine speech', referred to by Eliot in the quotation given above, Eliot is far more interested in its 'universal' than in its local quality). In the *De vulgari* the model language Dante is seeking turns out to be that found in the writings of the Italian poets – 'Hoc enim usi sunt doctores illustres qui lingua vulgari poetati sunt in Ytalia'[42] – rather than one based on any language *spoken* in any part of Italy, and as is explained in the following chapter the *Quartets* to a large degree conduct a campaign against the spoken word in order to maintain the standard of their own 'literary' language. Although Eliot is fond of talking of the way 'common speech' should feed into poetry, as in his comment above that poetry's music must be 'latent in the common speech of its time', he stresses that communication between the written and spoken is two-way: 'The poet who gave the English speech' is the title of one of his essays on Dryden (see note 5), and writing remains paramount in the hierarchy.[43] In spite of Eliot's support for the locality of art, then, the *Quartets* exemplify the reverse, just as in spite of his sympathy, politically speaking, with regionalism (discussed in chapter 3), *Four Quartets* is not a regionalist poem. These contradictions will be explored subsequently.

In Graham Greene's *England Made Me* of 1935 we have the constant polarization of cosy, dingy, 'slatternly' England, with its nostalgically evoked pubs and Lyons cafés, and glass-and-chrome capitalist Sweden, epitomized by the 'inhuman' fountain of monolithic green stone that features recurrently.[44] A similar debate between traditional England – this time in its pastoral guise – and the brave new world is found in an Orwell poem of 1934, as its title indicates: 'On a ruined farm near the His Master's Voice gramophone factory', the factory being a construct of 'steel and concrete' in 'dizzy, geometric towers'.[45] It seems to me that writers like Eliot, and to some extent Auden (see chapter 4), attempt to obviate this polarity between England and its traditions and the foreign and formalistic by harnessing their work to the new movements in design. I now go on to show in detail how Eliot does this with the English language, beginning with his changing attitude to a writer around whom questions of Englishness very much congregated in the 1930s and Second World War years, Shakespeare; in chapter 3 I then show how he and others do it with the English landscape too. It is true that there are poems of the 1930s that show a simpler acceptance of contemporary design than do the *Quartets*; Spender's 'The express' and 'The pylons' immediately spring to mind, but works like these hardly engage with the issues behind the new aesthetic as the *Quartets* and Eliot's *Quartets*-related essays do.[46] When he implies that his efforts towards a 'common' language and classic discipline are bedevilled by isolation (as above, p. 10), Eliot is I think minimizing the extent to which poets during the 1930s do share certain techniques and tricks of diction; indeed, as I argue in chapter 4, it is possible to speak of some measure of 'standardization' in the poetry of Eliot and his contemporaries which parallels the collectivism of contemporary design. Although the shared context traced in this chapter does exist for Eliot's later classicism, it is entirely to the *Quartets*' purpose to present themselves as a desolate enterprise brooding on their own failures and pervaded by a sense of isolation, as if Eliot is stressing his fate of being aligned to classicism in a so-called 'Romantic' age (see Introduction, p. 6). If then the poem can be described in further paradoxes than those it already abounds in, we might describe it as a monument to the isolated (and authoritarian) collectivist, to the unorthodox conformist, its programme, like all things temporal, vitiated by its own emphasis on earthly *vanitas*. It is doubtless this highly personal appropriation of a contemporary neo-classicism that weighs with those critics who claim the *Quartets* (erroneously, as I hope to show) as belonging to some 'Romantic' tradition.

2

ELIOT'S ENGLISH

ELIOT AND SHAKESPEARE

In moving towards the austerity of the classic style, Eliot was led to revalue some of his earlier poetical enthusiasms, and to discover that though Dante's 'astonishing economy and directness of language' remained a usable model, the 'extravagances' of the English Renaissance writers did not ('To criticize the critic', *TCTC*, p. 23). Echoes of Donne, for example, are totally absent from the later poetry, as Eliot began to discover in his work a self-dramatizing quality wholly at odds with say the utter absorption in his subject of Bishop Andrewes's writing ('Lancelot Andrewes', *SE*, pp. 351–2). In his assiduous search for meaning, rather than performance, Andrewes takes individual words and 'squeezes' a 'full juice of meaning' from them (pp. 347–8), rather as Eliot tussles with the many values of inconspicuous monosyllables like 'turn' or 'still' in the later work, instead of exploiting accumulations of imagery or verbal decoration. The 'genius of the language' is meant to be on show, in true common-style fashion, rather than the individual genius.

Eliot's 'disowning' of Donne is quite overt, and its stages can be easily traced through the 1920s.[1] Shakespeare, however, is a much more interesting and problematic case, and it seems that Eliot could never, in a sense, categorize his work satisfactorily, even though the adoption of the classic style would seem to warrant the jettisoning of his influence too. In 'Shakespeare and the stoicism of Seneca' (1927), Shakespeare's tragic heroes are seen as studies of 'individualism', of the 'vice of Pride', dying, like Othello and Hamlet, in a final bout of rhetorical self-assertion rather than in the humility warranted by the 'pretty considerable mess of things' they brought about (SE, pp. 130–2). Nothing could be further from Eliot's 'heroes of humility' in the 1930s, Becket and Harry, the martyrdom of the former only being possible after his overcoming the spiritual pride represented by the Fourth Tempter. It is natural to compare Harry in *The Family Reunion* with Hamlet, his interview with Mary in part I, scene ii – in the presence of ghosts which he sees but she cannot – recalling Hamlet's with Gertrude in her bedchamber, but surely the point of *The Family Reunion* is Harry's transition from Hamlet to Aeneas, so to speak, from the hysterical upbraiding of others to the spiritual rescue of the family through self-abnegation, 'Its bird sent flying through the purgatorial flame' (CPP, p. 333).[2] Questions of spiritual humility immediately take us back to ideas of poetic humility too, and to Eliot's attitude to Shakespearian style and diction.

'Anyone who attempts to write poetic drama, even to-day', Eliot noted in 1947, 'should know that half of his energy must be exhausted in the effort to escape from the constricting toils of Shakespeare: the moment his attention is relaxed, or his mind fatigued, he will lapse into bad Shakespearian verse' ('Milton II', OPAP, p. 150). At the back of Eliot's mind here are doubtless the lines describing Cleopatra quoted in the Dante essay of two decades earlier:

> she looks like sleep
> As she would catch another Antony
> In her strong toil of grace.
> (SE, p. 244)[3]

In that essay, Eliot was contrasting Dante's simplicity and economy with the complexity of Shakespeare's style: 'If you try to imitate Shakespeare you will certainly produce a series of stilted, forced, and violent distortions of language. . . . If you follow Dante without talent, you will at worst be pedestrian and flat' (p. 252). Eliot's early poetry is certainly caught up in the 'toils' of Shakespeare, and the implications of this can be considered by looking at *The Waste Land*.

These toils again originate with Cleopatra; at the beginning of the 'Game of chess' section of Eliot's poem we find the Cleopatra-inspired Belladonna figure surfeiting in a kind of descriptive excess, metamorphosed into artwork:

Huge sea-wood fed with copper
Burned green and orange, framed by the coloured stone,
In which sad light a carvèd dolphin swam.

                                                    (ll.94–6)

The inspiration behind this metamorphosis in *The Waste Land*
comes, however, from Ariel's song in *The Tempest*. It may be
worthwhile giving this in full:

> Full fathom five thy father lies.
>   Of his bones are coral made;
> Those are pearls that were his eyes;
>   Nothing of him that doth fade
> But doth suffer a sea-change
> Into something rich and strange.
>   Sea-nymphs hourly ring his knell. . .[4]

The third line here is that which seemingly mesmerizes
Belladonna's interlocutor in 'A game of chess'; the entire
section suggests that the 'Shakespeherian Rag', in all its
grandeur and magniloquence, contributes to the de-energized
and enervated state that characterizes the chess players; the
natural becoming the artificially beauteous but also becoming
dead in the process – 'Those are pearls that were his eyes'.
Ariel's statement is, of course, untrue; in *The Tempest* Alonso has
not drowned but comes back as it were to life; in *The Waste Land*
the song and the debilitating ornamentation it exemplifies
feature solely in the 'pre-resurrection' stages of the poem. In
part v we not only have figures like the risen Christ at
Emmaus, but we also get what can be seen as Eliot's earliest
sustained exercise in the spareness of the 'classic' style in the
'water-dripping song' (ll. 331–58), the only part of the poem
Eliot seemed satisfied with after its completion.[5] The poem
formally sloughs off the Shakespearian 'toil' then, having
identified its potent beauty throughout in Cleopatra-like terms;
something hypnotic, artificial, and polarized against 'life' and
rebirth.

Eliot never attempted anything like 'A game of chess' in his
later poetry, and there is no doubt that the section is in concept
as well as style deliberately Shakespearian. In an article of 1931
he offers a familiar interpretation of Shakespeare's supposed
comic relief scenes:

the comic is not really 'relief' at all, but on the contrary, at its best an intensification of the sombreness. The Porter in *Macbeth*, the Gravedigger in *Hamlet* . . . merely make the horror or tragedy more real by transposing it for a moment from the sublime to the common.[6]

This transposition is imitated in 'A game of chess' as we pass from Belladonna's salon to the Cockney pub. The dramatic contrasts and abrupt intrusion of different voices in this part of *The Waste Land* – with its original rubric 'He do the Police in Different Voices'[7] – are not conspicuous in Eliot's later drama, with its emphasis on the formality of the classic style, just as the racy American idiom achieved in 'Sweeney Agonistes' is sacrificed too (see below, pp. 144–5). In the 1930s, Eliot turned his back on his own dramatic gifts, in part, eschewing a variety of voices and idioms for the sake of an essential, tightly disciplined 'English'; the 'escape' from Shakespeare in the plays of that decade will be discussed later.

Another early poem that succumbs to, and yet satirizes, the extravagances of Renaissance ornamentation is 'Whispers of immortality', from the *Poems* of 1920 (*CPP*, pp. 52–3):

> Webster was much possessed by death
> And saw the skull beneath the skin;
> And breastless creatures under ground
> Leaned backward with a lipless grin.
>
> Daffodil bulbs instead of balls
> Stared from the sockets of the eyes!
> He knew that thought clings round dead limbs
> Tightening its lusts and luxuries.

The second stanza here is a passage singled out by Orwell to demonstrate the superiority of Eliot's early over his later manner, in the review quoted above (p. 9). But the poem clearly indicates its frustration with the Jacobean attitude to death and to 'dead limbs' with which, however, the poet identifies himself in the final stanza: 'But our lot crawls between dry ribs/To keep our metaphysics warm'. A glamorizing of the grave, a corpse-fixation expressed as a kind of poetic necrophilia whereby dead eyes become pearls or sprout daffodils, this is the type of 'bones-as-art-object', rather than true image of *vanitas*, which Eliot also picked up on in Donne.

For example, Eliot is fond of quoting in his early criticism lines like that from Donne's 'The relique' – 'A bracelet of bright hair about the bone' – as if they had some singular talismanic property; once the theory of classic form dismisses the value of the ostentatious individual line, however, such pieces of Donne are never mentioned again.[8] This line also falls from favour because of its sensuality, a prime instance of thought 'tightening its lusts and luxuries' around dead limbs. The 'bones' in Eliot's own poetry gradually become divested of any gratuitous mystique; in 'Ash-Wednesday' ii, their ability to 'shine' and to sing to the Lady is founded on their self-recognition as 'dry' and lifeless, rather than as potently talismanic. Body and personality are abnegated in 'Ash-Wednesday' ii as a prerequisite of spiritual growth.

The Renaissance theatre is opposed to this kind of humility in Eliot's eyes; its heroes vaunt themselves and the death that might remind man of his transience is a dramatic end in itself, dressed out as something 'rich and strange'. In an article on 'Dryden the dramatist', written in 1931, Eliot 'hazard[s] . . . an heretical and contestable opinion' on behalf of his neo-classical exemplar; namely that 'later blank verse dramatists have written better verse when they wrote more like Dryden . . . and worse blank verse when they were conscious of Shakespeare'.[9] He cites Shelley's *The Cenci* as an example of this latter consciousness,

> My God! Can it be possible I have
> To die so suddenly? So young to go
> Under the obscure, cold, rotting, wormy ground!

criticizing it as merely a 'feeble echo' of Claudio's speech in *Measure for Measure* (III.i.118–32), and adding: 'but Shelley is not the only poet who has been Shakespearian by the appropriation of worms and rot and such Elizabethan stage properties' (p. 681).[10] The Shakespearian element in Eliot's early poetry seems to lead us back, again and again, to Ariel's song in *The Tempest*; surely that is the inspiration behind Eliot's recurrent submarine scene-painting, where

> worried bodies of drowned men drift down in the green
> silence,

Dropping from fingers of surf
                    ('Mr Apollinax', *CPP*, p. 31)

or where

A current under sea
Picked his bones in whispers
                    (*The Waste Land*, 11.316–17, *CPP*, p. 71)

or even in Prufrock's fantasizing:

We have lingered in the chambers of the sea
By sea-girls wreathed with seaweed red and brown.
                    (*CPP*, p. 17)

Eliot's later exercise in the 'submarine' in 'The Dry Salvages' offers an instructive contrast, with its refusal to linger imaginatively in 'the chambers of the sea'; there the fate of drowned sailors is described quite starkly:

those who were in ships, and
Ended their voyage on the sand, in the sea's lips
Or in the dark throat which will not reject them
Or wherever cannot reach them the sound of the sea bell's
Perpetual angelus.
                    (*CPP*, p. 189)

Arnold's severe, rather prosaic 'Dover Beach', with its picture of the sea as the permanent but indifferent ebb-and-flow of a Godless world, is the model in 'The Dry Salvages', in which a similar conception of a world inhabited solely by 'chthonic powers' is faced up to and overcome; here there can be no question of the sea being invested with the fineries of coral, pearls, or mermaids. We are told indeed in the quartet that the 'sea has many voices', but its Renaissance voice, so to speak, is suppressed; its soft whispers and rich and strange transmutations are replaced by a more 'realist' set of noises including the 'whine in the rigging' and the 'distant rote in the granite teeth' (*CPP*, p. 185). In its presentation of the dangers of the sea as workplace, rather than as theatre, Eliot reminds us of the contrast he had earlier drawn between Dante's Ulysses episode in *Inferno* XXVI as 'a well-told seaman's yarn', and Tennyson's 'Ulysses', which primarily reveals 'a very self-conscious poet' ('Dante', *SE*, p. 250).[11]

The austere homogeneity of the classic style resists, as we

stressed in the previous chapter, the incorporation of different voices, and 'multi-voicedness' is generally appraised in Eliot's later work as synonymous with danger, or temptation, or evil. A full account of this will be given in the third section of this chapter, but the idea that the ostentatious Websterian imagery in 'Whispers of immortality' – 'Daffodil bulbs instead of balls / Stared from the sockets of the eyes!' – is a symptom of a kind of mental 'lust' or 'luxury' is one that is made quite plain in the later writing. 'The beautiful line for its own sake is a luxury', Eliot comments in the Yeats lecture of 1940 (quoted above, p. 9), and he does not use this latter noun idly; poetical excess is commensurate with any other kind of hyper-sensuality, and the equation between the purging of style and the purgation of self is always present; compared with the ornateness of the early work, for example, 'Ash-Wednesday' is clad in a kind of linguistic hair-shirt. In 'Burnt Norton' the exponent of the classic style is always seen as being called upon to renege, being tempted to don theatricality and to swerve from the path that runs between different types of verbal excess, his temptation paralleling that of Christ:

> The Word in the desert
> Is most attacked by voices of temptation,
> The crying shadow in the funeral dance,
> The loud lament of the disconsolate chimera.
>
> (*CPP*, p. 175)

If for Adolf Loos, to recall the discussion of chapter 1, ornament equalled crime, and if for Gropius it equalled 'concealment' or deception, then for their fellow 'puritan' Eliot it equalled sin and temptation.[12] This equation already seems to me implicit in early poems like 'Whispers of immortality' and *The Waste Land*, so that it should come as no surprise that as early as 1924 Eliot is severely castigating the extravagances of the Elizabethans, rounding on 'their artistic greediness, their desire for every sort of effect together, their unwillingness to accept any limitation and abide by it'.[13]

The later Eliot's questioning of Shakespearian influence is surely also one of the reasons why he does not participate in that conspicuous 1930s enthusiasm for the poetry of Gerard Manley Hopkins. Eliot's objection to the 'exaggerated' claims for Hopkins's influence on modern poetry, on the grounds that his work transgresses the canons of the common style – being 'very doubtfully adaptable to what anyone else has to say' – is probably directed at critics like Read, Grigson and Day Lewis.[14] The former reiterated the idea in 1935 that 'no poet of recent times is likely to exercise such a potent influence', and Hopkins (along with Eliot himself) is one of the heroes of Day Lewis's *A Hope for Poetry* (1934), being mainly responsible for the 'new arrangements and cadences of words' in the modern period.[15] Day Lewis stresses Hopkins's 'decorated verbal accumulation' (p. 6), and it is easy enough to find rather self-conscious examples of the Hopkinsesque in the early poetry of people like Auden, Rex Warner and Day Lewis himself, though it seems to me, as I show in chapter 4, that there is a reciprocity of stylistic influence between Eliot and Auden at least in the 1930s that far outweighs any potential division between them set up by Hopkins. The 'neo-Shakespearian' quality of Hopkins's language is discussed at length by Leavis in *New Bearings in English Poetry* in 1932; his interest in an Anglo-Saxon-based vocabulary would also contradict the stress in Eliot's common style on a 'Europeanized' English, as outlined in chapter 1.[16] Further account of the divergence between Hopkins and Eliot is given below (p. 129).

Thus far, it seems that Eliot's insistence on escaping from Shakespeare has been fairly straightforward: Dryden is a better model for later blank-verse dramatists, Shakespearian influence has led to 'distortion' and excess, and neo-Shakespearians like Hopkins meet with a very cool reception. And yet, in the 1930s and 1940s, Eliot's critical writing, if not his poetry and drama, is full of tributes to Shakespeare; more so, indeed, than his early criticism. Even in the Dante essay, where Dante's economy is being contrasted favourably with the verbal luxuriance that recurrently tempts English poets, we are reminded that 'only Shakespeare can be so "poetical" without giving any effect of overloading, or distracting us from the main issue' and are given in evidence of this the line from *Othello*, 'Put up your bright swords or the dew will rust them' (I.ii.60; *SE*, pp. 248–9). 'Great Wits sometimes may gloriously offend': there is, of course, a tradition for neo-classicists making the honourable exception.[17] The 'Milton I' essay of 1936 is similarly warm in Shakespeare's praise (*OPAP*, pp. 139–40).

As we approach the period of the *Quartets'* completion, however, Eliot begins to strive much harder to bring Shakespeare himself into the classicist camp. In 'Poetry and drama' (1951), Eliot makes use of two unpublished lectures delivered in the late 1930s on 'The development of Shakespeare's verse', and here he is concerned to stress, not Shakespeare's 'poeticality', but his ability to write lines of the utmost simplicity, to achieve, as in the opening scene of *Hamlet*, that 'transparent' quality that characterizes the common style (*OPAP*, p. 75).[18] In fact Shakespeare's career is seen as thus far following a similar pattern to Eliot's own; by the time he wrote the balcony scene of *Romeo and Juliet*, 'the stiffness, the artificiality, the poetic decoration, of his early verse has finally given place to a simplification to the language of natural speech' (p. 88). This is the Shakespeare who *can* be followed, if not necessarily strictly imitated, for 'no poet has begun to master dramatic verse' until he can write lines of a like transparency (p. 75). This was not, however, the end of Shakespeare's achievement, for in 'The music of poetry' (1942), Eliot sees the movement from 'artificiality to simplicity' as characterizing Shakespeare's first period alone, whereas the 'later plays move from simplicity towards elaboration', culminating in *Cymbeline, The Winter's Tale, Pericles* and *The Tempest* (*OPAP*, p. 36). 'The music of poetry' indeed sees poetry's function as a constant historical oscillation between two tasks; in some periods it must purge itself of outmoded ornamentation and aspire to the simplicity and naturalness of common speech, but once this has been achieved it must then explore the possibilities of elaborating and complicating this established poetic idiom. What this implies, of course, is that in 1942, the year of this essay and the year of the *Quartets'* completion, Eliot had come to understand the classicist purging towards a common style as part of a two-way process, a necessary prerequisite to a new elaboration of that style. The overall movement of ornamentation → simplicity → elaboration is again expressed in 'Poetry and drama':

> I also believe that while the self-education of a poet trying to write for the theatre seems to require a long period of disciplining his poetry, and putting it, so to speak, on a very thin diet in order to adapt it to the needs of the stage he may find that later . . . he can dare to make more liberal

use of poetry and take greater liberties with ordinary
colloquial speech.

(pp. 85-6)

This movement towards and then away from simplicity fully
explains the supposed inconsistencies between the two Milton
essays of 1936 and 1947. In a period like the 1930s, with Eliot
striving to establish the common style, Milton's poetic individualism could only be anathema; but what of the situation in
1947?

> If the poetry of the rest of this century takes the line of
> development which seems to me . . . the right course, it
> will discover new and more elaborate patterns of a diction
> now established. In this search it might have much to
> learn from Milton's extended verse structure; it might
> also avoid the danger of a *servitude* to colloquial speech and
> to current jargon.

('Milton II', OPAP, p. 160)

'New and more elaborate patterns of a diction now established':
what else could Eliot mean by this but the idea that the *Quartets*
(but not perhaps these alone – see chapter 4) *had* satisfactorily
established the common style, and that future freedom was
now possible within the formal constraints that they had laid
down? 'Little Gidding' announces the end of the classic quest,
in the lines quoted in the previous chapter (p. 10), inserting
those lines as parenthesis within the statement

> And every phrase
> And sentence that is right. . .
> Every phrase and every sentence is an end and a beginning,
> Every poem an epitaph.

(CPP, p. 197)

The *Quartets* are the realization of, and hence epitaph on,
modern classicism, the end, if you like, of stage one, and the
beginning of the movement towards elaboration in stage two.
Milton himself is referred to in 'Little Gidding' as now 'folded in
a single party', his previously 'outlawed' poetry now recuper-
ated within Eliot's overall strategy.[19]

Returning to Shakespeare, we see how his career represents
the necessary motion of poetry itself towards, and away from,

simplicity, and that in achieving this he 'carried out, in one short lifetime, the task of two poets' ('The music of poetry', p. 35); for Eliot himself there was to be no stage two, so to speak, no elaboration of the common style after the *Quartets*. Although then the direct echoes of Shakespeare became progressively rarer in Eliot's poetry, his influence, in Eliot's eyes, became much more important, to result in a debt to him akin to that to Dante, for 'the important debt does not occur in relation to the number of places in one's writings to which a critic can point a finger, and say, here and there he wrote something which he could not have written unless he had had Dante in mind'. The greatest debts, in fact, 'are not always the most evident' ('What Dante means to me', p. 126). I should stress here, however, that Eliot's acceptance of Shakespeare during the 1930s is founded on an understanding of Shakespeare himself as fundamentally exemplifying the 'classic' enterprise; even the elaboration of the late plays remains anchored within common speech ('The music of poetry', p. 31). And I should also note, to anticipate the next section of this chapter, that the *Quartets'* achievement of the classical goal is still, in Eliot's eyes, only relative on several counts; enough to stabilize an idiom, but not to achieve the 'absolute' classic.

Eliot's classicizing of Shakespeare in the 1930s makes more sense if we understand the entirely antithetical and often nationalistic requisitions upon him that Eliot was resisting, such as his being championed as the key figure and prime exemplar of the 'romanticism' that, in John Middleton Murry's eyes, *is* the English cultural tradition.[20] In Murry's later monograph on Shakespeare, that tradition is one that is seen as celebrating the multifarious and mysterious 'vortex' of 'life itself', that mocks conventional morality and order: 'to enter that vortex is to plunge into chaos: a chaos of the world of order and of moral law in which men long to believe. Of such a world Shakespeare eventually knows nothing, or spares nothing.' Thus Shakespeare, like life, 'has no pattern', a hero-anarchist defying, as it were, those like Eliot who mean to search for a pattern in him.[21] A similar though somewhat less anarchical Shakespeare is found in Herbert Read's essay, also of 1936, that introduces the volume *Surrealism*. Here there is an obvious attack on certain of Eliot's positions on Shakespeare, though at a date when Eliot's classicizing of him had yet to be fully worked out. For Read, Shakespeare is indeed the great 'anti-classical' rebel, classicism being identified throughout with political repression; 'any return to the standards which tended to exalt a Dryden or a Pope above Shakespeare' would be synonymous with the curtailing of liberty in general, and it is the Shakespeare who 'breaks all the academic rules' whose work operates as a kind of safeguard against the rule of the state.[22] 'The rehabilitation of Shakespeare's genius', Read continues, 'after the class and classical denigration of the seventeenth and eighteenth centuries, has been the work of specifically romantic critics, beginning with Coleridge and ending, for the moment, with Middleton Murry' (p. 47). Although Eliot on occasion seems to partake of this classical 'denigration' of Shakespeare – as, for example, in his declaration of never having seen 'a cogent refutation' of Rymer's objections to *Othello* (footnote to 'Hamlet', *SE*, p. 141) – and although, as we saw above, he is on record in 1931 as preferring Dryden to Shakespeare as a *model* for practising playwrights, he had never 'elevated' Dryden above Shakespeare as such, and Read would have been aware, in 1936, that any such denigration was more than offset by the recurrence of handsome enough tributes to Shakespeare throughout Eliot's writing (notably, again, in the 1929 'Dante' essay). Rather than exclude or denigrate Shakespeare, Eliot was to work from the late 1930s onwards, as we have seen, to bring Shakespeare into the classicist camp; and some stimulus to this must have come from the polemical 'romanticization' of him we find in the above two writers. Read indeed states quite simply the battle between a Shakespeare-inspired 'principle of life, of creation, of liberation' that is the 'romantic spirit' and of 'order, of control and of repression' that is classicism (*Surrealism*, p. 26). Classicism is 'the intellectual counterpart of political tyranny . . . wherever the blood of martyrs stains the ground, there you will find a doric column or perhaps a statue of Minerva' (p. 23); thus 'the norms of classical art' are for Read a means of political control or repression (p. 25) in the manner touched on in chapter 1. With Murry and Read, Shakespeare emerges as ungovernable, anti-establishment, illimitable, iconoclastic, carnivalesque, and it is easy to see why an introduction to surrealism should dwell on him for so long. Eliot's insistence that Shakespeare does gradually come to observe the norm of the 'common style' may not seem to be an enormously authoritarian requisition upon him until, perhaps, we realize the full ideological import of this notion of the common style, which the rest of this chapter traces via the *Quartets*.

The nationalistic implications in Murry's comment above, where Shakespeare exemplifies the specifically 'English', are extremely prominent in much writing on him at this time, though never embraced, of course, in Eliot's Europeanizing aesthetic. In the war-conscious 1930s and early 1940s Shakespeare took on for many something of the nationalist symbolic status that Dante had had in the Italian *Risorgimento*, as in G. Wilson Knight's assertion that 'our own deepest and most royal selfhood . . . [is] something we shall find in Shakespeare, and in Shakespeare alone – the voice of England'.[23] In chapter 3, I shall be looking more specifically at the nationalistic element attaching to English 'Shakespearian' landscape and Eliot's rejection of this, while in the remainder of this chapter I shall consider Eliot's own rather contrary understanding of 'the voice of England' by way of a more detailed examination of the classicism of *Four Quartets*.

'STILL AND STILL MOVING'

If the *Quartets* do arrive at the standards of 'classic' art, as Eliot understands the term, it is important to stress that the poem harnesses the notion of an achieved classical 'stasis' to a dynamic pressing onwards beyond this goal in accordance with the recurrent ornamentation → purification → elaboration pattern discussed in the previous section: 'We must be still and still moving' ('East Coker'). This 'dynamic classicism' finds parallels in the visual arts of the 1930s; if Eliot in adopting it is conducting a debate with various neo-Romantics, he is also arguing against other less subtle classicizing positions too.

In 'What is a classic?' (1944), Eliot is in fact expressing an ambivalence towards classic art which must seem, to many of his readers, a rather tiresome prevarication:

> My own opinion is, that we have no classic age, and no classic poet, in English; that when we see why this is so, we have not the slightest reason for regret; but that, nevertheless, we must maintain the classic ideal before our eyes.
>
> (*OPAP*, p. 59)

Virgil could reach the absolute fruition of the common style in the *Aeneid*, but only because Latin is a 'more homogeneous' language than English, which, 'being the most various of great languages in its constituents, tends to variety rather than perfection' (p. 66). 'Perfection' here, in the sense of 'finish', is a rather double-edged quality; in realizing the 'genius' of the language, Virgil left his successors little to do, and 'no great development was possible' in Latin poetry after him (pp. 63–4): 'it is not merely that a classic poet exhausts the language, but that an exhaustible language is the kind that may produce a classic poet' (p. 65).

There is no danger that the English language is as yet 'exhaustible' – it 'still contains, perhaps, more unexplored possibilities' (p. 66) – and therefore no danger that the mixed blessing of the absolute classic can at present be achieved. If 'Little Gidding' has arrived at the common style, 'where every word is at home', and so forth, this is not a style to dampen future exploration but rather, as we saw in the previous section, an idiom that Eliot prescribes to his successors as the basis for further 'elaboration'. 'Little Gidding' already anticipates 'next year's words' and the new 'voice' that will speak them. In the balcony scene of *Romeo and Juliet*, Shakespeare achieved 'a perfection of verse which, being perfection, neither he nor anyone else could excel – for this particular purpose' ('Poetry and drama', p. 88); but such 'simplification' having been achieved, the resources of the English language now permitted Shakespeare to begin the counter-movement towards elaboration, with no danger, as with Virgil's Latin, that this perfection was a dead-end. Eliot's preaching the classic measure in English is then a kind of liberal authoritarianism, providing a check on poetic individualism but encouraging freedom within prescribed limits. His doubts about Pope's classicism involving 'the exclusion of some greater potentialities of English verse' ('What is a classic?', p. 60) contrast with the much more straightforward pro-classicist position of a work like Sherard Vines's *The Course of English Classicism* (1930), where Pope is established as a kind of enduring centre: 'the further from Pope, the wider are floodgates opened to the tide of all that can excite the pens of cosmically disposed sciolists and mystagogues'.[24] The claim then that for Eliot Virgil occupied a similar centrality as 'the perfect poet in the perfect culture', as has been done, without realizing the limitations Eliot attached to the concepts of 'perfection' and centrality, is to misread 'What is a classic?'.[25]

This notion of a standard to be universally striven for, and at the same time never reached, is one that occurs in much of Eliot's social criticism and writing on culture of the late 1930s and 1940s, as well as in his literary work. In *The Idea of a Christian Society* (1939), the inability to establish the classic word is rephrased as the inability to establish the Word:

> we have to remember that the Kingdom of Christ on earth will never be realized, and also that it is always being realized . . . whatever reform or revolution we carry out, the result will always be a sordid travesty of what human society should be. . . . In such a society as I imagine, as in any that is not petrified, there will be innumerable seeds of decay.
>
> (p. 79)

Variations on the need to reach after the unreachable are played most exhaustively, however, in *Notes Towards the Definition of Culture* (1948), the strategy being summed up in the very title; 'definition', like 'perfection', is something to be moved *towards*, not achieved. Here, the ideal of an international 'world culture' is a necessary aspiration for all individual nations, though a 'nightmare' if ever reached: 'we should have a humanity de-humanised'. Rather, 'we must aspire to a common world culture, which will yet not diminish the particularity of the constituent parts'; and 'we are the more likely to be able to stay loyal to the ideal of the unimaginable world culture, if we recognise all the difficulties, the practical impossibility, of its realisation' (pp. 62–3). In a word, 'a constant struggle between the centripetal and the centrifugal forces is desirable' (p. 82); 'we need variety in unity: not the unity of organisation, but the unity of nature' (p. 120). Such thinking exactly reproduces the theories of classic style we have looked at thus far: the need to work towards a literary standard that should never be reached; the oscillation between simplification and elaboration, like a continuous centrifugal/centripetal movement; and the variety in unity of individual poets working in the common style.

Eliot's emphasis on this two-way motion towards and away from the 'centre', is what separates him from the classicism of a figure who obviously influenced him a great deal, Irving Babbitt. Babbitt's *Rousseau and Romanticism* (1919) is full of talk about 'centres' and 'peripheries', the former representing ethical and cultural consensus, the latter the Rousseau-inspired insistence on individual freedom and self-assertion that Babbitt deplores: the Romantic imagination 'is not drawn back to any ethical centre and so is free to wander wild in its own empire of chimeras'.[26] For Babbitt, 'the effect on a mature observer of an age so entirely turned from the One to the Many as that in which we are living must be that of a prodigious peripheral richness joined to a great central void' (p. 366). Babbitt is not concerned to project the central 'One' as any kind of religious principle but is concerned rather with notions of centrism in social and cultural life. He defines the classicist as one who

> having decided what is normal either for man or some particular class of men . . . takes this normal 'nature' for his model and proceeds to imitate it. Whatever accords with the model he has thus set up he pronounces natural or probable, whatever on the other hand departs too far from what he conceives to be the normal type or the normal sequence of cause and effect he holds to be 'improbable' and unnatural or even, if it attains an extreme of abnormality, 'monstrous'.
>
> (pp. 16–17)

Babbitt's support for this kind of 'centripetal' outlook, a consensus movement towards the normative and away from the 'wildness' of the periphery, has a confidence and clarity about it that differs markedly from Eliot's more cautious classicism. In *Rousseau and Romanticism* Babbitt seizes on the 'affront' to 'the good sense of mankind' involved in the more excessive paradoxes of Christianity: 'Pascal falls into this excess when he says that sickness is the natural state of the Christian. As a result of its supreme emphasis on humility Christianity from the start inclined unduly perhaps towards this type of paradox. It is hardly worth while, as Goethe said, to live seventy years in this world if all that one learn here below is only folly in the sight of God' (p. 246). Babbitt's humanism, his belief in the possibility of human amelioration through self-discipline, self-criticism and education, mixed, it is true, with 'an element of religious insight' (p. 380), is completely at odds with the kind of 'excessive' Christianity which he would see lying at the heart of the *Quartets*. Eliot's constant disillusion with human endeavour means that the various ideal centres he sets up can never be reached; the 'Catholic philosophy of disillusion' which he thought he shared with Dante ('not to expect more from *life* than it can give or more from *human* beings than they can give; to look to *death* for what life cannot give': 'Dante', p. 275) means a 'classicism' inevitably impaired by 'centrifugal' tendencies. As I said above, there is a more or less complete ignoring of Dante's own humanism in Eliot's assessment of him, of, for example, Dante's projection in the *Monarchia* of the earthly felicity that is conceivably achievable under an imperial peace for those able thereby to practise the moral and intellectual virtues without impediment. In *The Idea of a Christian Society* Eliot does indeed talk of a 'natural end of man', namely 'virtue and well-being in community', as well as of the supernatural end of beatitude (p. 62), but the rest of his account of this 'natural end' is a set of dampening provisos, as indicated above, as to its non-attainability.[27] It contrasts markedly with Dante's fervent Aristotelianism, his belief in the 'beatitudinem . . . huius vitae' (*Monarchia* III. xv. 7) which even in the *Commedia* is not wholly subordinated to the supernatural end of beatitude, in Eliot's phrase. Kenelm Foster has discussed at length the 'two' Dantes, the humanist and the Christian, and their imperfect reconciliation;[28] in Eliot's writing, and particularly in the *Quartets*, we not only have a Christianity largely devoid of any humanist element (which, in the guise of Puritanism, is at least a historically familiar phenomenon) but we also have a would-be 'classicism' divorced from humanism, as discussed in chapter 1, a far more peculiar development. I leave detailed discussion of the 'non-humanism' of the *Quartets* to my section on landscape in chapter 3.

Returning to Babbitt, we find that the solution he gives to the problem of 'the relation between humanism and religion' lies in 'looking upon them both as only different stages in the same path' (p. 380). The immense gulf and severance Eliot places between human achievement and true 'beatitude' leads him, however, to reject this position completely, and his attack on Babbitt and affiliation with Hulme are clearly stated at the

end of his essay 'Second thoughts about humanism' of 1929, in
which he stresses his belief in the 'radical imperfection' of man:

> I cannot help feeling that Mr Foerster and even Mr
> Babbitt are nearer to the view of Rousseau than they are
> to the religious view. For it is not enough to chastise the
> romantic visions of perfectibility, as they do; the modern
> humanistic view implies that man is either perfectible, or
> capable of indefinite improvement. . . . It is to the
> immense credit of Hulme that he found out for himself
> that there is an *absolute* to which Man can *never* attain.
>
> (*SE*, p. 490)

This 'absolute' is posited in Babbitt in terms of a 'centre' as we
have seen; in the above essay in which Eliot criticizes Norman
Foerster, he quotes a paragraph from Foerster's book *American
Criticism* which begins:

> This centre to which humanism refers everything, this
> centripetal energy which counteracts the multifarious
> centrifugal impulses, this magnetic will which draws the
> flux of our sensations toward it while itself remaining at
> rest, is the reality which gives rise to religion.
>
> (*SE*, p. 482)[29]

It seems we are back at the 'Chinese jar still / Mov[ing]
perpetually in its stillness', the emblem of classic form which
the *Quartets* themselves are emulating; what we now have to
consider, in looking at the poem, is the deliberate 'centrifugal'
countermovement Eliot also insists on, which marks his disagreement with the humanist belief in an attainable, temporal
absolute. In other words *Four Quartets*, whilst striving towards
that classic form which is the 'only' way to express the timeless
still point, is, like all temporal creations, radically imperfect; and
the poem is to some degree bent, in ways we shall now
examine, on a kind of deliberate non-realization of classic form
too.

On an obvious level it is clear that the *Quartets* combine
tightly 'chiselled' and rhythmically regular passages – the
'Garlic and sapphires in the mud' section from 'Burnt Norton',
for example – with much looser, 'prosy', discursive passages in
which 'form' has become rather more elastic:

48

> There is, it seems to us,
> At best, only a limited value
> In the knowledge derived from experience.
> The knowledge imposes a pattern, and falsifies,
> For the pattern is new in every moment.
>
> ('East Coker', *CPP*, p. 179)

Critics of the poem might be divided into those who see the latter type of passage as a symptom of poetic weakness, where 'the tension seems to drop unduly', in Derek Traversi's phrase, leading the reader to the 'occasional suspicion of imaginative exhaustion', and those who see such a dropping of tension as deliberate, with the introduction of 'designedly flat and arid passages' as G. Rostrevor Hamilton puts it.[30] I side very much with this second camp, as will be clear from the preceding part of this section; the formal regularity of the *Quartets* is subject to a recurrent dismantling in the interests of the manifold doubts relating to 'perfection', described above. 'East Coker' seems to be the key quartet here; more than any of the others, it assaults its own procedures, throwing up constant recriminations on the practice of poetry itself. In part ii it famously disclaims the formal opening lyric:

> That was a way of putting it – not very satisfactory:
> A periphrastic study in a worn-out poetical fashion,
> Leaving one still with the intolerable wrestle
> With words and meanings.
>
> (*CPP*, p. 179)

The opening of part ii of 'East Coker' is surely no more a 'periphrastic' and 'worn-out' study than that which opens part ii of 'Burnt Norton', which is allowed to pass unscathed; the second quartet proceeds, however, to the lines quoted earlier, on the falsity of experience, which

> imposes a pattern, and falsifies,
> For the pattern is new in every moment
> And every moment is a new and shocking
> Valuation of all we have been.
>
> (*CPP*, p. 179)

This statement has obvious important consequences for the *Quartets'* conception of their own form; the classic keynote of an overall structural emphasis rather than attention to 'local' decoration implies that the entire pattern of the poem must be envisaged, to some degree, at the outset, yet here we have the insistence that that pattern can be created only in the very process of the poem's construction, the result of constant and repeated interventions and modifications. Every moment in the poem is a new and shocking valuation of all it has been. 'It was only in writing "East Coker" that I began to see the *Quartets* as a set of four', Eliot has told us, and this realization has obvious significance for the relation between the second quartet and 'Burnt Norton', the bit of the 'pattern' already in existence.[31] The debate between the two parts, and the status of 'Burnt Norton', are discussed further below.

'East Coker' continues in its almost obsessive prosiness, its dismantling of any 'classic' formal finish:

> You say I am repeating
> Something I have said before. I shall say it again.
> Shall I say it again?
>
> (*CPP*, p. 181)

and it opens the concluding section with a kind of declaration of poetic hopelessness,

> Trying to learn to use words, and every attempt
> Is a wholly new start, and a different kind of failure
> Because one has only learnt to get the better of words
> For the thing one no longer has to say, or the way in
>   which
> One is no longer disposed to say it. And so each venture
> Is a new beginning, a raid on the inarticulate
> With shabby equipment always deteriorating
> In the general mess of imprecision of feeling,
> Undisciplined squads of emotion.
>
> (*CPP*, p. 182)

With its constant reminders of all the obstacles to achieving classic form, 'East Coker' arrives at the formulation that describes, not the classicism of perfect 'finish', but that of endless approximation, half-realization: 'We must be still and still moving'.

If in the process of 'East Coker' the *Quartets* arrive at an

understanding of a less finished classicism then, it follows that
such an understanding is not a feature of 'Burnt Norton',
published four years earlier, and that, as I say, 'East Coker' has
developed insights not present in its predecessor. It is true that
in 'Burnt Norton' we have the 'still' and 'moving' paradox, as in
the Chinese jar itself, but here it seems to me that the idea of
movement is much more easily accommodated within an overall stability of form; the motion of the jar inscribes a harmonious circle, so to speak, which can thus be equated with
stillness.[32] And indeed 'Burnt Norton' is a much more formal
poem and far more impersonal than 'East Coker'; it avoids the
extreme rhythmical looseness of its successor, and has a
homogeneity of tone and diction that does not admit the
internal debate and contrast of parts we spoke of above in 'East
Coker'. We might compare, for example, the final sections of
the two quartets: the regular, concise line-lengths of 'The detail
of the pattern is movement . . .', etc., with the less formally
disciplined 'Home is where one starts from. . .'. The obvious
reason for this contrast is of course that as far as we know
'Burnt Norton' was written as a single, self-contained poem,
arriving at a conclusion in part v that returns to the dilemma
outlined in part i of being simultaneously present in and absent
from the rose-garden. As it stands it has a circularity and
wholeness which do not necessarily require any further completion, whereas the ending of 'East Coker' with its commitment to further exploration through 'the vast waters' already
seems to envisage 'The Dry Salvages'. When 'Burnt Norton'
first appeared as the concluding poem in Eliot's *Collected Poems
1909–1935* (1936), its unitary quality emphasized that Eliot saw
it as an 'end'; with 'East Coker' it perforce changed status and
became a beginning, and its wholeness had to be harmonized to
a larger whole. 'East Coker' acts as a kind of tow-rope, pulling
the first poem into the larger assembly and in the process
unsettling positions and conclusions which it seems to have
regarded as 'finished'. Thus 'East Coker' questions, as we have
said, the confidence in formal pattern, within which movement
is safely inscribed in the opening of the conclusion to 'Burnt
Norton' quoted above; it also offsets the picture of stellar
harmony and reconciliation at the opening of 'Burnt Norton' ii
with an account of 'constellated wars' in the equivalent position. In 'East Coker' 'movement' is a much more sprawling,

untidy, less easily accommodated affair; indeed, much more 'centrifugal'.[33]

'Burnt Norton' is not, however, a more 'finished' poem solely because it was envisaged at the time of its creation as a self-contained whole; far more than the other three quartets it partakes of the prevailing aesthetic of abstraction current in the mid-1930s and discussed in chapter 1. In its insistence on 'the form, the pattern', in its impersonally 'abstract' subject-matter, in its evocation of the universal language of Rome through the deployment of the Latinate nouns listed above (p. 11) – a feature less in evidence in the later quartets – it has a homogeneity and severity typical of its historical moment. It protests too about language's unwillingness to subject itself to classic discipline:

> Words strain,
> Crack and sometimes break, under the burden,
> Under the tension, slip, slide, perish,
> Decay with imprecision, will not stay in place,
> Will not stay still. Shrieking voices
> Scolding, mocking, or merely chattering,
> Always assail them. The Word in the desert
> Is most attacked by voices of temptation,
> The crying shadow in the funeral dance,
> The loud lament of the disconsolate chimera.
>
> (*CPP*, p. 175)

By 'East Coker' the battle to make words 'stay still' has been largely given up, the form that would impose such stillness having become much looser, as described above. Eliot's essays from the time of the later quartets show a marked acquiescence in the mobility of language:

> a language is always changing; its developments in vocabulary, in syntax, pronunciation and intonation – even, in the long run, its deterioration – must be accepted by the poet and made the best of.[34]

In 1944 he criticizes Johnson and his contemporaries for their belief in some timelessly correct poetic diction, their ignorance of 'the notion of the language as perpetually in change', at the same time as he approves of their practice of a common style

('Johnson as critic and poet', *OPAP*, p. 185). By 1950, in 'The aims of education', he can state quite bluntly that

> the wobbliness of words is not something to be deplored. We should not try to pin a word down to one meaning, which it should have at all times, in all places, and for everybody.
>
> (*TCTC*, p. 65)

This seems to me to directly contradict the passage from 'Burnt Norton' quoted above, where the wobbliness of words is certainly deplored. If during the writing of 'East Coker' Eliot came to terms with this and a greater formal 'wobbliness' (to retain his word) is in evidence, we can understand why the last two quartets contain no animadversions on the difficulty or unsatisfactoriness of poetic language; indeed, 'Little Gidding' seems to exult at its arrival at the desired common style, where 'every word is at home' and so on. What it seems that Eliot learns during the writing of the *Quartets* is the untenability of the austere, uncompromising 'classicism' of 'Burnt Norton'; what he finally arrives at is a classicism that looks more sympathetically on change and movement, that accepts, in a sense, its relativity. I claimed at the end of the previous section that Eliot regarded the *Quartets* as having established a diction that sees itself not as 'finished' but as the basis for future elaboration, a diction caught up in a constant dialectical process; the poet's language can never be absolutely 'still', only periodically stabilized. When the necessary purification has been achieved, elaboration can begin; ends are thus automatically dissolved into beginnings. But this latter formulation enters the *Quartets* only with 'East Coker'; the notion of what I termed 'dynamic classicism' at the beginning of this section is not in evidence in 'Burnt Norton'. In 'The aims of education' Eliot treads a familiar middle ground between celebrating the plurality of the individual word, its different meanings in different contexts, in short, its 'wobbliness', and yet maintaining the need to be 'always trying . . . if we are to think at all, to fix a permanent meaning for every word' (*TCTC*, p. 75). Eliot's description of this latter attempt is accompanied by nostalgic glances at languages like Latin:

> It is one of the advantages of the study of a dead language

that it is more manageable, that the words in it have come
to the limit of their meaning: there they are in the texts,
and their meaning can be no more than what the authors,
during the time in which that language flourished, have
given them.

(TCTC, p. 74)

He immediately adds, however, that 'we do not want our
language to become a dead language' (pp. 74–5). Nevertheless,
the striving for a final definition of each word, like that for the
Kingdom of Christ on earth, or for world culture, is another
instance of that necessary 'centripetal' movement which must
constantly struggle with the equally necessary 'centrifugal'
forces of plurality, individualism and regionalism. 'Burnt
Norton's aspirations are all, so to speak, centripetal, yearning
frustratedly towards that still point where the Word is found
and towards that definitive form and language that can 'reach'
the stillness. Just as temporality is categorized as 'ridiculous' in
the final lines of 'Burnt Norton', so the temporality of language
– its change and 'decay' – is deplored, and not, as later, accepted.
The classic word, in its aspiration towards some still centre,
some final definition, is assailed by a plurality of 'voices': the
'merely chattering' voices of spoken discourse, insisting on
their own rights to appropriate language; and, as I suggested
above (p. 37), the 'voices of temptation' representing the earlier
poetic luxuriance that the chastity of Eliot's later style has
turned its back on. There is also the loud lament of the
'disconsolate chimera' assailing the Word; as Mikhail Bakhtin
(whose analysis of classicism is considered at some length in the
following section) notes, the chimera, in its fantastic eclecticism
(combining human, animal and vegetable forms) was formerly
'the quintessence of the grotesque' to the classicist poetic; in
the seventeenth century La Bruyère used it as a 'significant
symbol' to characterize the monstrueux assemblage of the work of
Rabelais:

> The chimera is grotesque; in classical aesthetics there was
> no place for it . . . La Bruyère . . . is used to conceive being
> as something finished, stable, completed, clear and firm.
> He draws a dividing line between all bodies and objects.[35]

The chimera is the enemy of finality, of definition. Yet even in referring to 'the loud lament of the disconsolate chimera', 'Burnt Norton' suffers no disruption to its decorum and even-ness of rhythm, for the line in no way creates the chimera's voice; the formal and Latinate diction, consistent throughout the poem, actually embodies the resistance to 'temptation' it discusses, and the same with the other voices referred to in the poem (including the 'sea voices' of 'The Dry Salvages'). The contrast with *The Waste Land* is instructive, for in that poem we have precisely the incorporation of plural disruptive voices (including beast/bird sounds: 'Jug jug jug jug jug jug', 'Co co rico co co rico') which makes that poem polyphonous in a way the *Quartets* cannot possibly be. As opposed to 'Burnt Norton' the later three quartets work much more with temporality rather than straining against it; there can be no final return to the Garden through timeless magical doors but only through the discipline of prayer and humility practised in time; and 'history' enters the *Quartets* from 'East Coker' onwards to give valuable exemplars of holiness, reconciliation and *vanitas mundi*. All temporal change, including the changes in language, 'must be accepted by the poet and made the best of', in the words of the 1942 essay quoted above.

'Burnt Norton', however, seems not to have arrived at this realization; indeed in its desire to discipline language into univocal order and its resistance to polyphony it provides a perfect example of a classicist poetic as formulated by Bakhtin:

> For classicism, only the word of language exists, 'no one's word', a material word which is part of the poetic lexicon, and this word passes directly from the treasurehouse of poetic language into the monologic context of a given poetic utterance. Thus a stylistics nurtured on the soil of classicism recognizes only the life of a word in a single self-enclosed context. It ignores those changes that take place in a word during its passage from one concrete utterance to another.[36]

The strain of practising such a thoroughgoing classicism is confessed to in 'Burnt Norton' itself, and it is no surprise that 'East Coker' modifies the positions taken up by the earlier poem in the ways described above nor that there is a fresh emphasis in the essays of the early 1940s on poetic language retaining vital links with the language of everyday speech (see the extracts from 'The music of poetry' quoted above, pp. 27–8). We should guard, however, against pushing Eliot too far into the opposite camp, as a writer actively embracing linguistic change and polyphony. As suggested above (p. 28), the diction of the *Quartets* remains founded on a 'placeless', unlocalized, bookish English, its homogeneity continuing to permit a heavy overall emphasis on form, the whole being underscored by nostalgia for classic languages like Latin where words 'have come to the limit of their meaning'.

Four Quartets attempts to incorporate a relationship then between 'centripetal' and 'centrifugal' forces, the necessity of the latter being recognized only in the post-'Burnt Norton' period. This 'dynamic classicism' is itself a significant departure from traditional classicist aesthetics, for one recurrent signification of classic art is its being identified as in some sense 'timeless', as representing a stasis and perfection absolved from, and often polarized against, the decay and imperfection associated with temporality. Keats's 'Grecian urn' and Browning's 'Old pictures in Florence' immediately spring to mind as treatments of this attitude towards the antique. Eliot himself adopts a similar attitude in praising the classicism of Valéry in 1924, and in particular the 'Cantique des colonnes' which manifests an 'indefinable difference' that guarantees its status:

> The indefinable difference is the difference between the fluid and the static: between that which is moving toward an end and that which knows its end and has reached it; which can afford to stand, changeless, like a statue.[37]

Similarly, in a *Criterion* Commentary of the same year Eliot defines a 'classic moment in literature' as 'surely a moment of *stasis*, when the creative impulse finds a form which satisfies the best intellect of the time, a moment when a type is produced'.[38] In his later classicism, as exemplified by the *Quartets*, stasis is acceptable only if involved in an interchange with movement, as we have seen, Eliot's brand of the classic seeking to incorporate that change and 'imperfection' that traditionally stand in antithesis to it.

Eliot's Christianity is a pertinent factor here. If the classic outlook is one that incorporates 'disillusion' and the recognition of original sin, then classic art, like all things postlapsarian, necessarily admits its imperfections too. However, the notion of a classic art or poetic diction as somehow absolved from temporality, which Eliot reprimands in Johnson (see above, p. 52), is one that continued to survive throughout the nineteenth and twentieth centuries, surfacing, for example, in the Keats and Browning poems referred to above. Tucker's *Life in Ancient Athens*, referred to in chapter 1, sees antique art as exemplifying the assertion of F. W. J. von Schelling that

> every growth of nature has but one moment of perfect beauty [and] . . . one moment of full existence. In this moment it is what it is in eternity. . . . Art, in that it presents the object in this moment, withdraws it from time, and causes it to display its pure being in the form of its eternal life.[39]

This idea of the momentary perfection of the temporal, caught by classic art, is one that Eliot's classicism cannot, of course, subscribe to; indeed, in *Four Quartets* the situation is rather the reverse. There, there are intrusions of the timeless into the temporal, and art remains a temporal institution which can only imperfectly record them through its formal 'pattern'; in so doing it reaches beyond its own limitations, and 'only through time time is conquered'. Whereas in von Schelling's formulation art can 'withdraw' its subject from time, itself thus becoming timeless, in Eliot's the 'timeless' subject is incorporated into time, the artwork confessing its own temporality. In architecture, the idea of a timelessly correct classicism continues to persist into the twentieth century and on into our own day. When Loos submitted the plan of a single, giant Doric column as his entry for the *Chicago Tribune* offices competition in 1922, he did so on the grounds that the unornamented severity of such a construction was a timelessly enduring tradition, whereas ornament was, so to speak, culture-specific, changing every few years at the whim of fashion, an assumption already present in 'Ornament and crime'.[40]

We saw in chapter 1 that the movement towards austerity and abstraction in modern design is often explicitly motivated by a desire to embody some underlying essence or reality beyond the flux of phenomena; by a progressive purging of ornamentation modern classicism is meant to finally arrive at pure, 'neo-Pythagorean' structure, becoming 'a-temporal' in the process, and thus in the eyes of some modern theorists ideologically value-free. This position is traced in the recent works of the architectural historian David Watkin by the critic Jules Lubbock, who contests Watkin's idea that architecture is ideologically innocent, and suggests that Watkin's admiration for the classical tradition is based on 'the ethical reason that it celebrates the Imperium of Western European and Catholic civilisation over Islam and all barbarisms'.[41] Such a description would tend to fit Eliot's classical enthusiasms, and the idea that classic art is a function of authoritarianism – already strenuously forwarded by Herbert Read (above, pp. 41–2) – is underlined in the discussion of the *Quartets* that concludes this chapter.

Although Eliot's classicism, especially in the *Quartets*, is harnessed to an extremely authoritarian world-view, his disbelief in the pretensions of secular power is at one with an aesthetic that can be said to undermine itself in various ways as discussed above. A suggestive parallel for the stasis-movement relation he is working with in the *Quartets* can be found in the theories of constructivism, at least as outlined in the English 'manifesto' of the movement, *Circle*, published by Faber in 1937. Mondrian's call is for abstract art to aspire to what he terms a 'dynamic equilibrium', the construction of 'a rhythm of mutual relations, of mutual forms or free lines'; as opposed to the 'static' equilibrium necessitated by portraying individual form, 'the equilibrium of which we speak in non-figurative art is not without movement of action but is on the contrary a continual movement'.[42] This 'still and still moving' aesthetic is perhaps best exemplified, however, by the theory and practice of Naum Gabo's 'kinetic sculpture', also represented in *Circle*. In discussing the *Victory of Samothrace* Gabo notes:

> in this sculpture the feeling of motion is an illusion and exists only in our minds. The real Time does not participate in this emotion; in fact it is timeless. To bring Time as a reality into our consciousness, to make it active and perceivable we need the real movement of substantial masses removable in space.[43]

Movement in Gabo's kinetic sculptures is not, however, uncircumscribed, but rather inscribed within an overall symmetry of form which has the kinesis pivoting about a constant centre (Plate 5). And in this 'limitation' of movement we come back to *Four Quartets*.

I have been maintaining in this section that the *Quartets* present in many ways a 'modified' classicism compared with traditional classicizing positions, and that in 'Burnt Norton' Eliot becomes aware of the problems attaching to the realization of 'absolute' classic art. The emphasis on form in 'Burnt Norton', with movement *controlled* by a still centre ('daylight / Investing form with lucid stillness / Turning shadow into transient beauty / With slow rotation suggesting permanence'), comes up against the 'centripetal' nature of language that will not submit to any final definition, that will not stay still. From 'East Coker' onwards the poem accepts much more fully the temporality of its own linguistic material, and conducts a kind of self-examination which results in the explicit confession of the impossibility of achieving any ultimate classic stasis. Yet it is clear that the *Quartets* are still committed to a *relative* classicism, and that this is celebrated in 'Little Gidding', the employment of the homogeneous, Latinate common style permitting the structural emphasis discussed at length in chapter 1. Ultimately, what I have been calling the 'centrifugal' elements throughout this section, movement and plurality of language and, as we shall see in the following section, regionalism, are safely accommodated within formal constraints that evoke the central still point, just as the movement of Gabo's sculptures is not random but centrally and harmoniously controlled. In the following section I discuss the *Quartets* in terms of Mikhail Bakhtin's work on the opposition between polyphony and plurality, on the one hand, and the 'monologism' of the classical outlook on the other, with the aim of emphasizing just how far, whatever his 'modifications', Eliot's work remains in the latter camp.

BAKHTIN AND THE POETICS OF CLASSICISM

I suggested above that the 'polyphony' of *The Waste Land* – 'He Do the Police in Different Voices', as parts i and ii were originally headed – is deliberately suppressed in Eliot's later poetry, in keeping with the classic emphasis on poetry being written in some normative common style, which displays, not the variety of the language, but its essential 'genius'. The tonal and stylistic homogeneity of the *Quartets* eschews, as Roman literature was held to have done in 'What is a classic?', a variety of tongues in sacrificing itself to realizing the one 'voice'; but it is a poem beset by a plurality of voices calling upon it to renege, from the 'voices of temptation' in 'Burnt Norton' to the 'sea voices' in 'The Dry Salvages'. Plural voices usually tend to be illicit and nefarious in Eliot's later poetry, as with the voices singing in the ears of the Magi, 'saying / That this was all folly' ('Journey of the Magi', *CPP*, p. 103), or as with the 'evil' spring in *The Family Reunion* that 'excites us with lying voices', in Harry's words (*CPP*, p. 309). Even when Eliot has to create a plurality of voices in the work of the 1930s, as of course in his dramatic writings with their different speakers, the result is hardly varied; *The Family Reunion* (1939), for example, possesses a stylistic homogeneity hardly less marked than that of the *Quartets*.

In his essay 'Poetry and drama' (1951), Eliot tells us how important it was for him to 'avoid any echo of Shakespeare' in writing his first play (*The Rock* aside) *Murder in the Cathedral* (1935) (*OPAP*, p. 80). We should certainly expect a work that is practically contemporary with 'Burnt Norton' (and indeed shares some lines with it) to shun such an influence, for the reasons given in the first section of this chapter.[44] Eliot felt that nineteenth-century verse dramatists had failed to approximate to the conversational idiom of their own day because their work was caught up in the toils of neo-Shakespearian blank verse; in order to remedy this, Eliot determined on 'an avoidance of too much iambic, some use of alliteration, and occasional unexpected rhyme' (p. 80). For *The Family Reunion* Eliot remained aware of the same danger; here the need to avoid Shakespeare and to 'find a rhythm close to contemporary speech' led him to devise

> a line of varying length and varying number of syllables, with a caesura and three stresses. The caesura and the stresses may come at different places, almost anywhere in the line; the stresses may be close together or well separated by light syllables; the only rule being that there must be one stress on one side of the caesura and two on the other.
>
> (*OPAP*, p. 82)

Whatever the success of this flexible but standardized line is in realizing the rhythm of contemporary speech, the result is certainly not the differentiation of contemporary voices. Eliot's line device leads in fact to the merging of all the characters together into one voice, or, as he himself put it, 'in retrospect I soon saw that I had given my attention to versification at the expense of plot and character' (ibid., p. 82). The following speech by Mary from part I, scene ii of *The Family Reunion* is illustrative of Eliot's theories in action:

> Well, there's something to be said for having an outsider;
> For what is more formal than a family dinner?
> An official occasion of uncomfortable people
> Who meet very seldom, making conversation.
> I am very glad if Dr. Warburton is coming.
> I shall have to sit between Arthur and John.
> Which is worse, thinking of what to say to John,
> Or having to listen to Arthur's chatter
> When he thinks he is behaving like a man of the world?
> Cousin Agatha, I want your advice.
>
> (*CPP*, p. 303)

Throughout the play, and indeed in the *Quartets*, there is a strong sense of the rhythmic dominance of the individual line: it is frequently end-stopped, often extremely caesura-conscious and rarely truncated, taking on a standardized quality that imposes uniformity on all the speaking parts. Eliot's avoidance in the play of prose sequences, or of any speedy interchanges of dialogue that might disrupt the rhythmic formality, emphasizes this homogeneity, as does his taking nearly all his characters from the same socio-economic background. The ritualistic quality that results from this standardization of voices is the ground-tone so to speak out of which, at moments of dramatic climax, the chant proper arises, as the four characters Charles, Amy, Violet and Gerald lose the individual voice completely in becoming merged into the Chorus. Of course each of these four speakers displays personal traits and even eccentricities which led one reviewer to praise the cast of aunts and uncles as being 'full of individuality', but this individuality is surely not found in their manner or tone of delivery.[45] One tends indeed to agree with Rostrevor Hamilton that *The Family Reunion* 'conveys an impression not far removed from that of monologue' (*The Tell-Tale Article*, p. 92).

In the *Quartets*, as in the play, the line tends to dominate as the rhythmic unit:

> deprivation
> And destitution of all property,
> Desiccation of the world of sense,
> Evacuation of the world of fancy,
> Inoperancy of the world of spirit. . .
>
> In the uncertain hour before the morning
> Near the ending of interminable night
> At the recurrent end of the unending. . .
>
> (*CPP*, p. 174, p. 193)

These two fragments from the first and the last quartet respectively would illustrate Hamilton's point that in the sequence as a whole the 'native energy of the verb [is] subdued', in keeping with Eliot's attempt to convey a meditative 'movement about a still centre, a static and deepening awareness' (p. 58). There is, overall, little variation of pace in the *Quartets*, in spite of 'East Coker's attempts, discussed in the previous section, to introduce a greater 'centrifugal' movement to the poem: although lyrics consisting of short lines are contrasted with lengthier, more discursive passages, individual lines of varying length are rarely intermixed; the poem is built up in sections of rhythmically similar line-units. The 'integrity' of the line is often emphasized by an avoidance of enjambment or the 'subduing', or indeed entire omittance, of the forward-pressing verb. Rhythmically then, as well as by means of its Latinate diction, the poem achieves a homogeneity that is necessary if 'form' is to be foregrounded, as the classic aesthetic requires. The idea of the importance of the 'standardized' line, as it applies to other poets in the 1930s besides Eliot, will be taken up again in chapter 4. We might note here that one of the possibilities of 'elaboration' of the *Quartets'* successful achievement of the common style that Eliot looked forward to was the subjugation of the line as the dominant rhythmical unit to the extended verse paragraph; this was one of the things that, in 1947, could now be learned from Milton, whose 'emphasis on the line structure is the minimum necessary to provide a counter-pattern to the period structure' ('Milton II', *OPAP*, p. 157). Any passage taken at random from *Paradise Lost* would show an exploitation of the rhythmic and grammatical opportunities enjambment provides in a manner that differs markedly from the *Quartets*.

The work of Eliot's classic period then is synonymous with a suppression of voices, of polyphony, and his setting up of the *Divine Comedy* as one of his great classic exemplars – there, 'if anywhere, we find the classic in a modern European language' ('What is a classic?', p. 60) – involves a complete obscuring of the many different voices and styles in Dante's work too, in the hypothesizing of the *Commedia* as a masterpiece of the homogeneous 'common style'.[46] Mikhail Bakhtin is surely correct in emphasizing, on the contrary, the pluralism of Dante's world, where what he calls 'multi-leveledness', the incorporation of different voices expressing different points of view, is seen as linking Dante with Dostoevsky: the latter's 'particular gift for hearing and understanding all voices immediately and simultaneously, a gift whose equal we find only in Dante, also permitted him to create the polyphonic novel'.[47] We have already seen, in 'Burnt Norton', Eliot's regret at the difficulties involved in imposing a monologic discipline on words, his protest at the multi-voicedness of language (see above, p. 52). The sentiment that art distils formal beauty out of the grossness of everyday plurality is also echoed in one of the choruses from *The Rock* (1934):

> Out of the meaningless practical shapes of all that is living
>   or lifeless
> Joined with the artist's eye, new life, new form, new
>   colour.
> Out of the sea of sound the life of music,
> Out of the slimy mud of words, out of the sleet and hail of
>   verbal imprecisions,
> Approximate thoughts and feelings, words that have
>   taken the place of thoughts and feelings,
> There spring the perfect order of speech, and the beauty
>   of incantation.
>
> (*CPP*, p. 164)

Just as in *The Rock* the church is built by the humble labour of Ethelbert and his stage-cockney workmates, so presumably their language typifies the necessary *prima materia*, or 'slimy mud', out of which the verbal artwork evolves. Notice here that Eliot is insisting, as he does in other essays (see above, p. 28), on the linkages between the 'perfect order of speech' that is poetry or incantation and everyday 'common speech', but the linkage remains that between two essentially different discourses, with no intermixture between them. In *The Rock* we have an absolute polarity between the exaggerated 'cockney' speech (in prose) of the builders and the formal choruses which alone survive to take their place in the complete edition of Eliot's poetry and plays. This is an instance of 'purify[ing] the dialect of the tribe' in action; the impurities of dialect have been burnt away; the classic common speech (never actually spoken) that lies at the heart of all specimens of the vernacular remains as poetry.

I suggested in the previous section that Eliot's acceptance of the fact that words should not be 'pinned down' to one meaning, that their 'wobbliness' is not to be deplored, enters the *Quartets*, to a limited extent, with 'East Coker', and that the striving towards the artistic ideal of classic 'finish' is modified accordingly; in Bakhtin's terms, the poem becomes less 'monologic' as discussed below. This realization is very far, however, from constituting a welcome to language's inherent polyphony, as described by Bakhtin:

> The life of the word is contained in its transfer from one mouth to another, from one context to another context, from one social collective to another, from one generation to another generation. . . . When a member of a speaking collective comes upon a word, it is not as a neutral word of language, not as a word free from the aspirations and evaluations of others, uninhabited by others' voices. No, he receives the word from another's voice and filled with that other's voice. The word enters his context from another context, permeated with the interpretations of others.
>
> (*Problems*, p. 202)

If 'Burnt Norton' actively protests about multi-voicedness 'assailing' the would-be 'stillness' of the word, the later quartets retain aspirations towards monologism with a few sops, perhaps, thrown in the direction of polyphony. Bakhtin explains that monologic language is the fitting expression of monist philosophy, of a belief, that is, in the kind of 'one' truth the *Quartets* illustrate:

> The monistic principle, that is, the affirmation of the unity of *existence*, is, in idealism, transformed into the unity of *consciousness*. . . . From the point of view of truth, there are no individual consciousnesses. Idealism recognizes only one principle of cognitive individualization: *error*. True judgements are not attached to a personality, but correspond to some unified, systematically monologic context. Only error individualizes. . . . In the ideal a single consciousness and a single mouth are absolutely sufficient for maximally full cognition; there is no need for a multitude of consciousnesses, and no basis for it.
>
> (*Problems*, pp. 80–1)

There is certainly no need, and no possible use for, a 'multitude of consciousnesses' in the *Quartets*, and it seems entirely fitting that the work's final word is 'one'. In polyphonic authors like Dostoevsky (and indeed Dante), 'the image of a unified spirit is deeply alien' (p. 27); the work of the former expresses 'not a polyphony of reconciled voices but a polyphony of battling and internally divided voices' (pp. 249–50). In 'Little Gidding', we indeed have a conception of 'battling' voices, in so far as the quartet with its blitzed landscape records warring nationalisms and hence languages; but it aspires to a final resolution 'When the tongues of flame are in-folded / Into the crowned knot of fire' and earth's Pentecostal variety of tongues is knotted into the lingua franca of the hereafter. If 'Little Gidding' perforce has to recognize, in the here and now, international disunity, it can at least contribute to the vision of final homogeneity by monologizing (and hence 'Europeanizing' (see above, pp. 11–12)) English into the common style; the idea of the poem and its language having 'overcome' its internal divisions (as adumbrated in 'East Coker') is the counterpart of the movement towards 'monologism' both in the course of English history (the antagonists of the Civil War now reconciled) and in the English landscape, as we shall see in chapter 3. In short 'Little Gidding' can now hypothesize, for the first time in the sequence, something called 'England' which is linguistically, historically and geographically united. Bakhtin himself might have been speaking of 'Little Gidding':

Even when one is dealing with a collective, with a multiplicity of creating forces, unity is nevertheless illustrated through the image of a single consciousness: the spirit of a nation, the spirit of a people, the spirit of history, and so forth. Everything capable of meaning can be gathered together in one consciousness and subordinated to a unified accent; whatever does not submit to such a reduction is accidental and unessential. . . . Semantic unity of any sort is everywhere represented by a single consciousness and a single point of view.

(Problems, p. 82)

Bakhtin consistently associates polyphony in its pre-Dostoevskian phase with the genre of the carnivalesque, which revelled, as in Rabelais, in a rejection of the canon of stylistic unity in favour of 'multi-toned narrative, the mixing of high and low, serious and comic . . . [the] wide use of inserted genres . . . [the] mixing of prosaic and poetic speech, living dialects and jargons' (*Problems*, p. 108). It would be difficult to imagine a more 'anti-carnivalesque' work, on many levels, than *Four Quartets*. In its reverence for asceticism and 'Ardour and self-lessness and self-surrender' ('The Dry Salvages'), it bears out, like the vast majority of Eliot's writing of the 1930s and early 1940s, his comment of 1930 that 'The need of the modern world is the discipline and training of the emotions'.[48] Such an attitude is in fact a recurrent feature of the 'classic' aesthetic at this time, as adumbrated in chapter 1; for example Gropius notes of modernist architecture that 'the repetition of standardized parts, and the use of identical materials in different buildings, will have the same sort of co-ordinating and sobering effect on the aspect of our towns as uniformity of type in modern attire has in social life' (*The New Architecture*, p. 30). Just as the 'carnival sense of the world' with its 'joyful relativity' seeks to resist any attempt to impose uniformity, or 'absolutize a given condition of existence or a given social order' (*Problems*, p. 160), so carnivalesque art, with its 'ambivalent and contradictory' images like the chimera is hostile to the decorum of classic 'finish', to 'ready-made, completed being' (one might add also to prefabricated building units).[49]

It might seem, in fact, that the *Quartets* do contain some of the features of the 'carnivalesque', as theorized by Bakhtin, but this turns out to be illusory. Consider for example the carnivalistic paradoxes in which 'symbols . . . include within themselves a perspective of negation (death) or vice versa. Birth is fraught with death, and death with new birth. . . . Carnival celebrates the shift itself, the very process of replaceability' (*Problems*, p. 125). 'The carnival sense of the world' therefore 'knows no period, and is, in fact, hostile to any sort of *conclusive* conclusion: all endings are merely new beginnings; carnival images are reborn again and again' (ibid., p. 165). This might seem to take us immediately to the opening of the final section of 'Little Gidding':

> What we call the beginning is often the end
> And to make an end is to make a beginning,
> (CPP, p. 197)

lines I have explained on one level as constituting an acceptance of the implication of art itself in temporality, so that the desired 'end' of classic simplification must also look beyond itself to the beginning of the period of elaboration (see above, pp. 39 and 43). Nowhere in the *Quartets*, however, is there a celebratory sense of temporal 'replaceability', and nothing to equate with the carnivalesque idea that 'death is not a negation of life . . . but part of life as a whole – its indispensable component, the condition of its constant renewal and rejuvenation' (*Rabelais*, p. 50). Temporal rejuvenation would seem to be a contradiction in terms for Eliot; the 'replaceability' described in the first section of 'East Coker' posits the earth as some vast midden in which generation after generation proceed aimlessly on their way towards 'Dung and death'. I suggested above that, after 'Burnt Norton', the *Quartets* as a whole convey the idea of working much more 'with' temporality than straining against it; even so, the idea of the 'ridiculousness' of temporality is never quite lost, and the aspiration towards some final release from it is ever-present, notably at the close of 'Little Gidding'. If Bakhtin's words on the 'deep ambivalence' of the image of fire in carnival, that 'simultaneously destroys and renews the world' (*Problems*, p. 126), also evoke the destruction-renewal motif of fire in the final quartet, we should also note that Eliot is celebrating throughout the apocalyptic 'pyre' of *final* destruction-renewal, after which there will be no further temporality. Bakhtin talks a good deal about the elevation of the 'horizontal line of time and of historic becoming' at the time of the Renaissance above 'the narrow, vertical, extratemporal model of the world, with its absolute top and bottom, its system of ascents and descents' that characterizes the hierarchical world-view of the middle ages (*Rabelais*, pp. 364, 403). In 'Burnt Norton' Eliot introduces images of verticality and horizontality, restoring, as it were, their pre-Renaissance values to them; man's proper spiritual movement towards God is up or down the 'vertical' axis, while the 'horizontal line of time' is expressed in part iii as blind 'appetency', the fixed running of the tube train 'on its metalled ways / Of time past and time future'. In short, the *Quartets* as a whole project temporality as a necessary evil, and seem to me to adopt a more or less uncompromising non-humanist, non-vitalist and non-immanentist position. I shall explain these last two terms when discussing landscape in the following chapter; there I shall substantiate how Eliot's employment of the peasant dancers in 'East Coker' i might indeed be read as a deliberate satire on the 'carnivalesque'.

I make the above obvious distinctions between Eliot and the carnivalesque because, since various quasi-dialogic features do exist in the poem, which I shall now discuss, it might be possible on a superficial reading to make the plea that the *Quartets* are in fact a less 'closed' text than is actually the case. For example, Bakhtin notes how 'in the presence of the monologic principle, ideology – as a deduction, as a semantic summation of representation – inevitably transforms the represented world into a voiceless object of that deduction. . . . A unity of viewpoint must weld into one both the most formal elements of style and the most abstract philosophical deductions' (*Problems*, p. 83). I shall discuss the various attempts made by the classic aesthetic in the 1930s, particularly in the visual arts, to present itself as 'voiceless' later in this section; that is, to present itself, not as a perception of 'truth', but as 'truth' itself. There seems at first sight, however, no elision of subjectivity in the *Quartets* themselves; indeed, with their foregrounding of the perceiving 'I' they remind us constantly that we are listening to an individual voice, and perhaps this is one of the factors that weighs with critics concerned to posit a 'Romantic' Eliot. This 'I' is, however, ruthlessly subordinated to the collective 'we'; on a simple numerical count the ratio I/my/me:We/our/us through the *Quartets* is as follows: *BN* 5:13; *EC* 17:26; *DS* 4:19; *LG* 22:24. The rejection of any authoritarian voice in the polyphonic approach to the world leads authors like Dostoevsky to refuse the possibility of such a status even to their own heroes; thus Bakhtin points to the device of 'parodying doubles' used in his novels, where 'almost every one of the leading heroes . . . has several doubles who parody him in various ways' (*Problems*, pp. 127–8). Thus Dostoevsky typically 'forces his heroes to recognize themselves, their idea, their own words, their orientation, their gesture in another person, in whom all these phenomena change their integrated and ultimate meaning and take on a different sound, the sound of parody or ridicule' (ibid., p. 217). I mention this here because it throws light on the use of the double in the famous second section of 'Little Gidding', in which nearly all the uses of the 'I' recorded in the above ratio for that quartet occur. The double in this episode is, of course, in no sense parodic; he is rather mirroring, or confirmatory, his scathing satire on 'the gifts reserved for age' more or less reproducing (with metaphysical sanction, so to speak) the *vanitas mundi* theme found throughout the *Quartets* and in particular reproducing the message of the disappointments of that 'Long hoped for calm, the autumnal serenity / And the wisdom of age' found in 'East Coker' ii. There needs in fact no ghost come back from the grave to tell us this.

Thus this dialogue in 'Little Gidding' is in no sense dialogic; the assurance of the 'we' transmutes into the 'I' in this section of the poem with no intention of quizzing the poem's voice, of adopting any unsettling polyphonic approach to it. The differences with Dante here are instructive, if we turn to Dante's encounter with Brunetto Latini in *Inferno* XV, on which Eliot's episode is based. In that encounter, Dante unmistakably meets another *voice*, a brisk, colloquial, excitedly denunciatory voice that, moreover, tells Dante *personaggio* not what he already knows but what he doesn't, in the forecasts concerning Dante's future he makes. Dante's undoubted sorrow in the encounter, and warmth towards Brunetto, is presumably the kind of thing Bakhtin has in mind in suggesting that the *Commedia* is truly polyphonic, i.e. that Dante gives, as it were, an equal status to all the voices in the poem, whether of the saved or damned (but see note 47 to this chapter). The encounter in 'Little Gidding' is empty of this type of dramatic resonance; a conversation exists between 'two' figures who use exactly the same formal, measured tone, rather as in the homogenization of voices in *The Family Reunion*. The 'we' of the quartet remains intact, temporarily transposed into 'I' and 'you'.

The other high incidence of the 'I' in the *Quartets* occurs in 'East Coker'. I suggested in the previous chapter that this quartet is the one in which doubts and reservations about the classical aesthetic position set up in 'Burnt Norton' are aired, in the interests of an aesthetic less committed to the monumentality of classic 'finish'. There is no doubt that 'East Coker' is the only quartet that begins to approach Bakhtin's definition of the dialogic:

> dialogic relationships are also possible toward one's own utterance as a whole, toward its separate parts and toward an individual word within it, if we somehow detach ourselves from them, speak with an inner reservation, if we observe a certain distance from them, as if limiting our own authorship or dividing it in two.
>
> *(Problems*, p. 184)

Manifestations of this attitude to one's own utterance take the form of

> self-deprecating overblown speech that repudiates itself in advance, speech with a thousand reservations, concessions, loopholes and the like. Such speech literally cringes in the presence or the anticipation of someone else's word, reply, objection.
>
> *(Problems*, p. 196)

Not only does 'East Coker' set up a dialogue with 'Burnt Norton', it also does with itself, 'repudiating', for example, the 'overblown' mode of the 'What is the late November doing' lyric, anticipating the objection voiced in 'You say I am repeating / Something I have said before', even, if you will, foregrounding its 'inner reservations', so that every poetic attempt is 'a different kind of failure'. I suggested, however, that this is not really an attempt to 'open up' the *Quartets*; it is rather a gesture to the inevitable 'centrifugality' of existence which, once made, allows the *Quartets* to proceed on their way towards the conclusive monism (on many levels) of 'Little Gidding' that polyphony rejects (see above, pp. 65–6). In any case, even in 'East Coker' itself we should not overestimate the dialogic elements, nor the projection of a voice assailed by internal division. It is indeed the most 'personal' quartet, but its opening sentence, 'In my beginning is my end', signals that the 'I' being ventured throughout is not a naked subject to be scrutinized but rather the mouthpiece of a collective; the use of Mary Queen of Scots' motto suggests that we are dealing not with personal confession but with the permanent, impersonal facts of collective human transience. Exactly the same tactic was used in 'Ash-Wednesday', where what was Eliot's most 'personal' poetic opening to date – 'Because I do not hope to turn again' – turns out to be 'lifted' directly from Cavalcanti. Even the sequence in 'East Coker' beginning 'You say I am repeating / Something I have said before' is not really an anticipation of *someone else's* objection, in Bakhtin's formulation above. The poet at this point is still talking to his own soul rather than hypothesizing another voice, and once more, as in the 'dialogue' of 'Little Gidding', the 'I' and 'you' of the sequence remain in perfect accord. The way further throughout 'East Coker' the impersonal 'one' is used (five times) to replace 'I' – 'It was not (to start again) what one had expected' – tends also to put the brakes on any movement away from authoritative, impersonal pronouncement.

In short, neither 'East Coker' nor the *Quartets* as a whole develop 'an active dialogic approach to one's own self' in Bakhtin's terms, partly because that 'self' never really emerges from cover; nor does the poem adopt a dialogic relationship to *itself* (*Problems*, p. 120). It remains bent on the essential monism of the classic enterprise, on reducing plurality to one. Although it frequently explores the possibility of combining contra- dictory judgements, as thesis and antithesis, it encompasses this within the 'single utterance of a single subject' which expresses that subject's 'unified dialectical position on a given question. In such a case no dialogical relationships arise. But if these two judgements are separated into two different utter- ances by two different subjects, then dialogic relationships do arise' (*Problems*, p. 183). These relationships are obviated in the *Quartets* by the classic exclusion of voices.

The rejection of subjectivity is very much part of the aesthetic of other phenomena of the 1930s which, in chapter 1, we discussed as partaking of a classic austerity in various ways: abstract painting and modernist architecture. Ben Nicholson in

Circle suggested that his white reliefs had sacrificed all that is accidental, or superfluous: ' "Realism" has been abandoned in the search for reality: the "principle objective" of abstract art is precisely this reality.' [50] Hinks in his review of *Circle* in the *Criterion* attacks the 'false logic' involved in the constructivist ideal of the work of art as a 'pure object'; art is necessarily what he calls a 'percept', mediated through a perceiving subject; there is no such thing as 'autonomous' painting and sculpture. [51] Gropius, with the typically modernist assumption that ornament is synonymous with concealment or illusion, is fond of declaring the new style to be one that is 'based on realities', or that is 'true to itself'; Frank Pick, in his Introduction to Gropius's book, supports this notion of a Bauhaus-inspired 'true' architecture (*The New Architecture*, pp. 7, 20, 56). The idea is enlarged upon by Pevsner, who associates modern design with a reaction against Impressionism: 'the world is not this fairyland of caressing air and tender lightness. There are things, hard and tangible, and there are persons, weighty and active. . . . What they essentially are, they will be in sunshine and in rain' (*Pioneers*, p. 80).

The attempt, by abstracting towards simplicity and monumentality, to take creations out of the flux of appearance and subjectivity is something that Worringer saw as characterizing the art of any age unable to empathize with the natural environment; he talks of 'the instinct for the "thing in itself" ' being of great importance for primitive man (*Abstraction and Empathy*, p. 18), and it is this instinct which Read, following Worringer, sees as operative in the art of his own day. [52] As I suggested at the end of the previous section, the classic ideal in architecture, in which chastity and grandiosity are frequently combined, often appeals to its theorists because of a quality of autonomy it supposedly represents, existing 'independently' rather than constructed socially or ideologically; hence 'timeless' and 'real'. Worringer is to an extent aware of the ideological site of such an outlook; that is, he locates it within particular historical contexts. In aesthetic discussion of the 1930s, however, interest and enthusiasm for what is seen as the 'nonconstructed' art-object is very strong. It is one of the reasons that accounts for the remarkable new-found popularity of the monoliths, Avebury, Stonehenge, and so on, photographs of both of which sites appear in *Axis* and *Circle* respectively, as if according with the principles of abstraction and con-structivism.[53] It is not simply that such monuments have a resemblance to the monolithic simplicity of modern architecture, nor that their construction exemplifies the impersonality of collective endeavour. It is rather that other records of that endeavour have now been lost, and that these remain as almost self-generated artefacts. When Wordsworth discusses his visit to Salisbury Plain in book xii of *The Prelude* (ll.312–53), he concentrates almost totally on evoking the Druidic rites that he sees as synonymous with Stonehenge's past, whereas in the constructivist reconstruction of Stonehenge there is no interest whatsoever in any possible social or historical context for the monoliths; they are presented as pure, formal absolutes.[54] In this they become objects cleansed, so to speak, of any traces of their makers, in an absolute dichotomy between enduring form and human transience, a dichotomy resembling that between the church and its makers in Eliot's *The Rock* (see above, pp. 63–4). We return to part v of 'Burnt Norton', where form is offset against 'that which is only living' which 'can only die'.

I shall return to the monoliths in the following chapter, where I discuss the construction of 'classic' landscape during this period. Returning now to the *Quartets*, I might recall the suggestion of the previous section, where Eliot's 'admittance' of temporality, particularly as it affected language, is seen as leading in 'East Coker' to a modification of the idea of absolutizing form. Devices like the fairly frequent use of the speaking 'I' in the *Quartets* would also seem to counter the aspiration towards autonomous, impersonal form that is manifested in the period by both skyscrapers and Stonehenge. However, with the help of Bakhtin, we have seen just how weighted the *Quartets* remain towards absolutizing its one voice; and the parallels with modernist design I suggested in chapter 1 emphasize the poem's drive towards monumentality, in its simplification, 'purification' and four-square structural emphasis. Other poems, contemporary with the *Quartets*, are indeed more 'voiceless', poems of the documentary movement in which no 'I' appears at all in the interests of a supposed total objectivity; the *Quartets* strive, not to eliminate the voice in this way, but to monumentalize it; not the voice of 'Eliot', but that of England and of 'classic' English.

Whilst striving to do this, Eliot also tends to homogenize

literary history in the interests of the classic tradition. In 'What is a classic?' he holds a view of ancient Latin literature as totally *Aeneid*-centred; a literature 'unconsciously sacrificing . . . the opulence and variety of later tongues' to 'produce' this one monumental work (p. 70); a literature therefore revealing the dangers of reaching an *absolute* classicism which does not allow for further development, for the post-Virgil poets are seen as doing little more than working in his shadow. But Eliot's picture here of the successes and failures of classic classicism is achieved only by ignoring completely the plurality of Latin literature; indeed, Bakhtin finds immense 'wealth and variety' in parodying, anti-establishment 'hetero-voiced' Roman forms like menippea and the entire Saturnalian tradition which is the ancestor of 'the medieval literature of laughter'.[55] His emphasis on 'Latin literary language in all its generic diversity' [56] is totally at odds with Eliot's 'de-polyphonizing' of Roman literature into the one central voice of the *Aeneid*. A similar attempt to canonize a highly polished literary Latin above more populist forms is noted by Bakhtin to be the endeavour of Renaissance stylists whose re-establishment of Latin 'in its classic antique purity transformed it into a dead language'; Cicero's Latin, for example, became a 'beautiful but dead' ideal (*Rabelais*, pp. 466–7). 'We do not want our language to become a dead language', Eliot noted, yet in the same essay he is aware of the 'advantages' that exist (for the linguistic authoritarian) when words 'have come to the limit of their meaning' (see above, pp. 53–4).

'Alongside the centripetal forces, the centrifugal forces of language carry on their uninterrupted work; alongside verbal-ideological centralization and unification, the uninterrupted processes of decentralization and disunification go forward.' [57] If I have described the *Quartets* as a major example of 'verbal-ideological centralization', in Bakhtin's phrase, that yet make a relatively minor allowance for the centrifugal forces, it may seem that I am being too one-sided in my interpretation of Eliot. After all, he himself talks throughout *Notes Towards the Definition of Culture* of the desirability of *variety* in unity, of his welcoming the 'constant struggle between the centripetal and the centrifugal forces' (p. 82). He had furthermore in 1933 attacked the belief in any attempt to 'unify peoples' through 'standardization', adding that he was 'instinctively in sympathy' with regionalist movements.[58] One such means of 'unification' he deplored within England itself was the growth of 'BBC' or standard English during the 1930s, and he hoped that the time 'may be long postponed' when everyone 'talks alike'; similarly, he is cool in his praises of any 'universal lingua franca such as Esperanto or Basic English'.[59] The *Quartets* are heavily underlain, however, as the prose writings are not, by the entire classical aesthetic of centralization expounded thus far, a centralization entirely appropriate in Eliot's eyes to the emergency of war, though not desirable in times of peace (*NDC*, p. 51).[60] Eliot's undoubted sympathy with regionalism does not enter into the *Quartets*; there, his attention is very much focused outwards towards the relation between England and Europe, rather than inwards. In gesturing in 'Little Gidding' towards the end of international division, towards the final unification of 'tongues', he suppresses any notion of internal division, and collapses diversity into the one unity of England and of classic English; a unified England becomes the type of a unified hereafter. We can indeed talk of the *Quartets* as a 'patriotic' poem, as imbued with an all-pull-together, 'wartime' spirit; yet as we shall now see, they disengage themselves from, and indeed attack, other current notions of England too, especially notions of England that raise patriotism to an absolute, rather than a severely relative, value.

Thus we finally come back to the *Quartets'* own announcement of their classicizing language programme in 'Little Gidding':

> And every phrase
> And sentence that is right (where every word is at home,
> Taking its place to support the others,
> The word neither diffident nor ostentatious,
> An easy commerce of the old and the new,
> The common word exact without vulgarity,
> The formal word precise but not pedantic,
> The complete consort dancing together). . . .
>
> (*CPP*, p. 197)

The privileging here of verbal conformity and the rejection of words that lie to either side of a hypothetical mean bear a striking resemblance to Nietzsche's attack on literary decadence in *Der Fall Wagner*, where, according to Alan Robinson, decadent style is seen as an ' "anarchy of atoms" in which the individual element, whether word, sentence or page, usurps an undue amount of attention at the expense of the aesthetic whole, a parallel to a decadent society in which, with the political theory of equal rights for all, the undisciplined masses arrogate to themselves undue individual importance'.[61] The classic style admits 'variety in unity', in so far as old, new, common and formal words are countenanced, but such variegation is subject to rigorous canons of exclusion that define a centrist and normative English against the wealth of voices and discourses exiled beyond the periphery.

Plate 1 Walter Gropius, Bauhaus, Dessau, 1925. Reproduced by permission of the Courtauld Institute of Art.

Plates 2(a) and 2(b) (a) Paul Ludwig Troost, Haus der Deutschen Kunst, Munich, 1933–7. Reproduced by permission of the Courtauld Institute of Art; (b) Jean-Claude Dondel, Musée d'Art Moderne, Paris, 1934–7 (Photo: John Sinclair).

PAESTUM, 600–550 B.C.

THE PARTHENON, 447–434 B.C.

When once a standard is established, competition comes at once and violently into play. It is a fight; in order to win you must do better than your rival in *every minute point*, in

HUMBER, 1907

the run of the whole thing and in all the details. Thus we get the study of minute points pushed to its limits. Progress. A standard is necessary for order in human effort.

DELAGE, "GRAND-SPORT," 1921

Plate 3 From Le Corbusier, *Towards a New Architecture*, 2nd edn (Rodker, 1931), pp. 134–5. Reproduced by permission of Birmingham University Library.

Plate 4 Charles Holden, Senate House, University of London, 1932–8. Reproduced by permission of the Courtauld Institute of Art.

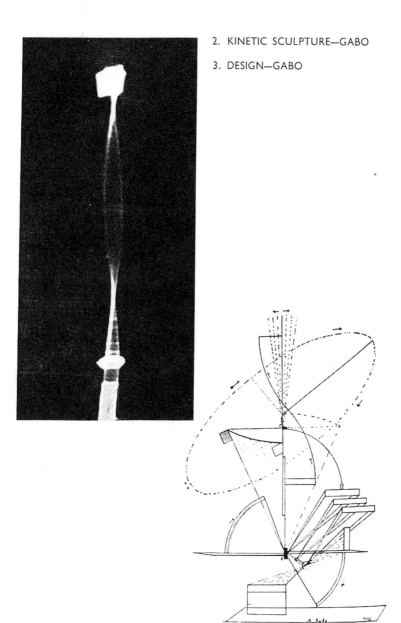

2. KINETIC SCULPTURE—GABO

3. DESIGN—GABO

Plate 5 Naum Gabo, illustrations from *Circle: International Survey of Constructive Art*, ed. J. L. Martin *et al.* (Faber, 1937), p. 112.

Plate 6 Paul Nash, *Wood on the Downs*, 1929, oil on canvas, 71.9×91.4 cm. Reproduced by permission of Aberdeen City Arts Department, Art Gallery & Museums.

Plate 7 Eric Ravilious, *Downs in Winter*, c. 1934, watercolour, 44.9×55.7 cm. Reproduced by permission of the Towner Art Gallery and Local History Museum, Eastbourne.

Plates 8(a) and 8(b) William Gilpin, illustrations, from *Three Essays: on Picturesque Beauty* . . .(1792), between pp. 18–19. Reproduced by permission of Birmingham University Library.

1900. The Humanized Landscape.

- First appearance of the "typical" English countryside.

- The trees have grown up.

- The vision of the eighteenth century is realized.

- The humanized landscape.

Plate 9 Robert Austin, *The Humanized Landscape*, from *Architectural Review*, 77 (1935), 91. Reproduced by permission of the Architectural Press and Birmingham University Library.

Plate 10 Brian Cook, dust-jacket for C. B. Ford, *The Landscape of England* (Batsford, 1933). Reproduced by permission of B. T. Batsford Ltd.

THIS IS ENGLAND

What is it like to be living in England at this moment? People overseas must surely often ask themselves that question. The series 'This is England', broadcast in the Empire Programme, set out to provide the answer by letting ordinary people, typical of modern England, talk about themselves, their work, their homes. But they needed introducing to listeners who had emigrated long ago, or who, maybe, had never been in the homeland at all. So Anthony Weymouth introduced each speaker, and gave before each talk some description of the countryside or town where the speaker lives, and of the part he or she plays in English life today. Extracts from these descriptions appear at the head of the talks

Plate 11 Illustration to 'This is England', *Listener*, 31 March 1937, p. 583. Reproduced by permission of Birmingham University Library.

Plate 12 Frank Dobson, *The Giant, Cerne Abbas, c.* 1934, Shell Petrol poster. Reproduced by kind permission of Shell UK Ltd.

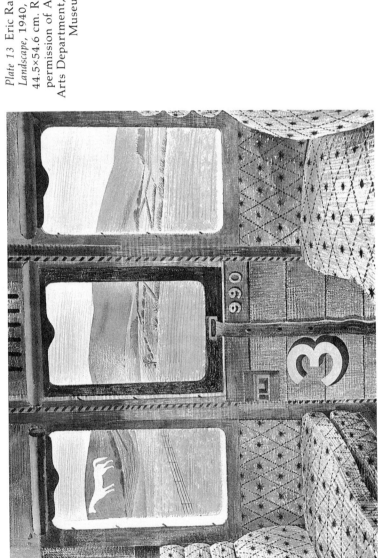

Plate 14 Leslie Moffat Ward, *The Long Man of the Downs*, *c.* 1930, woodcut, 27.9×23.5 cm. Reproduced by permission of the Towner Art Gallery and Local History Museum, Eastborne.

Plate 15 Paul Nash, *Landscape of the Megaliths*, 1937, watercolour, 50.2×75.6 cm, Albright-Knox Art Gallery, Buffalo, New York, Room of Contemporary Art Fund, 1948.

3

ELIOT'S ENGLAND

CLASSIC CENTRALIZATION

In this chapter I wish to discuss a neglected and it would seem largely forgotten context within which the ruralism of *Four Quartets*, and Eliot's construction of 'England' in the poem, can be better understood. If at times my historicist orbit seems to take me rather far from Eliot's poem, I can only enter my plea that the significance of the *Quartets* in these areas lies very much in a debate the poem stages with other texts, both verbal and visual, and that there is no clear demarcation between the relevant and irrelevant in dealing with concepts as culturally embedded as those of national identity. The classicism I have discussed in linguistic and aesthetic terms thus far seems entirely appropriate to Eliot's picture of England in the *Quartets* too, and in this first section I discuss classicizing strategies in other writers which afford some kind of parallel to Eliot's enterprise, before considering in the following section the 'landscape polemics' of the 1930s and 1940s within which we can situate the *Quartets*.

In his essay 'Anglican Eliot', Donald Davie takes Eliot to task for what he sees as the extremely limited projection of 'England' in *Four Quartets*, and thus questions Eliot's right to speak in the sequence as a 'patriotic' poet, as Eliot is on record as wishing to do (see his remark quoted above, p. 26).[1] Davie, however, takes no cognizance of Eliot's extremely circumspect handling of the idea of nationality, which I have been at pains to stress; that is, Eliot's distancing himself from a narrowly chauvinistic conception of England and attempting indeed to dismantle the opposition between the English and the 'foreign' in various ways (see above, pp. 26–7). Davie rather com-

partmentalizes the *Quartets* in a manner contrary to my understanding of them:

> Eliot, when he herded all his American references into
> 'The Dry Salvages', rather plainly meant, by thus honour-
> ing his transatlantic pieties in one delimited act of
> homage, to assert his right through the rest of the
> sequence to speak as an Englishman.
>
> (p. 181)

Eliot, however, who in the quartet preceding 'The Dry
Salvages' had featured a time and a place, in East Coker, that
preceded the Eliot family's emigration to America in 1669, for
whom art was 'racial and local' rather than 'national or international', and for whom consciousness of the nation was 'a very
recent and contingent experience' (see above, p. 26), is surely
not separating out the nations in this way in the *Quartets*, but
placing them in a 'timeless' perspective that suggests a common
origin and a common end. Certainly it makes no sense in a
poem of such close structural and thematic interlinkages to
believe that Eliot is speaking for one quarter of it as an
American and 'asserts his right' to be English in the remaining
three quarters. It is true that the American and English
landscapes that figure in the poem have widely differing
significations for Eliot, but the *Quartets* attempt to synthesize
the connotations of either side of the Atlantic into a unified
Christian outlook (discussed below, pp. 136–7). We should
remember that Eliot stated that 'the last *three* of my quartets are
primarily patriotic poems' (my emphasis), as if his 'Englishness'
in some way incorporates rather than excludes 'transatlantic
pieties'; Davie's notion of Eliot's England presumably only takes
account of what he sees as practically the 'Little England-ism' of
quartets one, two and four.

Davie is able to sustain this charge because Eliot's construction of England in the *Quartets* is so manifestly partial: 'it is
certainly to the point to ask how well he knew the country and
the people that he meant to speak for . . . the consensus is that
Eliot knew England and the English very imperfectly, after
thirty years' (pp. 181–2). Davie suggests in fact that 'Eliot's
sense of Britain is offensively metropolitan – and not of Britain
but of England too; his England is to all intents and purposes
London, or at most the home counties' (p. 182). It is true that

the *Quartets* themselves range further afield, into southern English village locations, but 'every one of these locations is presented in the poem as a place of pilgrimage, accordingly as seen from the outside by the visitor from London (or for that matter from St Louis, Missouri)'; to present such places as quintessential – that is 'Little Gidding's 'History is now and England' – is an insult in Davie's eyes to 'the industrialized Midlands and North', the areas that have been 'for one hundred and fifty years the heart, once throbbing and now ailing, of imperial and then post-imperial England' (pp. 182–3). In fact Davie is 'not sure there is any evidence that Eliot ever travelled in industrial England at all' (p. 183).

It is of course true that Eliot's projection of England in the *Quartets* is extremely reductive, and in the previous chapter I discussed the classical aesthetic of centralization – in linguistic, historic and geographical terms – which is fundamental to the poem. Where Davie's account is incomplete is in its criticism of Eliot for a narrow type of patriotic speaking that he never aspired to, and in its obscuring the fact that the *Quartets* constitute an attack on and debunking of the ruralism they partly embrace, in the face of a far more flourishing ideology of rural England in the 1930s; also questionable is Davie's reiterated suggestion that Eliot's 'ignorance' of England and the English can be put down largely to his foreign origin. We can throw far more light on Eliot's England by attempting some historical contextualization, in which the landscapes of the *Quartets* can be related to a widespread *native* fashion during the period to define England in similarly exclusive terms, side by side with a counter-movement that insisted on English plurality and diversity. What is at issue in the *Quartets* is not some solitary act of untravelled ignorance but a keen polemic, waged with particular vigour during the 1930s and 1940s, over what might constitute a definition of 'England'. In short, 'to speak as an Englishman' is not for Eliot the simple and blinkered act Davie construes it as, but one hedged about with much complexity.

Martin J. Wiener has shown in great detail how potent a force English ruralism has been in the writing of the late nineteenth and twentieth centuries, and certainly the 1920s and 1930s, which witnessed a great expansion in the use of the motor-car, as well as the relentless spreading of town into country in the form of ribbon development, were decades in which the search for what was sensed as a vanishing and threatened rural England was conducted with a particular intensity.[2] As Ian Jeffrey puts it, 'the idea of England' during the period was 'indissolubly connected with the idea of England's despoliation'.[3] The number of books published on the native countryside during the 1920s and especially 1930s was enormous, the most famous being the Batsford *Face of Britain* series, while organizations like the Youth Hostels Association and the Society for the Preservation of Rural England (founded in 1926) expanded rapidly. The movement in Eliot's work from the early metropolitan settings to the *Quartets'* 'pilgrimage' into rural parts is part indeed of what amounts to a countryside invasion during the period, and his hypothesizing of 'England' within a restricted area of the country is by no means unusual. For a whole host of twentieth-century writers, as Wiener says, 'the truly typical England was usually seen to reside in the historic and comfortably domesticated rusticality of the South', wherein the English village received particular attention as the embodiment of national values; after 1900 indeed, as Wiener notes, 'the idealization of the village came into its own'. The search for England conducted in the *Quartets* is of course of a rather less idealizing nature; England seems to be at once both found and dismissed in the southern half of the country.

In an essay of 1960, Eliot declared that 'English landscape has come to be as significant for me, and as emotionally charged, as New England landscape', and in the years during which the *Quartets* appeared Eliot takes a new interest in the settlement of that landscape.[4] Thus in a *Criterion* Commentary of 1938 he advances the belief that 'real and spontaneous country life . . . is the right life for the great majority in any nation', while later in the same year he deplores the increasing 'urbanization' of the English mind: 'it is necessary that the greater part of the population . . . should be settled in the country and dependent upon it'.[5] In *The Idea of a Christian Society* (1939) the complaint against urbanization and indeed 'sub-urbanization' continues, and here Eliot proposes the rural parish as the 'norm' of social organization, 'the idea of a small and mostly self-contained group attached to the soil' (pp. 58–9). In an article appearing in *Christendom* in 1940 Eliot suggests that industrialization and urban life are essentially alien to the English, whose 'natural habitat' is the 'small rural community': 'there is something about England which remains stubbornly attached to the parochial'. Here Eliot very much anticipates the matter of Martin Wiener's book in noting how 'the most highly industrialised country in the world' nourishes the most pervasive nostalgia for rural existence.[6]

The *Quartets* hardly contain any very enthusiastic picture of rural or parochial life, or of communities 'attached to the soil', and in the following section I shall attempt to explain how and why Eliot's poetry and prose seem to some extent to diverge over this issue. The 'emotional charge' the English landscape gives him remains inseparable, however, from his notions of settlement and of parochial organization: not for Eliot any Wordsworthian swooning over mists and mountain-peaks. A *Criterion* Commentary of 1934 is explicit in this 'anti-Romantic' emphasis:

> the beauty of England is not primarily that of the more remote hills and moors which men have not yet found it worth their while to disfigure, but is to be found in the ordinary countryside which is largely the work of generations of humanising labour.[7]

The term 'remote' begs the question, of course, 'Remote from where?' – the answer being necessarily London. The idea of the beauty and identity of England being synonymous with the 'ordinary countryside' is pure classicism, in its absolutizing of the norm: I refer readers back to Babbitt's comment quoted above (p. 46). In the 1930s the emphasis on the genuine and largely more 'normal' (southern) England inevitably becomes part of a classic-Romantic debate, given the cultural connotations of the northern landscape; thus Cyril Connolly, reviewing the recently issued Shell countryside posters in 1934:

> The moral of the landscapes here shown is that it is not the awe-inspiring or exceptional which now seems important, but what is most cheerful and genuine in our countryside – England is merry again – farewell romantic caves and peaks, welcome the bracing glories of our clouds, the cirrhus and the cumulus, and the cold pastoral of the chalk.[8]

Although there are some odd inconsistencies in Connolly's

appraisal, which I shall return to, his down-grading of the Romantic and elevation of the chalklands, which stretch in a great band across the southern part of the country, together with the tag from Keats's 'Grecian urn', illustrate well the new conceptualization of England I am tracing. A more explicit classicism is found in Thomas Sharp, writing in 1932, whose pleas for better appreciation of England's 'quiet, normal, humanised landscape' are accompanied by attacks on the 'childish love of the spectacular', and the 'Gothic romanticism' whose interests and energies can be marshalled only on behalf of 'the abnormal, the beauty spot'.[9] This questionable legacy from Wordsworth and Ruskin is a slight on the 'easy undulations' of the English countryside (p. 34) and on the agricultural lowlands which possess in fact the most 'scenic importance' (p. 30). England is 'the loveliest, the most humanised of all landscapes' (p. 15), and beauty and cultivation are indeed synonymous in Sharp's eyes. In architecture and town-planning Sharp's tastes are for the 'urbanity of Bath and Edinburgh', and like many writers of the period he is a severe critic of what he calls 'garden-city romanticism' (p. 165); in the Introduction to his book he calls for the re-establishment of a clear antithesis and demarcation between town and country, and fiercely opposes hybrid forms like the garden city and ribbon suburbs that straggle between one and the other.

Eliot's theories of classic English, expounded in previous chapters, set up a supposed 'common style' as the desired and authentic norm, hypothesizing linguistic individualism and plurality as abnormalities. Exactly the same procedure is involved in the creation of classic landscape with its emphasis on the 'ordinary countryside' or on some sort of centralized focus – like the village or the parish – where the 'real' England is to be found. Thus far, however, I have also been discussing the various reservations and distinctions that Eliot attaches to his classicism, and the procedure will be the same here in talking about 'classic landscape' in the *Quartets*.

The relation between the type of classicist positions we looked at in the first two chapters, and questions of landscape is raised by Anthony Ludovici, writing in 1911, who equates 'the sentimental gushing that is given vent to nowadays over rugged and wild scenery' with the democratic insistence on what he calls 'pointless freedom'; he finds an absolute con-

tradiction in the fact that 'the same man who honours government and an aristocratic ideal may often be found to-day
dilating upon the charms of chaotic scenery' (*Nietzsche and Art*, p.
122n.). This emphasis on form and control in government, art
and landscape is seen as 'faintly risible' by Alan Robinson in
quoting Ludovici's latter comment, on the grounds that controversy between supporters of the formalized and picturesque
landscape is really a dead letter by the twentieth century (*Poetry,
Painting and Ideas*, pp. 98–9). I show below, however, that
Ludovici's interest in the political correlations of landscape is
repeated by many writers in the 1930s, as is his rejection of the
picturesque; certainly the writers we have quoted above,
including Eliot himself, echo (though with rather more restraint) Ludovici's rejection of the 'thoroughly and unquestiona-
bly contemptible . . . love of the Romantic in Nature' (*Nietzsche
and Art*, pp. 156–7).

Much Georgian ruralism from the early part of the century
can be seen as a continuation of the picturesque tradition in its
love of complex scenic detail, variegation and what the classicist
might dismissively call, with Babbitt, 'the cult of local colour'
(*Rousseau and Romanticism*, p. 56), not only in its cast of
individualistic country characters but also in those secreted and
embroidered vignettes that feature, say, in the work of Edward
Thomas:

> There are a hundred little landscapes on the walls by the
> roadside – of grey or silver or golden stone, embossed and
> fretted and chequered by green and gold-pointed mosses,
> frosty lichens, pale round pennywort leaves, and the
> orange foliage of a cranesbill.[10]

In 1930s neo-classicism we might postulate a return in Sherard
Vines's phrase to the more 'essential and generalised' treatment
of nature that characterized the eighteenth century, before,
that is, Ruskin got to work on an exhaustive detailing of
particulars (*The Course of English Classicism*, p. 98). For Vines, 'a
certain botanical conscientiousness in the Tennysonian tradition' was a hallmark of Georgian writing, as opposed to his own
preferred 'more general method of the eighteenth-century
landscape school' (*Movements*, pp. 23–4); one might compare this
preference with Paul Nash's attack on the Victorian approach
to nature represented by the work of William Henry

('Bird's-Nest') Hunt, and on the obscuring of the 'elements of great formal design' in the English landscape tradition generally.[11] Especially in paintings by Nash like *Wood on the Downs* of 1929 (Plate 6), or by Eric Ravilious like *Downs in Winter* of *c.* 1934 (Plate 7), we have the eschewing of decoration in the search for form and structure that parallels the movement in poetry and architecture discussed earlier in this book. Both paintings might stand alongside the hateful 'unimproved' scene in Gilpin's famous comparison to indicate the 'anti-picturesqueness' of the tendency we are discussing (Plate 8). Eliot's *Four Quartets* similarly are totally devoid, it seems to me, of any picturesque detail, their moments of scenic beauty showing a kind of abstract severity rather than microscopic luxuriance:

> Midwinter spring is its own season
> Sempiternal though sodden towards sundown,
> Suspended in time, between pole and tropic.
> When the short day is brightest, with frost and fire,
> The brief sun flames the ice, on pond and ditches,
> In windless cold that is the heart's heat,
> Reflecting in a watery mirror
> A glare that is blindness in the early afternoon.
>
> ('Little Gidding' i)

With such visions we seem, however, to have moved far beyond any 'generalized' treatments of nature in the eighteenth-century fashion, towards indeed something akin to the austere 'stripped classicism' discussed in chapter 1, and returned to in the following section. For the moment, however, we shall return to Eliot's centralization of England around the village, as in 'East Coker', which does contain a kind of model of the 'small rural community' which is properly England, or even better, in 'Little Gidding', where the quartet's location represents the exemplary community of agricultural labour and prayer anticipated in Virgil's *Georgics* and established by monasticism (see 'Virgil and the Christian World', *OPAP*, pp. 125–6).

The village community features again and again in 1930s writing as the true locus of England, representing continuity, stability and order threatened by the alien values of technology and modern urbanization. Throughout the decade the *Architectural Review*, for example, parallels its call for a return to the restraint, simplicity and homogeneity of eighteenth-century design with applause for the 'look' of the countryside in the same period, before the disasters of romanticism and the Victorians. Thus in 1935 a series of articles by W. A. Eden shows the evolution of the ideal English settlement in a sequence of drawings, a vision of a country village in the year 1900 nestling comfortably amidst the folds of what is termed the 'humanised landscape' or ' "typical" English countryside'; here, we are told, 'the vision of the eighteenth century is realized' (Plate 9).[12] What this village has managed to do is to reach the year 1900 having bypassed, so to speak, the entire nineteenth century, for in Eden's second article we have an alternative development showing the corruption of Englishness that takes place when the village falls foul of industrialization and suburban development, its typicality now surrendered. The diagrams are accompanied once again by attacks on Ruskin and on nineteenth-century mountain-worship, and on the *laissez-faire* attitude to the ordinary countryside that imperilled what generations of agricultural labour had previously achieved.[13]

Just such a village is chosen by Virginia Woolf as the setting for her final novel, *Between the Acts*, published in 1941. Her village families go back centuries, and the village and its environment itself have, like Eden's exemplary settlement, managed to bypass the nineteenth century more or less successfully:

> 1833 was true in 1939. No house had been built; no town had sprung up. Hogben's Folly was still eminent; the very flat, field-parcelled land had changed only in this – the tractor had to some extent superseded the plough.[14]

Within this setting, 'in the very heart of England' (p. 16), the village community stages a pageant reviewing the various periods of English history, introduced by a small girl personifying the nation: 'England am I' (p. 60). Here then 'England' looks at itself, at its artificially romanticized past, at its uncertain and unnerving eve-of-war present, and at the technological future – 'the motor bike, the motor bus, and the movies' (p. 59) – that encroaches on its identity. Woolf thus centralizes England for the purpose of analysis, but this review of the state of the nation produces mainly a deep foreboding; the 'very heart of England' turns out at the very end of the book to be a 'heart of darkness' (p. 158). In her use of heart imagery throughout the novel Woolf seems to be extending and indeed questioning the rural mysticism of 'Burnt Norton'; she features a lily-pond as a symbolic centre in the book, where Mrs Swithin does experience a spiritual illumination akin to that of the protagonist of 'Burnt Norton' i (pp. 148–9), but such epiphanies are rendered incomplete and superficial by the sombre authorial insistence on the dark mud at the pond's heart, offsetting Eliot's 'heart of light' in the quartet's first section. Certainly in *Between the Acts* to move ever inwards towards the centre or heart of existence is not to discover a meaningful 'still point' or governing axis but a frightening absence. Thus another symbolic centre in the novel, the portrait of the lady that stands over the Olivers' mantelpiece,

> led the eye up, down, from the curve to the straight, through glades of greenery and shades of silver, dun and rose into silence. The room was empty.
>
> Empty, empty, empty; silent, silent, silent. The room was a shell, singing of what was before time was; a vase stood in the heart of the house, alabaster, smooth, cold, holding the still, distilled essence of emptiness, silence.
>
> (p. 31)

The vase seems to be countering here the import of 'Burnt Norton's 'Chinese jar' that represents metaphysical presence, rather than absence, at the still centre.

In Rex Warner's novel of 1941, *The Aerodrome*, the village setting is again a microcosm of England, with its tradition of liberal democracy, here threatened by the totalitarianism of the air vice-marshal and the aerodrome being built on the village outskirts. Though the crazed dictatorial ambitions of the vice-marshal 'that the world may be clean' collapse with his death, Warner is careful to stress the 'vices and virtues' of both the old and the new orders; traditional England may survive,

> but it was not as though he [the vice-marshal] had never been, for none who had met him could forget him; no corner of the country that had felt the force of his ideas could afterwards relapse wholly into its original content.[15]

Warner's novel has an abstract and schematic symmetry, his village representative but by no means 'realistic': 'I do not even aim at realism . . . in this book my two worlds, "village" and "aerodrome", are of course not intended to describe any village or air force in existence' ('Author's Note', p. 6). Not only then is the village not given a name (just as the village in *Between the Acts* remains unnamed), which might impair its representative function, but its inhabitants too are solely identified by the categories common to each and every village, the Rector, the Squire, and so on.

The title of C. Henry Warren's book of 1940, *England is a Village*, emphatically proclaims (as does his foreword) the metonymic strategy discussed above.[16] It is not simply that the village displays clear continuity through periods of historical change, but more that the identity of the English village is immediately apprehensible and familiar, circumscribed within a set of constant and unchanging social roles and locations: the inn, the church, the manor, the landlord, the vicar, the squire. The 'typical' English village thus becomes an easily synthesizable construct and from here it is a short step to proclaiming it as metonymic of typical or 'true' England, as the writers above do. One type of writing that thrived on this standardized and normative location in the 1920s and 1930s was the crime novel, for which 'by 1930 the pretty English village was considered the most effective setting'.[17] In Agatha Christie's first Miss Marple story, *The Murder at the Vicarage* (1930), we have stylized maps of the unnamed village, featuring the familiar landmarks, and a wholly expected cast of typical characters, vicar, retired colonel, spinsters, village doctor and so on. The vicar-narrator somewhat naively observes that 'to have someone like Colonel Protheroe murdered actually in the Vicarage study is such a feast of sensation as rarely falls to the lot of a village population'; a whole mass of village murder-novels written in the 1930s of course belies this assertion, as if what is being satisfied is a taste for the representative rather than the unique.[18] In *The Murder at the Vicarage*, as in many crime stories of its kind, we have a more or less complete exclusion of the working-class element of village life, or of the agricultural labourer, to generalize or 'standardize' whom raises problems; accent or dialect is after all locality-specific, whereas a middle-class spinster in one county is for fictional purposes much the same as one in another. Such a construction of rural England might again be seen, in the words of Davie's charge against Eliot, as 'offensively metropolitan'; indeed Colin Watson, in dubbing village-thriller writers of the 1930s the 'Mayhem Parva' school, notes how the setting generally suggests 'a commuters' village in the Home Counties where there's a church, a village inn, very handy for the odd Scotland Yard inspector and his man who come to stay for the regularly recurring crimes'.[19] The uncovering of the murderer in such a setting has not unreasonably been seen as a standardized parable offering reassurance about the survival of middle-class English values.[20]

One final, and slightly less rigid, example of village standardization in the 1930s might be mentioned here, Beverley Nichols's *Chronicles of Allways* trilogy (1932–4). The final volume, *A Village in a Valley*, opens with what might be a celebration of plurality and multi-voicedness:

> The accents of Allways are many and various, and nowhere are they heard to better advantage than in church. Especially during the singing of the *Benedicite* . . . as the chant progresses, it is difficult not to be struck by the extraordinary number of different sounds which different people make, on being confronted by the same vowel.[21]

If this seems to promise a novel of rural individuals who display a picturesque evasion of type, the book is brought back within the normative by its four full-page illustrations in Rex Whistler's familiar neo-classical pastiche manner, showing 'The Church', 'The Inn', 'The Store' and 'The Pond'. In any case, there is a limit to the number of 'voices' Nichols will incorporate, and once more his novel has almost no working-class element. 'The women of Allways', we are told, 'were putting up a magnificent fight against genteel poverty, against falling dividends and rising prices' (p. 229).

The centralization of England to a (southern) village is then a familiar feature of much ruralism contemporary with the *Quartets*. It will be apparent (and discussed further in the following section) that the relation of Eliot's writing to this tendency is an extremely ambiguous one: if Eliot's search for England eschews any Neo-Romantic locus, it also steers well clear of any idealization of the 'ordinary countryside'. Yet that very search binds Eliot and his contemporaries in a common fascination; in the 1930s, with the threat of the Second World War casting a long shadow back over the decade, with the emergence of militaristic nationalism on the continent, and with, as I have said, the ever-growing encroachment of town on country, the search for 'England' is probably more intense than at any other period of the twentieth century; as Samuel Hynes has noted, the word itself is endemic in the writings of the 'Auden generation' (pp. 112–13). This search could of course take on propagandistic overtones; thus in 1932 Sir Stephen Tallents called for more effort to be made in the art of what he called 'national projection', a throwing of images of England on to the screen of international consciousness. It is true that Tallents has a reasonably plural sense of the country and does not decry its industrial regions, though in his dedication to the book, 'without apologising for its title', he requests the citizens of Scotland, Wales and Northern Ireland to put their shoulders to the wheel too on behalf of England's projection.[22] The further north and west we get, the more England tends to become Britain, a rather less fashionable figure during the 1930s. When a nation's self-projection takes place in a climate of war or at least of fiercely competing nationalisms, the tendency arises to centralize or unite the nation via some easily assimilable and projectible emblem, like the English village; an insistence on internal diversity might be seen as a kind of counter-patriotic obfuscation. England's chalk (such a popular subject in the 1930s as discussed below) can be another such emblem, the white cliffs fronting the Europe from which the greatest threat to England comes, and which again involve locating 'England' in the south. A good example of this is found in an earlier text: 'If one wanted to show a foreigner England,' Forster opens chapter xix of *Howards End* (1910), 'perhaps the wisest course would be to take him to the final section of the Purbeck hills, and stand him on their summit, a few miles to the east of Corfe.'[23] From this centre 'the imagination swells, spreads and deepens, until it becomes geographic and encircles England' though any detailed topography beyond the features of Forster's lovingly documented chalklands, fades into a kind of imaginative mist: 'Frome was forced inward towards Dorchester, Stour against Wimborne, Avon towards Salisbury, and over the immense displacement the sun presided, leading it to triumph ere he sank to rest. England was alive, throbbing through all her estuaries' (p. 178). Any faint flavour of naval militarism here has been anticipated in Forster's earlier salute to Southampton, Portsmouth and the Isle of Wight: 'It is as if a fragment of England floated forward to greet the foreigner – chalk of our chalk, turf of our turf, epitome of what will follow' (p. 170). Another constantly recurring 'epitome' of England is Shakespeare, in whom 'alone', according to G. Wilson Knight, writing in 1940, we shall find 'the voice of England' (*This Sceptred Isle*, p. 35). Knight opens his book with what might be seen as a warning to any who would contest this monologic proposition: 'at such times [i.e., of war] we are aware . . . of our own unity, as a people, and the dire consequences of any discordancy among ourselves' (p. 1). Knight has chosen the title of his book from the key text of Shakespearian nationalism, quarried repeatedly in the 1930s, namely John of Gaunt's speech from *Richard II* (II. i). Hynes has briefly discussed the currency of this Shakespearian landscape – 'this precious stone set in the silver sea', and so forth – in the work of Auden and his circle (*The Auden Generation*, pp. 112–13), and there is a rather ironic reference to it towards the close of Evelyn Waugh's *Vile Bodies* (1930).[24] This latter instance is an aerial view, with the protagonists of the novel looking down on England from an aeroplane and being able as it were to take in the whole island, set in its 'silver sea', at once; the value of Gaunt's 'this England' speech lies in fact in its overview of the island, in a series of unproblematic, unitary images: 'this fortress', 'this little world', 'this blessed plot', 'this teeming womb'. The country, by being visually distanced, contracts into unity.

There are no echoes of the 'sceptred isle' vision of England in *Four Quartets*, and indeed as I argued above (pp. 31–43), to hypothesize a classic Shakespeare contributing to the development of the common style, nourished by the European bloodstream, is in effect to resist nationalistic requisitions upon him. The imperialism of Gaunt's speech, interpreted by Wilson Knight as 'suggesting a royal responsibility held by our own island home and race among the peoples of the world' (p.33), is also not on offer in Eliot's poem, despite his support elsewhere for the imperialist ideal (see 'Virgil and the Christian world', 'Rudyard Kipling', *OPAP*, pp. 130, 243). Stylistically the *Quartets* might proclaim their ancestry in the central Latin tradition (see above, pp. 11–12) but the poem envisages no future for secular imperialism, the 'England' there presented being much too tepid and enfeebled to function as a seat of empire. If we compare Forster's 'England was alive, throbbing through all her estuaries' with 'Little Gidding's

> So, while the light fails
> On a winter's afternoon, in a secluded chapel
> History is now and England,
>
>   (*CPP*, p. 197)

it is clear that to find England is, for Eliot, hardly a proclamation of national power. The verbal-ideological centralization conducted in the *Quartets* is not undertaken with the intention of launching 'England' at others but is preparatory to the dismissal of England itself, along with all other temporal constructs, from the perspective of the 'timeless moment' when we find ourselves, in 'Little Gidding's phrase, in 'England and nowhere'. England is neatly packaged then posted into oblivion. It therefore seems that Eliot's 'patriotism' in the *Quartets* takes the form of putting the brakes on the more effervescent patriotisms of others; on insisting on England as a relative rather than an absolute value.

What makes the England of the *Quartets* so complex is that despite the fundamental and pervasive emphasis on *vanitas mundi* the poem does contain a rather battered blueprint of what England should be, namely a network of 'small and mostly self-contained group[s] attached to the soil', as outlined in *The Idea of a Christian Society*. In other words, its approach to England is both constructive and destructive, and however much the latter perspective predominates, as I shall argue, in the settlements of East Coker and Little Gidding we are meant to see some kind of correct way of life, and of social organization, for the country; thus centralization does serve some secular purpose in the poem.

We can only fully understand the motives behind classic centralization in the 1930s if we realize that such a strategy is locked into debate with its opposite; that is, that it occurs precisely at a time when the sense of England's diversity and regional variegation is being fuelled by a vast internal travel literature. It is fuelled also by the new 'aerial' viewpoint made available by the aeroplane, which in Auden's work, for example, permits rapid cross-country transits that emphasize the plurality of British landscapes and localities. The use of the 'aerial view' in Auden is very different from that in John of Gaunt's speech referred to above, which miniaturizes the island into unity, even though, as Hynes notes, we find echoes of that speech in poems like 'O Love, the interest itself in thoughtless Heaven' (EA, p. 118–19; Hynes, p. 112). It is true, as I shall argue in chapter 4, that Auden feels the pull of the classic centre, and that some of his landscape poems seem to succumb to it; more often, however, as in the poem Hynes quotes, we find the notion of a quintessential England taken up only to be exploded into centrifugal fragments.

As an illustration of the pluralist-centrist debate we might consider Ivor Brown's book *The Heart of England*, published by Batsford in 1935. The phrase that makes up Brown's title has had a very wide currency in nineteenth- and twentieth-century countryside writing, and it usually serves an exclusive and centrist ethic as in Woolf's *Between the Acts* that posits a quasi-mystical quintessential English location usually in the southern half of the country – the Adlestrop or Little Gidding syndrome, so to speak. The phrase indeed is so pervasive that there is no need to posit Brown's book as a specific rejoinder to Edward Thomas's *The Heart of England* of 1906, though this work, in its topographically unspecific but obviously southern ruralism, represents everything Brown seems to want to challenge. Brown's book opens with a frontispiece showing Lancashire cotton mills and begins with a discussion of the London and Liverpool docklands and resorts like Southend and Blackpool (pp. 6–21). Chapter iii, 'The downs and moors', concentrates almost entirely on sheep-farming on the northern fells and moors, the southern downs featuring hardly at all (pp. 22–38). In showing that England's 'heart' is plural, popular and per-ipatetic, Brown seems to be consciously countering southern rural centralization; his book moreover carries an enthusiastic foreword by J. B. Priestley, whose own *English Journey* of 1934 paid particular attention to the industrial towns of the north and midlands.

In the 1930s furthermore an active regionalist literature did exist and has been traced by critics like Glen Cavaliero.[25] If centralization is one element in a binary interplay then it is clear that we can only understand the England of the *Quartets* by restoring what is its complex polemical context. The *Quartets* are a campaign to present England aimed as much at adversaries within as without, and this is the subject of the following section.

LANDSCAPE POLEMICS IN THE 1930s

In the abstract severity of its landscapes amongst other things, *Four Quartets* resists any tradition of romanticizing rural England or of creating picturesque scenic tableaux; indeed the poem is conspicuously devoid of picturesque detail, as if the search for England becomes the sacrifice of all incidentals. The 1930s witnessed a final flowering of the Georgian movement, or what Michael Roberts called 'the neo-Georgian world', into which the New Country poets were importing their updated images of railheads and reservoirs,[26] but the older ruralism survived in the work of writers like Edmund Blunden; witness his *The Face of England: in a Series of Occasional Sketches* of 1932. The book is an extraordinarily picturesque continuation of what J. C. Squire in his Introduction describes as the staple of Blunden's poetry, namely 'typical English scenes and typical English characters', though such typicality, by the 1930s, is very much that of a nostalgic past:

> In his poems every Englishman who has had anything of a country childhood can find his own early villages, inns, churches, flowers, birds' eggs, gipsies, woodland fires, streams, ponds, fish, cattle – all the seasons and labours which impress themselves so indelibly on the childish mind.[27]

We are confessedly not in contemporary England here, though there is still a tendency to offer this England as the true and ever-present locus of national identity, the nation's 'heart'; thus by 'concentrating mainly on one very typical corner of England' Blunden's book is, says Squire, 'suggesting the character of the general fabric by poring affectionately over the particular' (pp. vi–vii). That the list of particulars given above was still representative of the whole took some swallowing in the 1930s; certainly it must have come as a surprise to writers like Brown and Priestley whose reviews of the general fabric actually involved some travelling around it. *The Face of England* is again topographically unspecific; it adopts a familiar picturesque strategy in building up a composite portrait from features not confined to any particular place, which gives Blunden's England all the strengths of empirical unverifiability; and his manner of employing 'sketches' – 'our sketch-book, so to speak, has a dearer secret than our finished canvases' (p. x) – might have come straight out of Gilpin.

As late as 1944, in works like *Cricket Country*, Blunden is still purveying picturesque and pre-industrial rural England, though this work again confesses that such a country is by now located firmly in the past. In *English Villages* (1941), we have the picturesque in human guise, the traditional cast of 'Merrie England', a land repeatedly evoked by nineteenth- and twentieth-century ruralists, and frequently underscored, as with Blunden, by appeals to Shakespeare:

> In such a village as the one through which we have walked, some characters are to be found in whom a marvellous richness of the spirit of the place is concentrated. They are Shakespearean . . . To them, and in them, life is many-coloured.[28]

It is true that Blunden seems conscious of writing towards the end of this merry Shakespearian tradition, and closes his book with a brief review of rural writing in which latterly a rather less 'many-coloured' figure has come to the fore: 'the authors of village books have been more and more inspired by the figure, one might almost say of Piers the Plowman. . . . The text is "See yonder stubborn lump of flesh who sings behind his spade" ' (p. 47).

If the *Quartets* are sparing with scenic decoration they are also of course devoid of 'rich' English characters; indeed the utter depopulation of the poem's England has often been noted and will be discussed below. The more recent and dourer vision of the rustic that Blunden records might have included the anonymous ghost labourers of 'East Coker' (1940), whose flesh goes to feed the earth they till. Even *English Villages* ends with a tailpiece reproduced from Thomas Bewick's *British Birds* (1805), showing a hoary-headed village elder staring at a headstone inscribed *'vanitas vanitatum omnia vanitas'* (p. 48), as if Blunden's book has been gradually overtaken by what he posits as the new ruralism. The sombre world-weariness of the book of Ecclesiastes, from which the inscription is taken (I. 2), is fundamental to 'East Coker', and even in the earlier *The Face of England* Blunden ends by wrestling with a vision of *vanitas*. This takes the form of a confrontation between Blunden's rustic heroine 'Tatty' and 'the common level of uninformative churchyards' into which such obscure characters, despite their immense vitality, finally sink (pp. 173–8). Throughout the *Quartets* we are constantly reminded of churchyard burial, from the 'old stones that cannot be deciphered' of 'East Coker' through the 'significant soil' – 'Not too far from the yew-tree' – of 'The Dry Salvages' to the 'illegible stone' of 'Little Gidding', the one fact of death echoing down a vast timescape; whereas Blunden battles to put life and not death at the heart of his village, Eliot's poem like Thomas Gray's emphatically insists on the transience of generations; we never forget that England is a necropolis.

When 'life' is on the rural agenda then as I say Shakespeare is often summoned. Thus Blunden has an account of the Bampton morris-dancers who bring with them their ' "all-licensed fool", equipped according to eternal law with a bladder on a stick', being 'one of the most popular parts of the entertainment'. Blunden notes that their dance is 'an ancient flower-ritual, by all appearances, and exists not by revivalism but by continuity of tradition' (*English Villages*, p. 34). In Edward Thomas we have characters like the neo-Shakespearian Watercress Man, who carries 'a basket of wild flowers on his back' and whose faculty for punning conversation strongly recalls the clown of *Twelfth Night* (cf. act III, scene i with *Heart of England*, p. 13). Possibly the most pervasive use of Shakespeare in conjuring Merrie England at this time occurs in John Moore's *The Brensham Trilogy* (1946–8), which describes a 'typical' West Country village between the wars, featuring characters named Pistol, Bardolph and Nym among its colourful cast, with a 'little Falstaff' of a village inn-keeper and 'the uncorrupted speech of Shakespeare' tripping from the villagers' tongues throughout.[29] The section headed 'And Ginger shall be Hot i' the Mouth too' (*Twelfth Night* II. iii) epitomizes how the Shakespeare largely drawn on in the trilogy is intended to serve a carnivalesque, anti-authoritarian ethic (see *Brensham Village*, pp. 385–6), rather as Herbert Reed claimed (see above, pp. 41–2). Another landlord in *Brensham Village*, Joe Trentfield, specializes in displaying phallic-shaped vegetables behind his bar, together with a wood-carving of the Long Man of Elmbury, 'in some ways an even more impressive figure than the better-known Long Man of Cerne Abbas'. The laughter that thereby circulates in the bar 'was the laughter, surely, of Chaucer and Rabelais; for it was of the earth earthy, like the comic misshapen vegetable in Joe's hand' (pp. 318–19). It is against this background that we are better able to understand the *Quartets'* resistance, discussed above (pp. 66ff.), to the carnivalesque in all its forms, social, rural, linguistic, and also Eliot's insistence on Shakespeare as a model of classic simplicity rather than colloquial richness. It is after all a short step from the *Falstaffian* Englishman to the Falstaffian *Englishman*, and thence once more into a highly nationalized Shakespeare. The *Quartets* indeed might be said to play the role of Malvolio to an inter-war literature of country riot; certainly the dancers of 'East Coker', whom I shall discuss shortly, get a pretty final come-uppance in 'Dung and death'. There is still, I suppose, an assumption that the stock-in-trade of rural literature will be the colourful 'character', his or her edges unrounded by the impersonal life of the city, and 'of the earth earthy'. In the period under discussion writers were faced with the options of defiantly proclaiming such a figure's existence – as in Moore's novels, or in works like Francis Brett Young's *Portrait of a Village* (1937) or C. Henry Warren's *England is a Village* (1940) – or indicating its likely demise, as in Blunden, or openly rejecting it altogether, as in Eliot and other writers.[30]

Around the peasant dancers of 'East Coker' i a great deal of critical controversy centres concerning Eliot's ruralism; not surprisingly, given the somewhat contradictory functions they perform in the poem. That they are, first and foremost perhaps, a satirical inversion of the carnivalesque and Merrie England tradition discussed above should not be in doubt; certainly the 'Dung and death' they end in has little of that affirmatory response to the cycle of fertility and rejuvenation described by Bakhtin:

> In grotesque realism and in Rabelais's work . . . excrement was conceived as an essential element in the life of the body and of the earth in the struggle against death. It was part of man's vivid awareness of his materiality, of his bodily nature, closely related to the life of the earth.
>
> (*Rabelais and His World*, p. 224)

The *Quartets* as a whole are largely silent on the idea of Godhead present *within* the creation as a sustaining *logos*, other than in the visionary 'timeless moments'. In other Eliot works like *Murder in the Cathedral* (1935), the extremely dour picture of the life of the rural peasantry is at least offset by a hymn of praise to God for the natural habitat where 'Thy glory [is] displayed in all the creatures of the earth, / In the snow, in the rain, in the wind, in the storm; in all of Thy creatures, both the hunters and the hunted'; thus 'all things affirm Thee in living; the bird in the air, both the hawk and the finch; the beast on the earth', and so on (*CPP*, p. 281). Any glorying in creatures, elements or seasons is muted totally in the *Quartets*, though 'East Coker' i has figured to many critics as essentially a celebration of the rustic seasonal cycle:

> Round and round the fire
> Leaping through the flames, or joined in circles,
> Rustically solemn or in rustic laughter
> Lifting heavy feet in clumsy shoes,
> Earth feet, loam feet, lifted in country mirth
> Mirth of those long since under earth
> Nourishing the corn. Keeping time,
> Keeping the rhythm in their dancing
> As in their living in the living seasons
> The time of the seasons and the constellations
> The time of milking and the time of harvest
> The time of the coupling of man and woman
> And that of beasts. Feet rising and falling.
> Eating and drinking. Dung and death.
>
> > (*CPP*, p. 178)

Surely the most illuminating text we can put beside this is, however, the opening chorus from Eliot's pageant-play *The Rock* (1934):

> The Eagle soars in the summit of Heaven,
> The Hunter with his dogs pursues his circuit.
> O perpetual revolution of configured stars,
> O perpetual recurrence of determined seasons,
> O world of spring and autumn, birth and dying!
> The endless cycle of idea and action,

Endless invention, endless experiment,
Brings knowledge of motion, but not of stillness;
Knowledge of speech, but not of silence;
Knowledge of words, and ignorance of the Word.
All our knowledge brings us nearer to our ignorance,
All our ignorance brings us nearer to death,
But nearness to death no nearer to GOD.
Where is the Life we have lost in living?
Where is the wisdom we have lost in knowledge?
Where is the knowledge we have lost in information?
The cycles of Heaven in twenty centuries
Bring us farther from GOD and nearer to the Dust.

(*CPP*, p. 147)

Critics who feel that in 'East Coker' i we have primarily a nostalgic vision of a lost natural harmony, or divinely appointed cosmic pattern into which humanity once fitted, unduly elevate what seems to me a totally subordinate and severely qualified significance in the passage. It is true that in the almost-contemporary *Idea of a Christian Society* Eliot upholds a return to the soil as the direction such a society should take; life must be lived 'in conformity with nature', and modern industrialism represents 'a wrong attitude towards nature [which] implies, somewhere, a wrong attitude towards God' (pp. 80–1). In the slightly later Kipling essay of 1941 Eliot applauds Kipling's 'vision of the people of the soil' displayed in his Sussex stories:

> It is not a Christian vision, but it is at least a pagan vision – a contradiction of the materialistic view: it is the insight into a harmony with nature which must be re-established if the truly Christian imagination is to be recovered by Christians.
>
> (*OPAP*, p.250)

In 'East Coker' it seems that any affirmations about such a vision are totally subordinated to the Ecclesiastes-type moralizing on *vanitas vanitatum*, and that Eliot is setting up his dancers as exemplary of the desired social fabric only to take the greater satisfaction in laying them low again. Retrospectively the Tudor peasants may be five or six centuries 'nearer' to God in *The Rock*'s numerical count; yet the seasons they live in have still taken them fifteen centuries 'farther from GOD and nearer to the Dust'. There is no room for bucolic satisfaction here.[31]

'Burnt Norton' has already told us that 'that which is only living / Can only die'; that the peasants have life denied to the modern urban-dweller is not much compensation compared with, again in *The Rock*'s phrase, the true 'Life' that is 'lost in living'. In *The Idea of a Christian Society* Eliot makes it plain that the ordinary, staple inhabitants of his rural communities will show no particularly advanced apprehension of the Christian life: the religion of 'the people' would be 'largely a matter of behaviour and conformity', where 'social customs would take on religious sanctions'; in short, Christianity for most will be 'a matter of behaviour and habit' (p. 62). It is quite enough then for country folk to carry on the immemorial seasonal round, while accepting as habitual observances Christian sacraments like 'matrimonie'. The peasants of 'East Coker' are then, like Kipling's, essentially a pagan folk too, but surviving into Christian society as its foundation.

That they are pagans serves partly to explain Eliot's extra-ordinary doubleness of attitude towards them. The necessary 'conformity with nature' had been nowhere better presented than in Virgil's *Georgics*, where the correspondence in particular between the cycles of the constellations and the care of the land is detailed (see book I, ll.204–30), and as I mentioned above Virgil had also provided the blueprint for agricultural monasticism (see p. 84). The 'pagan vision' of 'East Coker' i may be seminal but it is at the same time harshly curtailed, kept in its place and even derided; there is for instance no attempt to bring out the splendour or majesty of the calendary constel-lations, as we find in Virgil or for that matter Dante. However constitutive this community might be, it is sacrificed to the far greater thrust of the poem's apocalyptic satisfactions, which stress time and history throughout not as a realm of human achievement (certainly not communal/social achievement) but as a period of exile, a cyclic demonstration of the vanity of human wishes, with the destruction of the war exemplifying the ceaseless rise and fall of houses and civilizations in the poem long before the Blitz actually features in 'Little Gidding'. But perhaps the major reason why Eliot so fiercely debunks his own supposed rural programme, in 'East Coker', lies in the context of the competing rural ideologies I am attempting to trace. Other writers already noted had taken rural England to excessive and, as we shall see, even heretical proportions; Eliot seems so concerned to resist contemporary expressions of nationalism, vitalism, or 'natural religion' in 'East Coker' that his small group 'attached to the soil' becomes less a positive idea than a satire on ruralism itself, or, to use Worringer's term, on any creed of 'empathy' with environment. Even in *The Idea of a Christian Society*, Eliot is anxious to show how, in taking such a group as a 'norm', he wishes to avoid presenting 'any idyllic picture of the rural parish, either present or past' (p. 59).

Critics who have noted the 'doubleness' of 'East Coker' have often handled it in a highly tendentious manner; one such is George Bornstein, whose study of Eliot anticipates that by Edward Lobb in positing Eliot as essentially a 'romantic' poet, 'romantic against the grain' whatever his protestations of classicism.[32] The *Quartets* themselves are seen as recurrently betraying a 'drive into romantic patterns' that 'counter[s] the thrust of the poem'; one such episode according to Bornstein is precisely 'East Coker' i (pp. 156–7). Thus

> the natural description contradicts . . . [Eliot's] denial of the world elsewhere in *Four Quartets*. Lingering in the natural world provokes an outburst of poetic power. . . .
> In a brilliant thematic defense against his own fears, Eliot makes the vision embody order – a dance around a fire betokening concord. . . But shortly the poem begins to go to pieces, as Eliot's work often does under the pressure of sex as subject. Return to the meters of Ecclesiastes signals a coming failure in vision, which after paralleling human and bestial copulation arrives at a natural nadir, 'Dung and death'. That final phrase accords with the intellectual needs informing the general structure of the entire poem but betrays the extraordinary appeal of the rich vision in an often desiccated work.
>
> (pp. 157–8)

Really Bornstein is here dismembering the passage himself via a series of shameless value judgements which attribute poetic 'power' to the bits of 'East Coker' whose philosophy he thinks he can agree with. His foregrounding the 'brilliance' of the bonfire and matrimony section of the passage is overstated and purely arbitrary, a self-appointed romanticization of Eliot into a 'rich vision' which enables Bornstein to make the charge that thereafter the poem goes 'to pieces'. Why the lines of natural description and the 'concord' passage should automatically be labelled 'Romantic' is in any case a puzzle, given as we have seen that visions of seasonal harmony are by no means unknown in the Latin classics. The whole section describing the dancers is introduced by the bird of death, the 'early owl', and for me the would-be 'rich vision' never frees itself from an ominous and sombre consciousness of mortality that satirically insists on the death at the heart of life; the dancers have 'Earth feet' and 'loam feet' even before they go 'under' the earth. Leavis was right when he talked about the 'inevitability' with which 'that whole assured visionary contemplation of the "open field" . . . comes to rest in "Dung and death" '.[33] I would suggest in fact that even Eliot's quoting from Sir Thomas Elyot's *The Governour* in its original spelling is not free from a satirical intent:

> Two and two, necessarye coniunction,
> Holding eche other by the hand or the arm
> Whiche betokeneth concorde.
>
> (*CPP*, p. 178)

What is to Bornstein the apogee of the passage's romanticism is to me as much a dig at neo-Tudor revivalism as are the outcries of the time against the multiplication of 'Ye Olde Tea Shoppe' and of 'arterial Tudor semi-detachment'. Elyot's 'quaint' and picturesque language seems to totally belie the mud and mire of rural Tudor life.

Another noted *Quartets*-baiter, C. K. Stead, anticipated Bornstein in finding the odd 'fine passage' of natural description in the poem, indeed claiming that the lines only 'take life' when they are 'permitted to rest for a moment in the physical world, permitted to express "the love of created things" '.[34] Again, 'East Coker' i is held to afford just such an instance:

> Now the light falls
> Across the open field, leaving the lane
> Shuttered with branches, dark in the afternoon,
> Where you lean against a bank while a van passes,
> And the deep lane insists on the direction
> Into the village, in the electric heat

Hypnotised. In a warm haze the sultry light
Is absorbed, not refracted, by grey stone.
The dahlias sleep in the empty silence.
Wait for the early owl.

(*CPP*, p. 177)

This passage may well display 'the love of created things', though what it loves about them is precisely a mystical, even sinister, 'death-in-life' aura rather than any simply natural vitality or vigour. We have darkness in the midst of light, stillness amid motion, emptiness amid habitation, sleep amid waking, the whole scene static and 'hypnotised', waiting for the early owl.[35]

Of course, there have been plenty of critics who have no illusions about any would-be romanticism on Eliot's part in the *Quartets*, and foremost among these would be Leavis: Eliot cannot be accused of inconsistency, but he can be accused of an utterly negative 'reductivism' towards the natural world and towards the 'rural English populace' featured in 'East Coker' whom he 'clearly thinks' of as 'yokels', 'clumsy, crude, gross and incapable of the spiritual or cultural graces' (*The Living Principle*, pp. 195–6).[36] This seems to me a far more tenable reading than that of the opposite extreme, represented by Bornstein, yet it is still an incomplete one. *The Idea of a Christian Society* makes it plain that, however slightingly treated, the rustic dancers are the nearest Eliot comes in the poem to an ideal of staple communal organization, available in the past but now vanished; certainly no other English community, save that of 'Little Gidding' (discussed below), is even considered, unless it be that of the London Underground. A. D. Moody finds it 'unmistakable' – though he indeed notes that 'many readers want to have it otherwise' – that Eliot's vision in 'East Coker' i is of a 'dance of death', and finds the poem's anti-humanism exemplified by the contrast with the Elyot work that the text has raided; the humanism of *The Governour* is 'jarringly at odds' with the new context in which the work finds itself (Moody, pp. 208–10). Again, while I totally concur in seeing Eliot's passage as a 'dance of death', we should note that the death is meant to have *some* constitutive function 'nourishing the corn', and that the contrast with the fruitless dissolution of metropolitan death in 'Burnt Norton' – 'eructation of unhealthy souls / Into the faded air' – is marked. What we have in 'East Coker' is, as Davie has remarked ('Anglican Eliot', p. 183), a Maurrasian vision of England inhabited by a land-based peasantry firmly fixed in their neo-feudal station; dour, anonymous, transient and de-romanticized, they can simultaneously fulfil the twin functions of harmonizing with nature, and, more importantly, emphasiz-ing the power and omnipresence of death, in accordance with an unromantic 'of the earth earthy' tradition which always stresses the land-worker's eventual absorption by the land he works on. There is, in short, not much life in the *Quartets*, but what there is the dancers of 'East Coker' are at the centre of.

In *The Idea of a Christian Society* Eliot's plea for a return to the land and to 'conformity with nature' is occasioned more by a loathing of 'a mechanised, commercialised, urbanised way of life' than by the prospect of finding divinity present within the rhythm of the seasons and constellations (pp. 80–1). The *Quartets* never lose sight of the fact that the realm of nature is 'fallen' and provisional, and that conformity with it hardly narrows the abyss that separates temporal and eternal. It is all too easy for critics who contest the emphasis on *vanitas* in 'East Coker' that Leavis insists on to exaggerate the splendours of the 'cosmic family' scenario supposedly found there. Thus P. H. Butter in his reply to Leavis rejoices at the picture of 'men, beasts and nature all being parts of a rhythmical life, in which the men join with "rustic laughter" and "mirth", by ritual accommodating themselves to the cycle and making it accep-table . . . we are being invited, by the rhythms as well as the connotations of the words, to regard the whole process as natural and acceptable'. Though Butter is quick to add that religious values must supplement this picture – 'Men will not find fulfilment solely by accommodating themselves to the rhythm, though they are right to do so' – the whole tone of his observation elides the distinction in kind, rather than merely degree, the poem insists on between the natural and supernatural, and posits far too benign an Eliot looking on the 'mirth' of the rural world as some input of divine grace.[37]

It is extraordinary how rapidly critics at the sound of the word 'nature' resort to an immediate coupling with 'Romantic' (and thence, frequently, 'Wordsworthian') even with a work like the *Quartets* that represents the absolute antithesis to any Romantic nature-worship. We should expect to find this position in Lobb (see Introduction, pp. 4–5), even though he is not able to adduce much supporting detail from the poem and goes no further than evasive generalization:

> We tend to forget that Eliot's poetry is more tied up with the sense of place and the *genius loci* than that of most modern poets. The quiet tone of his 'landscape' poems surely owes much to Wordsworth, despite all the differences of temperament, belief, and style.
>
> (p. 74)

It seems to me, as I discuss below (pp. 139–40), that Eliot in the *Quartets* has no interest whatsoever in the *genius loci*, and that the term suggests precisely the type of nature spirit or pantheism he discounts in the poem. A more detailed attempt to substantiate Lobb's position has recently been made by Julia Maniates Reibetanz, who aspires to show that 'Four Quartets stands squarely in the tradition of English romantic landscape poetry'.[38] What this means for both her and Lobb is no more than the shared practice of spiritual meditation in country locations, and this common 'quietness' of tone is supposed to override the absolute difference in the ends such meditation serves; in Wordsworth, of course, the reaffirmation of the poet as 'A worshipper of Nature' in a poem like 'Tintern Abbey', in Eliot the patient endurance of temporality while 'another day / Prepares for heat and silence' ('East Coker').[39] For Reibetanz 'Four Quartets does not deny, but rather accepts and celebrates, man's emotional ties with the beauty of the earth; and this is one of the poem's great strengths' (p. 530). Again she can find little that is quotable in the poem to illustrate Eliot's sense of these emotional ties with 'the beauty of the earth', and has to resort instead to the New England seascape of 'Ash-Wednesday' vi, or to the 'beautiful natural imagery' of 'Marina' (p. 531). The title of Reibetanz's discussion as reprinted in her book, 'This grace dissolved in place', is taken, of course, from the latter poem, but is appropriate, she feels, to the prominent position granted to the Incarnation in the *Quartets*; the argument goes that since the locations of the *Quartets* are intersected by the 'timeless' in the form of spiritual epiphany (following on from the major epiphany of the Incarnation) then the poem becomes a typical Romantic document of landscape invested with the rosy glow of divinity, or, as Reibetanz puts it, 'time

and place are framed in the light of redemption' (p. 531). But
this 'framing' is extraordinarily fitful; in the *Quartets* we have no
pantheistic or immanentist idea of divinity permanently present with the creation, which might indeed lead a religious poet
towards celebrating 'man's emotional ties with the beauty of
the earth'; rather we have a sense of natural landscape as
fundamentally and chronically devoid of divinity, apart from in
those special moments of revelation that thereby emphasize
the gap that normally pertains between time's covenant and the
timeless. Thus with the opening of 'Little Gidding':

Midwinter spring is its own season
Sempiternal though sodden towards sundown,
Suspended in time, between pole and tropic.
When the short day is brightest, with frost and fire,
The brief sun flames the ice, on pond and ditches,
In windless cold that is the heart's heat,
Reflecting in a watery mirror
A glare that is blindness in the early afternoon.
And glow more intense than blaze of branch, or brazier,
Stirs the dumb spirit; no wind, but pentecostal fire
In the dark time of the year. Between melting and
    freezing
The soul's sap quivers. There is no earth smell
Or smell of living thing. This is the spring time
But not in time's covenant. Now the hedgerow
Is blanched for an hour with transitory blossom
Of snow, a bloom more sudden
Than that of summer, neither budding nor fading,
Not in the scheme of generation.
Where is the summer, the unimaginable
Zero summer?

(CPP, p. 191)

Here it seems that heaven and earth are running on completely
different timetables, so to speak, with heat, fruition and
fecundity all being posited as a total metaphysical inversion of
the natural 'scheme of generation' that peaks in the summer. In
the sestina of 'The Dry Salvages', the Annunciation is seen as
the only means whereby a 'way out' can be found from the
ceaseless recurrence of the natural cycle with its 'silent wither-
ing of autumn flowers', as if disjunction rather than confluence

between divine and secular is again emphasized. In fact Reibetanz has brought the Incarnation into play without realizing what a hotly debated issue it is, and how susceptible to differing interpretations. In the final section of this chapter I explore Eliot's theology in the *Quartets* and in particular the relation between his approaches to the Incarnation and to landscape, set against the background of a vigorous contemporary debate on just these issues.

One further feature of Reibetanz's necessarily somewhat threadbare catalogue of natural beauties in the *Quartets* might be mentioned here, and that is the rose-garden of 'Burnt Norton' itself, 'first experienced in perplexity and uncertainty', though 'its beauty and integrity lead the poet to search for a clearer understanding of its nature' (p. 539). The garden has also been examined at some length by Nancy Duvall Hargrove, in the only full-length study of Eliot as a landscape poet; she too posits the setting as one of natural bounty and beauty, though for her Eliot's mentor in this is not Wordsworth but Tennyson, in whose work decorative gardens abound 'filled with rose bushes and apple trees, the former symbolizing human love and the latter innocence and purity'.[40] In taking too little note of the distinction, one might say, *between* grace and place, she rewrites Eliot's setting to make the natural garden itself Edenic, rather than the vision that takes place there:

> the garden [at Burnt Norton] is filled with rose bushes and birds, and falling autumn leaves litter the ground [rather an interpolated Tennysonian touch, this!]. Further, Helen Gardner, referring to Section iv, points out there 'are sunflowers in the borders and clematis hanging from the wall and clipped yews'.
>
> (p. 135)

In 'Burnt Norton' we have rather the sparely described *disiecta membra* of such a garden, here pleasingly composed by Ms Hargrove, with Dame Helen's help, into an affecting scenic picture, though at this rate we should expect to find garlic (if not sapphires) growing in the border too.[41] The specific details of the garden we are given tend to deflate Tennysonian expectations, to produce a sense of desolation that is anything but picturesque:

106

Along the empty alley, into the box circle,
To look down into the drained pool.
Dry the pool, dry concrete, brown edged . . .
(*CPP*, p. 172)

Such mundane intrusions are common in the *Quartets*:

when you leave the rough road
And turn behind the pig-sty to the dull façade,
(*CPP*, p. 191)

and might be instanced again by the 'clumsy' peasants of 'East
Coker'. In fact in the garden at 'Burnt Norton' Eliot seems to
me to be resisting the traditional and consoling significations of
such a venue, as found, for example, in Ford Madox Ford: 'You
will find nowhere a *mise-en-scène* so suggestive of the ancient and
enduring as in an English rose-garden, walled in and stone
pathed, if it be not in an English cathedral close.' [42] Even the
brief glimpse of beauty in the 'kingfisher's wing' passage in
section iv of the quartet is there to remind us of the impassable
gulf between the natural light of the sun, liable to recurrent
clouding and setting, and the unfailing light that is always 'still',
'At the still point of the turning world'.

In insisting that the *Quartets* are anything but 'squarely in the
tradition of English romantic landscape poetry', I do not wish to
be regarded as claiming them simply for a supposed antithetical
category of 'classic landscape'. If romanticism and classicism
mean anything at all in landscape terms then the former must
suggest primarily an evocation of the powers of wild and
untamed landscape, the latter the beauties of cultivation and
human intervention in the natural cycle. Eliot's England, as
discussed in the preceding section, eschews favoured romantic
localities, and though 'The Dry Salvages' with its 'chthonic
Powers' of ocean might seem an exercise in the sublime, Eliot's
response to the sea has a marked severity and discipline
compared to that in his earlier poetry (see above, pp. 35–6). In
elevating the 'ordinary', parochially settled and southern countryside as the true locus of England Eliot indeed hypothesizes a
classic norm, but his handling of such a norm in the *Quartets*
shows a marked departure from anything we might recognize
as traditional landscape classicism. Such a tradition has always
stressed, in Worringer's term, humanity's 'empathy' with

environment, when 'Man was at home in the world and felt himself its centre' (*Abstraction and Empathy*, p. 102). For Sherard Vines a cardinal feature of seventeenth- and eighteenth-century landscape, in poetry and art, is precisely its 'homocentric' quality, its stressing 'the importance of man' and his possession of 'the right and the power to improve upon nature' (*The Course of English Classicism*, pp. 45, 54). Eliot's Virgilianism needs to be discussed here, which like his Dantism tends to the dour and puritanical, as the grudging quasi-Virgilianism already discussed in 'East Coker' i might indicate. In earlier chapters I drew attention to Eliot's use of the *Aeneid* in 'What is a classic?' as an exemplum of austerity in both a poetic and an ethical sense, the poetry's sacrifice of 'the opulence and variety of later tongues' corresponding to its hero's sacrifice of personal love to public duty (above, p. 11). This severe reading of the *Aeneid* sets the tone as we saw for Eliot's understanding of Latin literature as a whole (above, p. 74). If Virgil underlies both the imperialism and the agrarianism of Eliot's prose writings, as Gareth Reeves has shown,[43] then the *Quartets'* apocalyptic deflation of the former (above, pp. 90–1) is not unexpectedly accompanied by a complete absence of any fervour for rusticality such as we find in the *Georgics*. The connection between imperialism and rusticality, between 'a nobly filial love of country, and a love of the country', held a special appeal for apologists of British imperialism, as John Holloway has noted;[44] while Caesar is abroad giving 'justice to docile peoples' the citizen stays at home tending his flocks and fields.[45] Here the (southern) 'garden of England' becomes the entirely fitting seat of empire, rather than Davie's industrial north (see above, p. 79), whereas the desolate and curiously empty garden of 'Burnt Norton' might feature as a prefatory emblem in the poem of the vanity of imperial ambition. In a *Criterion* Commentary of 1928 Eliot noted how Britain might function politically as 'the middle way' between Europe and the rest of the world, 'by virtue of the fact that she is the only member of the European community that has established a general empire'; but in the *Quartets* there is no vision of this constructive role, the concept of 'the middle way' in 'East Coker' ii rather taking on the Dantesque connotations of bewilderment, loss and travail from the beginning of the *Inferno*.[46]

In noting how Greek and Latin writers have 'a positive

shrinking from wild and uncultivated nature', Irving Babbitt quotes sentiments from J. R. Lowell as expressing 'an attitude towards nature that an ancient would have understood perfectly': 'The green pastures and golden slopes of England are sweeter both to the outward and to the inward eye that the hand of man has immemorially cared for and caressed them' (*Rousseau and Romanticism*, pp. 270–1). This Babbitt calls the 'Virgilian attitude' to nature, and we see in it a balance between the beauty *and* effort of cultivation. The *Quartets* has as little place for such an attitude as it has for any enthusing over the wild and uncultivated; in 'East Coker' i the cycle of settlement and cultivation are presented with no emphasis whatever on any beauteous return in the form of 'green pastures and golden slopes'. Eliot's discussion of Virgil's *Georgics* concentrates almost entirely on the theme of agricultural labour, which is seen as anticipating the Christian monastic life of 'labour and prayer'; this spartan emphasis has no place for any vision of the land as the *Saturnia tellus*, such as we find in book II of the *Georgics* (ll. 136–76, 325–45).[47] And Eliot's interest in the *Eclogues* relates not to any notion of pastoral ease but solely to the famous 'prophecy' of Christ's birth in the fourth, divorced, however, from any prospect of a returning 'golden age' there described (see 'Virgil and the Christian world', *OPAP*, pp. 121–6).

The 'golden age' strain of ruralism is conspicuous, of course, in much Georgian writing; thus Thomas's *The Heart of England* makes repeated use of the phrase itself, and his travelogue records constant encounters with Apollo, Pan, Amaryllis, Daphnis and so on in field and woodland. Though Thomas's extraordinarily picturesque descriptions of farms, gardens and villages do not elide altogether the notion of work, his 'happy and proud' workmen like Richard the Ploughman either 'never become tired' or are presented within such a roseate mythological glow as to annul the distinction between pre- and postlapsarian landscape entirely:

> I have seen the radiant cart-horses coming with grave nods through the farmyard at dawn as if they were to be yoked to the chariot of the sun; the red-haired carter was at least a Phaeton, a son of Apollo, if not Apollo himself.
>
> (pp. 25–6, 94)

The neo-classical strain in Thomas's writing lies not simply in

the liberal sprinkling of mythology but in his attraction towards cultivated, homocentric landscape; although *The Heart of
England* is in no sense topographical, it is clear its author never
ventures beyond the golden-age hedgerows of southern
England into any more 'sublime' landscape that might threaten
or question humanity's tenure.[48] When Eliot asserts (to repeat
the quotation above, p. 81) that 'the beauty of England' is

> not primarily that of the more remote hills and moors
> which men have not yet found it worth their while to
> disfigure, but is to be found in the ordinary countryside
> which is largely the work of generations of humanising
> labour,

it might seem we have a view akin to Thomas's, but in the
Quartets the emphasis is not on 'beauty' but on two words in
Eliot's final phrase here, 'generations' and 'labour'; to look at
the slowly changing land is not to see the legacy of beautifi-
cation but to see the vast number of transient lives that have
gone to feed a soil 'Which is already flesh, fur and faeces, / Bone
of man and beast'. If the *Georgics* acknowledge both the beauty
and effort of cultivation, we might say that a book like
Thomas's tends to discount the latter in producing a 'golden-
age' scenario which to Babbitt was merely romanticism in
classic disguise (see *Rousseau and Romanticism*, pp. 79ff.); but we
should certainly note that the *Quartets*, in discounting the
former, represent a classicism as partial and unbalanced. We are
faced at bottom with the difficulties of a man making use of the
humanism of a classical tradition, handed down through Dante,
who combines with 'a Catholic cast of mind' what he himself
described as a 'Calvinistic heritage' and a 'Puritanical temperament' ('Goethe as the sage', *OPAP*, p. 209).

In *Four Quartets* we have a depopulated England where the
only visions of rural settlement are set deliberately in the past,
in sixteenth- and seventeenth-century East Coker and Little
Gidding; we might say that the poem elegizes rural life, did that
verb not imply too positive a salute to the way of life that has
disappeared. As far as the present day is concerned, Davie is
right to note of the *Quartets'* settings that 'no sense is conveyed
of what it is like in the twentieth century to *live* in these places'
('Anglican Eliot', p. 182). In this Eliot is far from alone in the

period around the 1930s and 1940s, and although many writers
are keen on the phrase 'the humanised landscape' as a challenge
to Romantic and Ruskinian tastes in scenery, as in the
comments quoted from Sharp and Eden (above, pp. 82, 85), and
as in Eliot's declared preference about England's beauty, the
fact is that countless reproductions of landscape at the time – in
poetry, painting, photographs, posters, book-jackets, prints –
show scenes completely devoid of human figures. One example
would be the stills from Paul Rotha's film *The Face of Britain*
which the *Architectural Review* chose in 1935 to illustrate again
'the humanised landscape'; we have a typical idyll of village,
clouds, fields and haystacks, but totally empty of any workers
or inhabitants.[49] The book-jackets Brian Cook produced for
Batsford (Plate 10), the (southern) landscape paintings of Eric
Ravilious and Paul Nash, a vast number of posters produced by
the railway and petrol companies – all suggest rural England to
be as it were a vast hills-and-fields *Marie Celeste*.[50] We might see
Ravilious's *Downs in Winter* (Plate 7) as a typical record of work
done rather than of workers doing it, the humanized landscape
with no humans. The six Shell posters featured in the 1934
Architectural Review, for example, that formed the basis of
Connolly's article referred to above (p. 81), show between them
just one human figure; the artists responsible, including Nash,
Rex Whistler and Graham Sutherland, are here clearly providing a tourist England to be looked at through car or train
windows rather than lived in. As all tourists know, however,
fellow tourists have the habit of getting in the way of solitary
views, though the Shell posters do all they can to suggest that
the increased access to the countryside the car gave was not, in
fact, the major threat to the beauty that was the point of the
whole enterprise. The petrol and railway companies offer rural
England not as a mass-sought-after commodity (which in some
regions it certainly was) but as an individual experience
exclusive to each viewer. The experience, whether scenic or, as
in the *Quartets*, mystical, which the country provides, is thus
authenticated. We might note the contrast with previous
presentations of scenery like that in the picturesque movement, where some humanity, if only token *banditti*, was generally included in the foreground of compositions, or even the
painters themselves. We might say that there were just too
many visitors to the country in the 1930s to take the chance of

suggesting the hordes who at any moment might drop in on a view.

As far as actual land-workers are concerned, there is no doubt, of course, of their decline in number in the twentieth century, yet even where the chance arises to depict them – as in cultivated rather than abandoned landscape, where crops and farm implements indicate their continuing presence, or as on many posters where well-tended fields and villages are purveyed – they are frequently omitted. The photograph with which the *Listener* fronts its 'This is England' issue of 31 March 1937 shows a marvellous constructivist-type landscape of two large haystacks on the bare Wiltshire Downs, with not a hay-maker in sight, even though the farmer whose land is photo-graphed notes that he employs 'about thirty men and boys' (p. 583) (Plate 11). Such treatments show a marked difference from Victorian depictions of harvest, where the labourers themselves remain a subject of importance, whereas a glance through some recent publications on twentieth-century British landscape painting confirms the frequent elision of the land-worker, and the work of Paul Nash and Ravilious in particular testifies to it.[51] Of course, many landscapists continued to treat the human figure, no doubt earning the approval of the Auden of 'Letter to Lord Byron' (1937) for whom 'Art's subject is the human clay, / And landscape but a background to a torso' (*EA*, p. 185). What we have is clearly some kind of polemic involving the 'emptied landscape' and its opposite, and the motives for the former, other than placating crowded tourists, need now to be discussed.

Four Quartets, inhabited solely by ghosts and spirits, is a prime instance of emptied landscape, and the poem consistently refuses to elevate the human subject, even when the oppor-tunity provides itself; thus the cold anonymity of 'Little Gid-ding' makes no mention by name of Nicholas Ferrar, though for some commentators to think of the place was immediately to think of the personality behind it.[52] 'You are here to kneel / Where prayer has been valid'; all individuals are gathered into the impersonal process of time and history. The charges of 'anti-humanism' levelled against the new tendencies in archi-tecture (above, pp. 22, 25) might easily be directed at this fashion for marginalizing or eliding the human figure in landscape, especially in the case of the works by Nash or by

Ravilious where nature is 'invested . . . with the functional look of modern design' in Ian Jeffrey's words (*The British Landscape*, p. 14). Again it was the southern half of England, with its great stretches of bare smooth chalkland, that permitted the importation of functionalist design into landscape, and it is no accident that the monoliths and earthworks such country bears, as Stonehenge, Avebury, Maiden Castle, increase in popularity as pictorial subjects at the same time as modern architecture is proclaiming its 'monolithic' emphases, nor that the final number of *Axis* (1937) should print photographs of Silbury Hill and Avebury opposite some constructivist work by Miró (pp. 8–9). It seems to me that many writers and artists who feature the chalklands in their work do so with the aim of communicating a vision of the land which is in many ways, though not entirely, similar to Eliot's in the *Quartets*. Connolly (inadvertently I believe) betrays this kinship in his comment on the Shell posters quoted above (p. 81). Although their 'cheerful and genuine' character suggests to him a farewell to Romantic brooding, now that 'England is merry again', that merriness is communicated through a rather odd list of spartan images rather than the traditional greenwood ones: 'welcome the bracing glories of our clouds, the cirrhus and the cumulus, and the cold pastoral of the chalk'. The chalk is indeed beautiful and unchanging, like Keats's Grecian urn, but the corollary of the quotation is here an unformulated sense of what is again the transience of generations: the chalklands with their ancient monuments will continue to remain when 'old age shall this generation [and all others, we might add] waste'.[53] Connolly's sense of 'merriness' is doubtless based on the bright, bold colours of say the Cerne Abbas poster which compensate, we might think, for the empty abstraction of the landscape; the fact that the giant's penis is censored by the cloud-shadow increases the sense that this 'merry' landscape has in fact had all its earthy or Rabelaisian qualities taken out of it (Plate 12). Similarly the ghost-labourers of East Coker, a mere ten miles or so from Cerne Abbas, might express 'rustic laughter', but we pretty soon see that the joke is on them, as it is on all transient humanity. Raymond Williams's comment on Hardy's landscapes, which include of course the Cerne Abbas figure, has a striking aptness here; Hardy saw 'the closeness of man and the land being broken', so he sometimes projected his insistence on closeness and continuity into the finally negative images of an empty nature and the tribal past of Stonehenge and the barrows . . . . Even these, however, in their deliberate hardness – the uncultivatable heath, the bare stone relics – confirm the human negatives, in what looks like a deliberate reversal of pastoral. In them the general alienation has its characteristic monuments though very distant in time and space from the controlling immediate disturbance.[54]

In fact Williams's comment seems to me far more illustrative of 1930s landscape practices under discussion here and below than of Hardy, since Hardy still peoples his landscapes with figures like Tess and Henchard who themselves have a monumental quality qualifying them to be the heroic site of that process of alienation. In later landscape we might say that there is often no Lear to rage upon the heath, merely the heath itself. Thus although 'East Coker' i might indeed be called a 'deliberate reversal of pastoral', Eliot unlike Hardy never has any originary pastoral to start with.

Eric Ravilious's *Train Landscape* of 1940 springs out of a 'summer project' he set himself in 1939 to paint many of the chalk figures on the southern downs (Plate 13).[55] Again this is a 'humanized landscape' of long standing, as the horse shows, again without actual humans. It is an extraordinary irony that Ravilious includes an empty third-class railway carriage as the other major component of this painting. Bakhtin, in discussing the opening of Dostoevsky's *The Idiot*, which takes place in such a carriage, notes how 'the third-class railway car, like the deck of a ship in the ancient menippea, is a substitute for the *public square*, where people from various positions find themselves in familiar contact with one another' (*Problems*, p. 174). In such a vision of England where has all the third-class public gone, one might ask, and 'East Coker' would doubtless reply with satisfaction, 'Under the hill'.

It is difficult to decide on the rhetoric of a painting like *Train Landscape*, of course, whereas it seems clear that the suppression of the human subject in the *Quartets* is part of the major emphasis on secular *vanitas* the poem wishes to inculcate, and of the total 'de-romanticization' of man's relation with the natural environment. Certainly it is unlikely that the painting 'glories in the ingenuity of modern man', as Freda Constable claims, by contrasting the beautifully designed carriage interior with the miniaturized primitive landmark.[56] In spite of the carriage's hogging of the foreground, we might feel that the painting reminds us what a brief tenure the ingenuity of modern man has on the immemorial age of the hills, and how unlikely he seems to leave something behind him as durable and as in keeping with the landscape as the chalk figure. We may also be being told how civilizations 'rise and fall, crumble, are extended, / Are removed' in 'East Coker's words. Certainly it is clearer with writers on the chalklands, whom we shall come on to, that the vast and changing timescape of human settlement they offer is a reminder of the follies of temporal pretensions. A satisfaction is taken in the chalk's formal absolutes – the hills of East Sussex, 'as they pass on to the sea, become purified and, as it were, abstracted from all that is trivial or obscures their structural integrity'[57] – which encourages descriptions that echo Gropius on his architecture or Eliot on his poetry, and which often suggests that humanity is to be included in that which trivially obscures such momentous abstract power. The only race which is seen as harmonizing with such a setting is ancient man, whose works are built on a similar monumental scale. One celebrant of just such power is Vaughan Cornish, in his *The Scenery of England* (1932), with its sub-title *A Study of Harmonious Grouping in Town and Country*, published by the Council for the Preservation of Rural England. Cornish not only has an emphatic southern bias in his choice of scenic locations, but his England is utterly depopulated, not only of rural inhabitants but of any fellow onlookers; the climaxes of his tour are elevations of abstract form, as in the environs of Stonehenge:

> On the rolling, treeless Downs there is a special splendour of the sky when great masses of cumulus are suspended in the blue. The sharp summits of mountains are incompatible with these rounded forms, and the great cumulus is too large to group with tree-tops, but when these clouds spread above the broad billows of the Downs, heaven and earth are united in one great harmony of form.
>
> (p. 40)

On setting out, in April, on his 'pilgrimage' from 'Collegiate Oxford to the Cotswold villages', Cornish cannot resist quoting the opening of Chaucer's *General Prologue*, though he seems to have no notion of the irony involved in equating the journey of that vanished community with his own solitary pursuit of scenic form (pp. 35-6). Certainly there is no nostalgia for merrie England here; Cornish's ghosts, like those of 'East Coker', have been safely laid.

The southern chalk downs, in their 'economy and reserve', had been noted by Hilaire Belloc in 1904 as being the English landscape's counterpart to 'the classic in verse or architecture',[58] and such landscape had indeed received a good deal of attention in late Victorian and Edwardian writing, notably the Wiltshire of Richard Jefferies and W. H. Hudson. With these writers, however, the attention remains centred on the human subject, be it shepherd or agricultural labourer; indeed with the latter writer we are often introduced to figures like the 'Apollo of the downs' we meet in *A Shepherd's Life*, a young rustic with 'powerful and perfect physique and marvellously handsome face – such a face as the old Greek sculptors have left to the world to be universally regarded and admired for all time as the most perfect'.[59] Although Hudson notes the severe and 'undecorated' nature of downland, indicating its unsympathetic character to lovers of the picturesque like Gilpin (p. 2), he then goes on to decorate it himself with such golden-age figures. It is not until the 1930s, however, and the arrival of functionalism, that the severity of the chalk truly comes into its own, and the visions it often inspires of humanity in its not very significant place are perhaps the nearest parallels we can find for Eliot's England in the *Quartets*. One writer whose treatment of chalk country has a very Eliot-like emphasis is H. J. Massingham, in his *English Downland* of 1936; witness his description of Butser Hill in Hampshire, 'at once so elemental and so finished', with

> an antiquity so great that the hill-grass was browsed by a million generations of herbivores before it was pressed by the foot of man. It is on the winds of Butser that floats the consolation of those words, 'As it was in the beginning, is now and ever shall be.' The scorings of ancient man have creased this Samson's limbs and shoulders, while man of to-day has peeled strips of their skin for his tennis-lawns.

Yet Butser's head will still be raised over the hills of the
east and the west when rebel man is no more.

(p. 72)

One is reminded of various tableaux of human desolation in *The
Rock*:

Where My Word is unspoken,
In the land of lobelias and tennis flannels
The rabbit shall burrow and the thorn revisit,
The nettle shall flourish on the gravel court,
And the wind shall say: 'Here were decent godless people:
Their only monument the asphalt road
And a thousand lost golf balls'.

(*CPP*, p. 155)

There is also Massingham's description of Bow Hill, near
Chichester:

The perfect unison between the trees contorted with age
and the memorials of vanished man on the hillside above
them; the even deeper harmony, dramatised by contrast,
between the shadowy patriarchs and the timeless bare
crown of Bow, bring forth a joy to arm me against
temporal things.

(p. 79)

Notice here that we have no dwelling on the mysterious or
titanic powers of nature herself, as in the 'sublime' landscapes
of the Romantic period; the southern chalk, in its austere and
elemental outline, is treated as an impassive, 'timeless' witness
of the puny habitations of temporality other than those of the
ancients whose memorials are in 'perfect unison' with the
environment. It is precisely a 'humanized landscape' that
dwarfs modern humans.

Massingham's admiration of the ancients and their monumental environs might seem to have a quasi-fascist ring to it, a
power-worship that scorns modern dwarfs sitting on the
shoulders of ancient giants; certainly some pictorial represen-
tations of the downs might be read in this way (Plate 14). That
the ancients were indigenous and racially unmixed – existing,
that is, before the recorded waves of Roman, Scandinavian and
French invasion – forms part of Massingham's positive

117

response; certainly the Roman legionaries, 'a polyglot assembly from all over Europe and Asia', were 'less highly civilised than their conquered' (p. 44; see also pp. 23, 81). This indicates one reason of course why the chalklands never feature in Eliot's own work; however much their classic austerity might suit his didactic ruralism, as landscapes they are in effect inscribed with an anti-Latin nationalism that is anathema to him. They may be a useful bludgeon to beat the present age with, but it is no use for an underminer of all secular kingdoms having some ancient English settlement set up as a 'Mecca of the downs', in Massingham's phrase on Stonehenge (p. 46).[60]

Massingham does, however, show a realistic awareness throughout his book that the downs civilization cannot be recovered, and the key-note generally is a gloomy satisfaction in man's declining further and further towards a time when, as Butser Hill proclaims, he will be 'no more', a world-weariness akin to that of the *Quartets*. The same cannot be said of another attempt, via the chalk, to hypothesize England, that by F. J. Harvey Darton in his *English Fabric* of 1935. The book has a good deal in common with Eliot's attempts to dissociate rural community from any prevailing idyllic or picturesque mood:

> I should hate to add to the number of books which discover the beauty of England and describe new paths to explore it. Still more depressing to me would it be to be bright and cheery about rustic characters and quaint customs.[61]

Darton stresses instead the dour anonymity and struggle of rural life, under the aegis of the Cerne Abbas Giant, who appears in the Shell poster version on the book's dust-jacket:

> In fact as well as in fantasy, in endurance and in origin, he stands for the principle of life eternally renewed but constant in one place from century to century, to be observed, perhaps, nowhere in more stubborn continuity than in a thousand English villages.

> (p. 35)

Darton has no interest in detailing individual villages, but as a resolute centrist concentrates on providing a taxonomy of the various social types to be found in all villages and in categorizing the 'common elements' of village culture (p. 20). Thus the

Dorset villages he features exclusively become the central node of the 'English Fabric', the Cerne Giant in their midst becoming its 'true emblem' (p. 60) and nearby Maiden Castle appearing as 'the foundation of England' (p. 312). Darton is of particular interest in combining the standardized village as definitive of England, discussed in the previous section, with an interest in the ancient monuments traced above. His refusal to single out any 'colourful' village rustic from his place within the 'stubborn continuity' of the anonymous generations tallies with the ruralism of 'East Coker', exemplifying Blunden's 'stubborn lump of flesh who sings behind his spade' (above, p. 94), as does his insistence on the vanity of at least modern human endeavour, initiated again by the vast timescape the monuments open up. Thus the 'cobweb columns' of the elec-tricity pylons set up in the vicinity of Maiden Castle become 'so little, so impotent' by contrast with something that 'will still be unharmed when the grids are a handful of rust'; from here indeed Darton goes on into a kind of rhapsody over the 'absurdity' of 'all human skill' and the 'brutish contempt' nature feels for humanity's achievement (pp. 316-37). The difference with Eliot (or for that matter Massingham) is that Maiden Castle itself, as a product of 'human skill', is available as a symbol of potential renewal which the English are exhorted to attain: the earthwork 'lay[s] bonds upon the earth magnificently. If all the life of our country could be informed with that splendour of imagination, England would be renewed' (p. 317). Darton's admiration for, and alarm at the decline of, the empire and its 'laying bonds upon the earth' is evident at several points in the book, and underlies his choice of epigraph, 'Tantae molis erat Romanam condere gentem' (*Aeneid* I.33) though we possess 'an empire in which Rome's would be but one large field' (p. 314n.). Dorset thus becomes a kind of global citadel, and this instance of imperialist centraliza-tion might illustrate by contrast just how far Eliot is from centring England for this purpose in the *Quartets* (see above, pp. 90-1).[62]

If the *Quartets* are a work emptied of people, they are also a work which creates an English setting curiously empty of historical events, other than the Civil War in 'Little Gidding', though even here the lesson to be learned from periods of secular crisis is a passive attending on political issues until ultimately all shall be 'folded in a single party'. The down-grading of history in the poem, of the establishment of present England out of successive waves of colonization or layers of past event and periodicity, is accomplished under the motto 'history is a pattern / Of timeless moments' ('Little Gidding' v); we might say that there are only two real events, the Fall and the Incarnation, and a sweeping dismissal of the whole period AD seems implied no less than in *The Rock*: 'The cycles of Heaven in twenty centuries / Bring us farther from GOD and nearer to the Dust' (quoted above, p. 98). The *Quartets* may feature village England, but there is nothing of the village pageant about them, in the manner of *Between the Acts*. In this sense we can talk about the strategy of centralizing time as well as place, and contrast it with those apprehensions of England that insist on seeing plurality and variegation in the temporal as well as the physical landscape. With writers like Massingham an admiration for the ancients involves a rather drastic polarization between England on the one hand and the 'post-ancient' on the other, lumped with all its diversity into a simple temporal bloc exemplifying decline. With Ravilious's *Train Landscape* we have ancient and modern confronting each other with any sense of an intervening history totally elided.

This neglect of our 'rich cultural heritage' can be inferred to have some sort of anti-nationalistic impetus behind it even where such a stance is not proclaimed, an England dissociating itself from the popular nationalism fed on Alfred, Arthur, Good Queen Bess, Shakespeare, Francis Drake, the Glorious Revolution, and so on. That even the ancient chalk figures can be sited firmly within such a heritage is shown by G. K. Chesterton's *The Ballad of the White Horse*, published in 1911. The poem records King Alfred's victorious campaign against the Danes, the fight 'for the Christian civilization against the heathen nihilism', though Chesterton self-confessedly 'telescopes history' in including in Alfred's army Roman and Celtic contingents to indicate that the work of Christian civilization was 'really done by generation after generation' ordering and settling the land.[63] Although the chalk-figure in Berkshire's Vale of the White Horse is mysteriously dated by Chesterton to some immemorial origin,

For the White Horse knew England
When there was none to know

(p. 2)

its survival through ages and civilizations represents the
triumph of humanity over nihilism, and Chesterton reminds us
that such figures need to be constantly re-cut, that the 'large
white commonweal' of England has to fight off the mosses and
weeds of barbarism and darkness generation after generation.
Here then the white horse and English landscape are inscribed
with historical continuity and not centralized to affirm the
power of any past political or metaphysical logos, though as
Harvey Darton and Chesterton himself show, a 'living' chalk
figure is more likely to support imperialist ideology than a dead
one.[64] A similar sense of England as a kind of archaeological
timescape is found in Kipling's work, which Eliot was taking such
an interest in at the time of writing the last three quartets. Thus
Puck of Pook's Hill offers to children of modern England a record of
the picturesque and heroic efforts that have gone into building
up the land performed by different races of the past – Romans,
Saxons, Normans – working, so to speak, in unison; the power of
present England needs always to be invigorated by memory of its
great forebears. In discussing Kipling's 'historical imagination'
Eliot notes how it gives us both 'an awful awareness of the
extent of time' and 'a dizzy sense of the nearness of the past', a
sense of 'the antiquity of England, of the number of generations
and people who have laboured the soil and in turn been buried
beneath it, and of the contemporaneity of the past' ('Rudyard
Kipling', *OPAP*, p. 248). Although Eliot is clearly aware that
Kipling intends this sense of the 'antiquity of England' as part of
an imperialist emphasis on present-day England living up to its
great and hard-won heritage, in the *Quartets* he takes completely
the opposite path, eliding all traces of heritage and using the
generations who have laboured and been buried as a reminder, in
the emphasis 'East Coker' gives, of the weariness of temporality.

I suggested in the previous section that Eliot's conceptualization of England in the *Quartets* and the prose writings contemporary with them could be related to a widespread
emphasis in the 1930s on finding the essential site of the
country in southern and 'homocentric' village landscape. I
wanted to show here, however, how this classicist strategy is

itself examined and subverted by Eliot, and how the 'ordinary'
settled countryside of the *Quartets* is the focus of a stern and
unaccommodating vision where rural humanity is kept firmly
in its place; homocentric landscape with humans radically
decentred. It seems to me that the term 'stripped classicism'
might again be applied to such a ruralism, as it was to the
formal austerity of modern design in chapter 1 above, and I
have sought to show its elements in other writers and artists of
the period. What remains now is to study the confluence
between religion and landscape in Eliot and others, to under-
score some of the points already made as well as introducing us
to further polemic concerning 'England'.

LANDSCAPE AND RELIGION

One useful way into the theology-landscape nexus in the
Quartets is through the neglected path of V. A. Demant's *The
Religious Prospect* of 1939, a book Eliot applauds in a *New English
Weekly* article of the same year and one by a writer whose work
Eliot frequently pays tribute to.[65] Demant considers that the
modern world is particularly beset by two types of heresy, one
that over-emphasizes God's place *within* the creation, the other
over-stressing His absence from it. The latter Demant labels
'unmitigated salvation-dualism', where the Redeemer indeed
'enters the cosmic process from the Eternal Places' though
otherwise natural and supernatural are held to be entirely
distinct; the result is, in Demant's words, a view of the world
order as 'a completely alienating or alienated existence in
relation to God' and a non-recognition of 'the creative and
gracious hand of God in the world' (pp. 199–202). It is the other
heresy, however, that causes Demant more concern as 'the
characteristic heresy of to-day', a liberal Christianity that
'denies the reality of an eternal world behind the cosmic world
of becoming' and 'tends to confine God's action to His immanent activity in creation' (p. 203). Thus the Incarnation is
devalued into 'a dogma of Christ as a particular instance of a
general revelation given by the immanent process itself' and
Christ becomes 'the crowning part of natural religion' (p. 206).
'In such a dogma the Incarnation is the very opposite of an
event which comes to man and confronts him with the one
decisive fact, the absolute Word from beyond the created order

by which he can evaluate the process itself. On this view the Incarnation becomes an aspect of creation' (p. 204). Thus for Demant 'the main task of Christian teaching to-day is to rescue the secular religious mind of modern man from its habit of identifying what belongs to the cosmic order with the divine. This habit has led by inevitable dialectic movements from liberal progressivism to ecstatic blood and earth cults' (p. 211). And so, Demant argues, we get the heresy of immanentism lending its force, at the present moment, to 'vitalistic totalitarianism in Germany' (p. 206). Sooner or later an inevitable Christian backlash will result and 'the wave of apocalyptic pessimism will grow in the Churches' own thought, proclaiming the catastrophic judgment of God upon all things human and counting every religious striving to inform civilization as idolatrous pretension' (p. 224). The stages by which liberalism leads to modern totalitarianism are endorsed by Eliot in his discussion of *The Religious Prospect*.[66]

Demant does not deny the immanent Christ; what he seeks is a *via media* between the two 'heresies', a simultaneous insistence on Christ's immanence and on his transcendence: 'the redemptive work of Christ depends upon its being the act of God transcendent, who, because He is transcendent, is not involved in the misdirection of the world of which He is nevertheless the immanent force'; we need refurnishing with 'the dogma of Christ the Saviour as also the sustainer and restorer of the world process' (p. 211); in short, 'the fact of Christ that does not explain away the reality of the eternal or the reality of the temporal' (pp. 201-2). In support of the Incarnation's sustaining these two realities and of its giving 'the possibility of a meaning to history' (p. 217), Demant quotes lines from the seventh chorus of *The Rock*:

Then came, at a predetermined moment, a moment in
    time and of time,
A moment not out of time, but in time, in what we call
    history: transecting, bisecting the world of time, a
    moment in time but not like a moment of time,
A moment in time but time was made through that
    moment: for without the meaning there is no time, and
    that moment of time gave the meaning.
                                        (*CPP*, p. 160)

The Rock itself, however, hardly endorses the status of the time that 'was made' through the Incarnation, nor does it ever assert the natural beauty that might lead to a recognition of 'the creative and gracious hand of God in the world', in Demant's phrase. Temporality is seen as a constant struggle to build form out of primal formlessness, order out of that which is primitive, uncouth and inchoate, 'Out of the sea of sound the life of music, / Out of the slimy mud of words, out of the sleet and hail of verbal imprecisions, / . . . the perfect order of speech, and the beauty of incantation' (*CPP*, p. 164). I noted above how the choruses themselves represent the 'perfect order of speech' seemingly created out of the 'slimy mud' of the everyday converse of Ethelbert and his workmates, a discourse not surviving to become part of Eliot's *Complete Works* (pp. 63–4), and throughout *The Rock* the state of nature is continually stressed as 'waste and void'. Thus part ii of the play opens with an account of the Creation that totally ignores the natural beauties produced in the six days and hurries straight into an account of man's alienation:

> In the beginning GOD created the world. Waste and void.
>   Waste and void. And darkness was upon the face
>   of the deep.
> And when there were men, in their various ways, they
>   struggled in torment towards GOD
> Blindly and vainly, for man is a vain thing, and man
>   without GOD is a seed upon the wind.
>
> (*CPP*, p. 160)

The same chorus concludes in bringing its account of history down to the present day where (despite the Incarnation) nothing seems to have changed:

> Waste and void. Waste and void. And darkness on the face
>   of the deep.
> Has the Church failed mankind, or has mankind failed the
>   Church?
>
> (*CPP*, p. 161)

Both *The Rock* and the *Quartets* seem in fact to be emphatic illustrations of Demant's first heresy, 'unmitigated salvation-dualism', showing, that is, again in Demant's words above, the world as 'a completely alienating or alienated existence in

relation to God', and stressing in 'Burnt Norton''s phrase the
'waste sad time' of historical exile. Although the lines Demant
quotes from *The Rock*, when taken in their proper context,
hardly serve his purpose, there was of course nothing in 'Burnt
Norton' (the only extant quartet at the time he was writing)
that would have served him better; rather than upholding the
reality of the eternal *and* the temporal, 'Burnt Norton' is explicit
in its devaluing of the latter to the status of the unreal. Thus
throughout Eliot's work there is no approach to the Creator
through His creation, or if there is it is only in those visionary
intrusions of the supernatural into the natural which act as
reminders of the negligibility of the latter. Thus with the
'epiphany' at the opening of 'Little Gidding':

When the short day is brightest, with frost and fire,
The brief sun flames the ice, on pond and ditches,
In windless cold that is the heart's heat,
Reflecting in a watery mirror
A glare that is blindness in the early afternoon.
And glow more intense than blaze of branch, or brazier,
Stirs the dumb spirit: no wind, but pentecostal fire
In the dark time of the year. Between melting and
    freezing
The soul's sap quivers. There is no earth smell
Or smell of living thing. This is the spring time
But not in time's covenant.

(CPP, p. 191)

The fact that Eliot chooses to feature one of the spiritual high-
points of the poem at the 'very dead of winter' enforces as
noted above (pp. 105–6) a complete disjunction between
natural and spiritual modes of fruition and rejects the idea of
any sort of staged ascent from the former to the latter.
Intuitions of the spiritual come to us, of course, through
'nature' and time, but Eliot always makes sure that natural
scenes and emblems are sufficiently understated, or devalued,
or ironized as to never themselves usurp the status of that
which they point towards and hint at. In *The Rock* a correspondence is indeed indicated in the final chorus between the 'Light
Invisible' and the sun, as if a difference in degree rather than
kind is being assumed, yet the celebration of natural light is

expressed in such diluted and counter-ecstatic images as to
dampen entirely any movement towards 'nature worship':

O Light Invisible, we praise Thee!
Too bright for mortal vision.
O Greater Light, we praise Thee for the less;
The eastern light our spires touch at morning,
The light that slants upon our western doors at evening,
The twilight over stagnant pools at batflight,
Moon light and star light, owl and moth light,
Glow-worm glowlight on a grassblade.
O Light Invisible, we worship Thee!

(*CPP*, p. 166)

It is especially in *Four Quartets* that we have Eliot's relegation
of the natural creation not only to a secondary status, but to
one totally sundered from the spiritual except in the epiphanic
moments of consciousness. In this he is following Hulme, who
insisted on the 'discontinuity' or 'chasm' between the natural
and the divine and again attacked modern liberalizations that
would 'attempt to restate the whole of religion in terms of
vitalism':

Biology is not theology, nor can God be defined in terms
of 'life' or 'progress'. . . . It is necessary to realize that
there is an absolute, and not a relative, difference between
humanism (which we can take to be the highest
expression of the vital), and the religious spirit. The *divine*
is not *life* at its intensest. It contains in a way an almost
anti-vital element.[67]

This leads again into Hulme's description of classical art as that
in which a formal, geometrical austerity attempts to approximate to the divine, an art springing 'not from a delight in life
but from a feeling for certain absolute values, which are
entirely independent of vital things' (ibid., p. 9). Eliot applauds
Hulme's 'theory of discontinuity' in his essay on Pascal, where
Pascal's own statement of an absolute division between the
orders of the natural and the divine – 'the higher is not implicit
in the lower as in an evolutionary doctrine it would be' – is
affirmed (*SE*, p. 416). We have already seen Eliot supporting
Hulme's anti-humanist insistence that 'there is an *absolute* to
which Man can *never* attain' (above, p. 48).

In the *Quartets* a Hulme-Pascal model of discontinuity between the human/natural and the divine is adopted, the barrier between them intensified by thàt Jansenist emphasis on the 'degraded and helpless state of man' which Eliot traced in Pascal (*SE*, p. 414).[68] It might be inferred that the poem's opposition to vitalism is shared by many exponents of a depopulated England in the 1930s discussed above, and that the primary desire is to dissociate the home landscape from that of the European totalitarian states, with their frequent glorification of the heroic land-worker. Eliot was in fact sceptical as regards the revival of what Demant calls 'ecstatic blood and earth cults' in Germany, but he is scathing about what we might call vitalist infiltrations into revealed religion in both Germany and England, 'the religion of the blue sky, the grass and flowers' (see *ICS*, pp. 86–7). Warnings about 'natural religion' and against an excessive immanentism that asserted every man's 'natural kinship with the divine with too little qualification' were being voiced in the *Criterion* at the same time.[69] At bottom Eliot's stand against romanticizing nature in the *Quartets* suggests that he shared Demant's view that the 'main task of Christian teaching to-day' is to 'rescue the secular religious mind of modern man from its habit of identifying what belongs to the cosmic order with the divine'. It is not to be wondered at, given Eliot's own account of the creation in *The Rock*, that works which salute the beauty and design of the cosmic order as evidence of the existence of God, like Blackmore's *Creation*, are dismissed as expressions of 'pure deism' (see 'Johnson as critic and poet', *OPAP*, p. 171).

One instance of English vitalism whose influence (albeit negative) on 'Burnt Norton' has never received its due is the final section of Day Lewis's 'The magnetic mountain' of 1933:

> Now raise your voices for a final chorus,
> Lift the glasses, drink to-morrow's health –
> Success to the doctor who is going to cure us
> And those who will die no more in bearing wealth.
> On our magnetic mountain a beacon burning
> Shall sign the peace we hoped for, soon or late,
> Clear over a clean earth, and all men turning
> Like infants' eyes like sunflowers to the light.
>
> Drink to the ordered nerves, the sight restored;

A day when power for all shall radiate
From the sovereign centres, and the blood is stirred
To flow in its ancient courses of love and hate:
When the country vision is ours that like a barn
Fills the heart with slow-matured delight,
Absorbing wind and summer, till we turn
Like infants' eyes like sunflowers to the light.

For us to dream the birthday, but they shall act it –
Bells over fields, the hooters from the mine,
On New Year's Eve under the bridegroom's attic
Chorus of coastguards singing Auld Lang Syne.
Now at hope's horizon that day is dawning,
We guess at glory from a mountain height,
But then in valley towns they will be turning
Like infants' eyes like sunflowers to the light.

Beckon O beacon, and O sun be soon!
Hollo, bells, over a melting earth!
Let man be many and his sons all sane,
Fearless with fellows, handsome by the hearth.
Break from your trance: start dancing now in town,
And, fences down, the ploughing match with mate.
This is your day: so turn, my comrades, turn
Like infants' eyes like sunflowers to the light.

Here, the dawning of a purely secular new order characterized
by health, strength, cleanliness and rural sports is saluted,
instituted by some unnamed and visionary 'doctor who is going
to cure us', a prospect that certainly merits John Lehmann's
alarm about the 'potentially fascist tendencies' in the poem.[70]
The chorus line here, 'Like infants' eyes like sunflowers to the
light', representing a renewed humanity turning joyfully to this
new day, is the type of vision 'Burnt Norton' iv deliberately
rejects:

Time and the bell have buried the day,
The black cloud carries the sun away.
Will the sunflower turn to us, will the clematis
Stray down, bend to us; tendril and spray
Clutch and cling?
Chill
Fingers of yew be curled

Down on us? After the kingfisher's wing
Has answered light to light, and is silent, the light is still
At the still point of the turning world.

(CPP, pp. 174–5)

Here we have not only the contrast between the intermittent
diurnal light and the eternal light, but also a rhetorical question
– 'Will the sunflower turn to us?' – that surely challenges the
homocentric secular dawn of Lewis's vision. The section of
'Burnt Norton' also encapsulates Eliot's disagreement with
Hopkins, other features of which have been touched on above
(p. 38). 'Immanentism' pervades Hopkins's poetry, a view of
divinity as constantly present within a 'never spent' creation as
a revitalizing force, hatching the world anew:

There lives the dearest freshness deep down things;
And though the last lights off the black West went
 Oh, morning, at the brown brink eastwards, springs –
Because the Holy Ghost over the bent
 World broods with warm breast and with ah! bright
wings.[71]

'Christ plays in ten thousand places, / Lovely in limbs, and
lovely in eyes not his', Hopkins elsewhere puts it, and Eliot's
utter lack of interest in this understanding of 'incarnation' is at
one with a classicism that shows no response whatsoever to
any antique ideal of the body, discussed above (p. 22). The
sonnet from which the latter lines are taken, 'As kingfishers
catch fire' (p. 129), takes us straight back to 'Burnt Norton' iv;
Hopkins's paralleling of Christ-in-man with the fire imbuing
the kingfisher is totally rejected in Eliot's distinction between
ephemeral natural beauty and spiritual permanence:

After the kingfisher's wing
Has answered light to light, and is silent, the light is still
At the still point of the turning world.

(CPP, p. 175)

In introducing Hopkins here to stress, by contrast, what A.
D. Moody has referred to as Eliot's 'dark' reading of the
Incarnation, which eschews 'the perfection of human nature
we like to think of, and which ideas of Incarnation usually allow
scope for' (p. 195), we come back once more to Eliot's quarrel

129

with humanism. Although Demant regards vitalism and its over-valuation of the secular as the most pressing threat to orthodox Christianity, because 'the characteristic heresy of to-day', he has a far more humanist outlook than Eliot or Hulme; his main worry seems to be that such a tendency will provoke reaction in the form of 'apocalyptic pessimism' (above, p. 123) and *The Religious Prospect* ends on a plea for a properly regulated immanentism which 'is the condition of recovering that status of persons the threat to which in our time is a threat to Christendom' (p. 192). Demant's desire to find a balance between transcendence and immanence echoes the work of another writer whom Eliot claimed influenced him a good deal, Jacques Maritain. Maritain too holds out a religious 'prospect', a 'new epoch in the history of christian culture' in which the creature 'will neither be belittled nor annihilated before God' nor assert its being independently of God, in what Maritain calls 'anthropocentric humanism'; rather with the 'rehabilitation of the creature in God' we shall have 'humanism indeed, but a theocentric humanism, rooted in what is radical in man: integral humanism, the humanism of the Incarnation'.[72] In this new epoch 'progress towards God will, it seems, before all be in the preparation of such conditions of earthly life for men that the sovereign love may rather be able to *come down* and make in man and with man a work that is divinely human' (p. 67). It is this study, *Humanisme intégral*, that Eliot professes being 'deeply indebted to' in the preface to *The Idea of a Christian Society* (p. 42), yet here there is little affirmation of humanism, and certainly no repetition of Maritain's enthusiastic vision of 'a veritable socio-temporal realisation of the Gospels', albeit 'in the degree to which that is possible here on earth and in given historical circumstances' (p. 86). For Maritain the Christian 'conception of the city'

> holds in it of its very nature the wish to adjust the conditions of this vale of tears so as to procure a relative but very real earthly happiness for the assembled multitude; a polity in which all can find a good and decent living, a state of justice, of amity and prosperity making possible for each the fulfilment of his destiny.
>
> (p. 131)

We do not find phrases like 'divinely human' nor 'very real

earthly happiness' in *The Idea of a Christian Society;* the word 'love' itself scarcely figures. Indeed the boundaries to Eliot's prospect are firmly and soberly marked:

> It is very easy for speculation on a possible Christian order in the future to tend to come to rest in a kind of apocalyptic vision of a golden age of virtue. But we have to remember that the Kingdom of Christ on earth will never be realised, and also that it is always being realised; we must remember that whatever reform or revolution we carry out, the result will always be a sordid travesty of what human society should be – though the world is never left wholly without glory.
>
> (p. 79)

If Eliot's attacks on the modern cult of individual personality and the literary inflation of the human subject throughout his critical writings of the 1920s and 1930s find an echo in Maritain's rejection of 'anthropocentric humanism', with its 'typical figure' of the Renaissance hero (p. 66; compare Eliot's castigation of the 'vice of Pride' in Othello *et al.*, discussed above, p. 31),[73] Maritain is still able to salvage notions of human value and status to a far greater extent than can Eliot through his concept of 'theocentric humanism', whose 'type' is the saint. And for Maritain the saint displays in particular a cherishing of creatures 'as loved by God, and made by Him as fair and worthy of our love. For to love a being in and for God . . . [is] to love and cherish their [*sic*] being as an end, because it *merits* love, in the degree to which that merit and their dignity spring from the sovereign love and the sovereign loving-kindness of God' (p. 65). To love God is to love God's love for his creatures; we could hardly have a greater contrast with the role of the saint-anchorite in 'The Dry Salvages', whose job is certainly not to adore God in His creation but to 'apprehend / The point of intersection of the timeless / With time' – that is, the unique intrusion of Christ into the temporal process.

The severity of Eliot's treatment of the temporal and natural realm owes a great deal to what Demant calls the 'Neo-Calvinist transcendental supernaturalism' of the theologian Karl Barth (see Demant, pp. 179ff.), a writer whose 'primordially anti-humanist' demand for the 'annihilation of man before God' is also discussed and rejected by Maritain (p. 63). In a short article adumbrating Barth's influence on Eliot, Ian Glenn has expressed justified surprise that Eliot's source-hunters seem to have passed Barth over in silence, though there is occasion for an extensive treatment of the relationship between them; Glenn himself does not supply this nor can I do it here, the points made below being intended to supplement the start he has made.[74] Barth's Commentary on Paul's Epistle to the Romans (translated into English in 1933) is as Glenn notes pervaded by references to the timeless 'Moment' of Christ and its difficult relation to temporality and history, as well as by the 'I am what I am not', 'he knows what he does not know' paradoxes attendant on the 'new man's faith in Christ ('Seen from the human side, he is incomprehensible, a mere negation; and yet, it is this which marks him out for what he is') and rehearsed in 'East Coker' iii.[75] It is, however, Barth's devaluing of the creation and of secularity other than as a foil to the absolute 'otherness' of God with which I am mainly concerned here: 'the whole course of this world participates in true existence when its non-existence is recognised' (p. 91). All 'improper notions of immanence', every 'non-radical idea of transcendence' that might open the door to a belief that men and their experiences 'are in themselves, apart from their subjection to the judgement of God and apart from their awaiting His justification, great and important' are simply 'incomprehensible and meaningless' (pp. 107–8); God is not a 'historical element in the midst of other elements' and the 'chasm' separating this world from the *Futurum aeternum* has only one bridge in Christ's death and resurrection (pp. 112–13). Barth's rigorous rejection of 'the process of humanizing . . . the assertions of Christology' (p. 296) is at one with various emphases on 'the vanity of the creature', 'the frightfulness of corruption' and the 'groaning' Creation (pp. 308–12), all such recognitions implying the hope of resurrection, the turning from death to life. Thus 'seen in the light of the Resurrection every concrete thing that we appreciate as life and fullness, as great and *high*, becomes primarily a parable of death; death, however, and everything that is related to death . . . become a parable of life . . . each daily occurrence in our lives is weighed down by this shadow' (p. 462). It seems to me that the peasant dancers of 'East Coker' are there precisely to exemplify this sort of position, in an emblematic landscape, 'dark in the afternoon', that thus points beyond itself, rather as the opening scene of 'Little Gidding' offers an intuition of life again through the death of nature – 'There is no earth smell / Or smell of living thing'. As Barth puts it, 'The life of the Spirit shines forth in the light which displays the death of the body' (p. 286). The 'new man', living in the midst of temporal death, will thus find that his faith is, in 'East Coker's words, 'all in the waiting'; for Barth 'Men are compelled to wait, and only to wait . . . by faith, however, their waiting is a waiting upon God alone' (p. 151). 'Are we not', asks Barth, in a striking anticipation of 'East Coker' iv, 'all patients in one hospital?' (p. 465).

Whatever Catholic devotional elements and iconography might have rendered *Four Quartets* unsympathetic to Barth, it seems that on the question of the status of the creature and the creation the two men are agreed, and that the poem is ample evidence for Eliot's self-confessed 'Puritanical temperament' and 'Calvinistic heritage' (above, p. 110). Barth's contribution to the volume *Revelation* (1937) follows on immediately from Eliot's introductory essay, and may have afforded Eliot his first opportunity of getting to know Barth's work; there Barth explicitly rules out the capacity of 'perceiving the Word of God in God's creation', finding there instead a series of illusory 'voices' which might bear comparison with the voices stigmatized in the *Quartets* (see above, pp. 59ff.); 'the man who has received grace' will confess that in the natural sphere

> he has always heard and always will hear nothing but the voices of the gods, that is to say, the God-created elements of this world; the voice of earth and of animal life; the voice of the apparently infinite heavens and, sounding through this voice, the voice of the heavens' apparently inescapable fate; the voice of his own blood and of the blood of his parents and of his ancestors flowing in his veins; the voice of the genius and of the hero in his own breast: voices all falsely endowed with divine dignity and authority, and for that very reason, not the eternal Word of God![76]

Robert H. Canary, in his excellent digest of Eliot criticism, provides a brief résumé of the long-running argument over the status Eliot attaches to 'time' and history in the *Quartets* and, whilst admitting that much of the poem 'may seem taken up with regret at the wastage of historic time', he finally declares the poem to be an affirmation of both temporal and eternal values, especially in 'Little Gidding'. 'The better readings of *Four Quartets'*, he adds, 'have always recognized the dual character of this affirmation, linking it often to the Christian doctrine of the Incarnation, but readings which concentrate on the poem's mystical sources sometimes lose sight of it. . . . Readings which stress the poet's acceptance of time are therefore useful.'[77] Canary's assumption that the Incarnation is necessarily to be read as a dual affirmation certainly ignores Eliot's own way of reading it, as did the similar assumption of Reibetanz (above, pp. 104–6). There is in any case an enormous difference between accepting time and 'affirming' it; in 'Little Gidding' 'history' does provide to those enduring one war valuable lessons of previous wars that have ended in unity:

> These men, and those who opposed them
> And those whom they opposed
> Accept the constitution of silence
> And are folded in a single party,
> > (*CPP*, p. 196)

but this reconciliation, like that envisaged at the very end of the poem,

> All manner of thing shall be well
> When the tongues of flame are in-folded
> Into the crowned knot of fire
> And the fire and the rose are one,
> > (*CPP*, p. 198)

takes place only on the further side of death or apocalpyse; the political or secular perspective on events is a purely passive one, 'all in the waiting', as it were. Indeed, of all the quartets 'Little Gidding' seems the most emphatic in its demonstration of earthly *vanitas*, with its opening upstaging of the natural cycle of fruition (above, pp. 105–6), its apocalyptic visions, its bitter message on 'the gifts reserved for age', its definition of history itself as 'a pattern / Of timeless moments' and its urgent waiting on the hereafter. Canary's assessment of which are the 'better readings' of the *Quartets* certainly does not inspire confidence when we find him recommending Nathan A. Scott Jr's argument that the poem shows us a potential way back to

the happy *civitas terrena* and the 'Good Place'.[78] Although as we
saw 'East Coker' does contain some kind of blueprint or 'idea' of
a prospective Christian society organized into small rural
settlements, such a prospect is so thoroughly disengaged from
'golden-age' prognostications and so subordinated to an anti-
temporal perspective as to practically disqualify it as a secular
intervention, at any rate as one encouraging notions of earthly
felicity.

We can, however, find some further residue of Eliot's 'Idea' of
a Christian society in the *Quartets*. In his essay he sees as already
remarked 'conformity with nature' as an essential aspect of a
Christian society, as opposed to the ruthless 'exploitation of the
earth' practised by industrial capitalism, and he can justify 'the
life of the savage', and with it D. H. Lawrence, as being imbued
more deeply with religious values than is 'the mechanised,
commercialised, urbanised way of life' (*ICS*, pp. 80-1). A
Christian society is bound to 'the struggle to recover the sense
of relation to nature and to God' as well as to 'the recognition
that even the most primitive feelings should be part of our
heritage':

> we need not only to learn how to look at the world with
> the eyes of a Mexican Indian . . . and we certainly cannot
> afford to stop there. We need to know how to see the
> world as the Christian Fathers saw it; and the purpose of
> reascending to origins is that we should be able to return,
> with greater spiritual knowledge, to our own situation.
> We need to recover the sense of religious fear, so that it
> may be overcome by religious hope.
>
> (p. 81)

In 'The Dry Salvages' this triumph of religious hope over a
primitive fear is enacted, with the furies of the 'daemonic,
chthonic / Powers' that drive the sea and the 'brown god' of the
river being evoked and overcome by the refuge the Incarnation
– here first introduced into the sequence – provides. Having
sailed the sea of 'primitive terror' and doubt the poem thus
comes safely to land in 'Little Gidding', a quiet rural location
which permits the practice of meditation on the world's end,
rather than on the elemental powers; these, in wiping out
humanity's vain efforts at cultivation, prepare solely for their
own apocalyptic demise:

There are flood and drouth
Over the eyes and in the mouth,
Dead water and dead sand
Contending for the upper hand.
The parched eviscerate soil
Gapes at the vanity of toil,
Laughs without mirth.
   This is the death of earth.
                (*CPP*, pp. 192–3)

When Eliot notes in *The Idea* that 'we need to recover the sense of religious fear, so that it may be overcome by religious hope', it is clear that the 'we' he has in mind is that of the 'Community of Christians' who in the same essay provide the society with its intellectual and spiritual backbone (pp. 62–5). Primitivism as Eliot understands it is not a component of the mentality of the ordinary rural populace, who, exemplified in 'East Coker', have as we saw a largely unreflecting and habitual existence where religion is 'a matter of behaviour and conformity' (above, p. 99). Primitivism is rather an intellectual recognition, reserved for those like the narrator of the *Quartets* and his addressees, and in 'The Dry Salvages' the cosmic and the divine are not simply 'discontinuous' but actively polarized against each other. It is significant, however, that Eliot has gone to the transatlantic seaboard for the necessary element of the primitive that forms part of the thinking Christian's heritage; in the other three quartets Eliot's England remains the classic centre of significant and settled soil, rather than itself a venue for chthonic powers; the Atlantic may have 'many voices' but England is not to have, and it is doubtful whether our rivers are 'strong brown gods' like the Mississippi. Here perhaps we may note a further dimension to the *Quartets'* quarrel with regionalism (see above, p. 75). Outside the *Quartets*, Eliot's support for regionalism is prominent; thus in an article of 1933 he notes that he is 'instinctively in sympathy' with regionalist movements 'after we have deducted the political nonsense and the sentimental-retrospective-literary nonsense', and at the same time attacks the notion that the peoples of the world might be unified through 'standardization'.[79] Rojer Kojecký has discussed Eliot's debt to Charles Maurras in this 'antipathy to centralization' and 'belief in the importance of the region', and such antipathy is prominent in *Notes Towards the Definition of Culture* (1948), where the constant stress on 'variety in unity' means not only the preservation of the nation within an envisaged 'world culture' but also the preservation of the region within each nation (see especially chapter 3).[80] But the *Quartets* take no cognizance of English regions, bent as they are on the programme of linguistic and geographic centralization discussed in this study. I have suggested that the poem is essentially a waiting on the end of nationhood and national language, 'when the tongues of flame are in-folded / Into the crowned knot of fire / And the fire and the rose are one', and as a preparatory stage to this, the internal variety of England's tongues, its regions, its dialects, its dissensions, its civil wars, are peaceably composed (see above, pp. 75, 91–2). This unification is easier to achieve if the chthonic, elemental powers are deferred to the other side of the Atlantic, since to acknowledge their presence at home seems to open up the entire question of England's racial and political identity. The fact is that a strong regionalist movement did exist in England at the time of Eliot's writing proclaiming precisely that 'primitivism' Eliot keeps his England free of. I am referring to the so-called 'Neo-Romantic' movement which has just begun to receive some attention, and which, gathering force during the latter half of the 1930s and in many ways reaching a peak during the Second World War, can be said to represent everything Eliot was most opposed to. This would include what Grigson called the 'vitalism' of Henry Moore, the elevation of an anti-Latin and indigenous Celtic tradition as the true line of British art, the concomitant focus on the 'Celtic fringe' of the country as in the Welsh landscapes of Sutherland, Craxton and Piper, and calls, as with Michael Ayrton, for a 'chthonic art' that would spring 'from the deep mysteries of the land itself'; as David Mellor argues, Ayrton's own *Mrs Chittenden* of 1943 can be seen as 'one more in a stock of British Neo-Romantic Earth Mothers'; a smack in the eye, we might add, for *aficionados* of depopulated landscape.[81] Such a movement of course made its own requisitions of ancient British monuments like Stonehenge and Avebury. In doing this it can be seen as attempting to dismantle the notion of fixed borderlines between England and Britain, as I shall argue Auden's work also does in the following chapter. Eliot's acknowledgement of nationhood as 'a very recent and contingent experience' meant as discussed above, a dissolving of the frontiers in the *Quartets* between England and Latin Europe (pp. 26ff.), but a veritable Hadrian's Wall continues to exist all round England's northern and western borders, so to speak, with the Celts and Britons firmly shut out. This in spite of the fact that as a Faber editor Eliot was extremely supportive of writers like Dylan Thomas and Vernon Watkins, who through their 'Welsh extraction' might supply English literature with fresh qualities and resources not available elsewhere (*NDC*, pp. 56–7).

In a *Criterion* article of 1931 C. M. Grieve ('Hugh McDiarmid') complained at length of what he called, to quote the title of his essay, 'English ascendancy in British literature', lamenting the fact that 'English literature is maintaining a narrow ascendancy tradition instead of broad-basing itself on all the diverse cultural elements and the splendid variety of languages and dialects, in the British Isles'.[82] 'English dialect' literature, as well as Gaelic, Scots Vernacular, Scottish, Irish and Welsh, is for McDiarmid a welcome part of this diversity (p. 600). It is deeply ironic that in support of the value of vernacular forms he quotes the following comment by Herbert Read: 'it is just a possibility that the music-hall song and its allied forms – music-hall patter and revue libretto – contain the germ of a new popular poetry. It is significant that the only poems which suggest such an art are some of Mr T. S. Eliot's recent poems' (p. 608). Read is doubtless referring to 'Sweeney Agonistes' at the very moment when Eliot is turning his back on such work to move towards the very 'English ascendancy', in the *Quartets*, McDiarmid is complaining of (see below, pp. 144–5). There may be house-room for McDiarmid in the *Criterion* but not (so to speak) in the *Quartets*.[83]

One artist of the 'Neo-Romantic' school referred to above is worth special mention here, namely Paul Nash, the foremost English landscape painter of the twentieth century. If an essentially formal or 'functionalist' interest in England's ancient monuments results in landscapes like Ravilious's that call to mind the severe ruralism of the *Quartets*, as discussed in the previous section, or if as with Massingham and Harvey Darton they indicate a civilization that proclaims the vanity of all others, there remains a mystical appropriation of these monuments in the works of an artist like Nash that Eliot can share nothing with but that highlights further features of his England. A work like *Wood on the Downs* of 1929 (Plate 6) has indeed already been quoted as a perfect illustration of the severe formalism that characterizes 'stripped classicism', but in spite of Nash's interests in the eighteenth century[84] and in the internationalism of the abstract movement, he is keen to cling on to a vision of England that is to all intents Romantic in ancestry. Thus in *Unit One* he declares his search for the *genius loci* behind the 'false reality' of nature, and has recourse to Blake's Albion as its prototype, as if what is being proclaimed in his Avebury paintings is some kind of apotheosis of the national spirit itself (pp. 80–1). I suggested above (p. 104) in denying Eliot's Wordsworthian identity that the phrase *genius loci* seems inappropriate in connection with the *Quartets*, given that the 'genius' or spirit that matters is not permanently resident within nature or in any given place but arrives there 'from the Eternal Places' in Demant's phrase (above, p. 122). The 'chthonic powers' are summoned from over the sea, and even as a venue for divine illumination England has no special privilege: 'There are other places / Which also are the world's end', 'Little Gidding' tells us, though it happens to be the nearest. Nash's art, however, works to absolutize a chthonic England in which the Avebury monoliths with their rugged and unsmoothed forms seem not so much erected and positioned by human agency as rooted in some cycle of cosmic growth, manifesting indeed all the awesome traits of Romantic sublimity (Plate 15). I have suggested that other writers and artists respond on the contrary to the human traces in those monuments, representing them as embodying authoritarian political power.

In his book on Nash, Andrew Causey suggests that his work is an endorsement of the tragic vision of Hardy, not only in his paintings but in books like *The Shell Guide to Dorset* of 1936: 'Nash sought out images that illustrated the greater strength of nature over man's creation and symbolizing the fraility of even man's best achievements'; thus monuments like Maiden Castle and Badbury Rings are now 'repossessed by nature', and 'speak for the emptiness of human endeavour'.[85] Despite Nash's obvious interest in Hardy in the *Shell Guide*, it seems difficult to believe that the paintings themselves do offer any 'tragic vision', or that tragedy is possible without heroes and heroines in the manner of Hardy to act as its victims. Even if one does accept that Nash's paintings of ancient monuments do 'speak for the emptiness of human endeavour' then the position would still be far removed from that of writers like Eliot and Massingham, who do indeed speak of that 'emptiness', but with no sense of tragedy; rather with a positive desire to inculcate, indeed celebrate, earthly *vanitas*. In fact one could practically establish the degree of romanticism and its reverse in landscape writers of this period by the extent to which they embrace or reject Hardy; Massingham has no mention of him in his chapter on Dorset (pp. 39–55), and Harvey Darton in *English Fabric* manages a whole book on Dorset with hardly a Hardy reference.

We might conclude this chapter by referring back to *The Idea of a Christian Society*, where Eliot is insistent that 'the allegiance of the individual to his own Church is secondary to his allegiance to the Universal Church', and that 'no one to-day can defend the idea of a National Church, without balancing it with the idea of the Universal Church, and without keeping in mind that truth is one and that theology has no frontiers' (p. 76). In the same work he expresses his horror at the idea of an 'English National Religion' and at the 'sanctimonious nationalism' religion can be confused with (pp. 94, 78). In the *Quartets* we see Eliot constructing an essential England it is true, but only as a preliminary to a vision of reality 'without frontiers', the 'England and nowhere' formulation which, together with common misinterpretations of it, I shall discuss at the end of the concluding chapter.

4

ELIOT AND AUDEN

I said at the outset of this book that there has been a tendency among critics writing on the 1930s to displace Eliot from that decade, to ignore or obscure the connections between his work and that of the rising poetic generation. Eliot's approval of Dryden and of his influence, together with his search for a common style such as the eighteenth century enjoyed (see above, pp. 10–11), seem, however, to link him with some of the poets of the *New Signatures* group, for example, whose 'respect for eighteenth-century ideals' and poetic technique is pointed out by Michael Roberts in introducing the anthology (pp. 17–18). In also pointing to the 'Augustanism' of the 1930s poets, Geoffrey Grigson compared the Auden–MacNeice relationship with that between Dryden and Pope, and it is indeed arguable that the English Augustans had a greater influence on the poetry of the younger generation than they had on Eliot's own work.[1] Detailed social documentation, wit and satire are not in abundance in Eliot's later poetry; he had already tried (and abandoned) in *The Waste Land* manuscripts the type of Popean scene-painting we find in, say, two of Julian Bell's contributions to *New Signatures* (pp. 33–47).[2] Eliot's classicism has very little that strives to be humorous or entertaining; like modern design it posits the classical tradition as standing for spareness and austerity, and it is infused with a religious dourness such as we hardly find in eighteenth-century poets, Johnson not excluded.

Although in 'Letter to Lord Byron' Auden looks back on the late 1920s as a time, in Oxford, of the 'dogma' that 'Good poetry is classic and austere' (*EA*, p. 195), his following, in the 'Letter' itself, a Byron much influenced by eighteenth-century satire is a measure of his distance from poetic austerity.

However, the epigraph to *Poems 1931–1936* seems to suggest that Auden did see himself as a participant in the movement we have been describing:

> Since the external disorder, and extravagant lies,
> The baroque frontiers, the surrealist police;
> What can truth treasure, or heart bless,
> But a narrow strictness?

(EA, p. 111)

By opposing a desired 'strictness' to the various failings associated with more florid aesthetic manifestations, Auden seems as if he may be throwing in his lot with 'stripped' classicism. What we should consider is how far, in comparison with Eliot, Auden observed a 'narrow strictness' in his work, in accordance with contemporary design, and, of equal importance, how much these two poets, who certainly watched each other's work very carefully, exercised a mutual influence.

In Day Lewis's *A Hope for Poetry*, published in 1934, we seem to witness Eliot's 'classicizing' principles – austerity, the purging out of poetical ornament, the movement towards a greater and greater starkness – being applied generally across the whole field of contemporary poetry. Thus the work of Auden and his circle is committed to 'pruning' the 'associational luxuriance of words' and to keeping a check (rather in the manner of Eliot's Dante) on their metaphorical mobility (p. 70); 'the majority of post-war poets' are seen as employing words 'in their denotative rather than connotative use', attempting, that is, to tie them down to their referent and to discipline any surplus of poetic evocation (p. 69). The procedure might be compared with Eliot's desire to get words to lie 'still' in 'Burnt Norton'. Day Lewis points to Auden's non-exploitation of the associations of words, in his selection of 'phrases flat and precise on the surface' and predilection for 'separate words hard-edged and non-committal as diamonds' (pp. 69–70). The whole of this discussion in Day Lewis's book should be compared with Eliot's Dante essay of 1929, where the elevation of the Dantesque model above the Shakespearian, on the grounds of its simplicity and translucency (as opposed to the 'opacity', poeticality and plural associations of English words) is set out at length.

By 1934, however, Eliot had not got very far in the *practice* of a classic diction (as later manifested in the *Quartets*) and certainly

Day Lewis has no intention of attributing the above tendencies in Auden *et al.* solely to Eliot's influence. Indeed, any specific origin for the fashion of pruning English of its luxuriance is not posited. Although literary historians (including, incidentally, Day Lewis himself) tend to make a good deal of *The Waste Land* as a kind of sacred text for the younger generation of 1930s poets, we can indeed make the case that it is the later, more austere, more 'classic' Eliot, as he starts to evolve in 'The hollow men', whose influence is most discernible on the young Auden. Compare, for example, the clipped terseness of Eliot's poem, as in

> Between the conception
> And the creation
> Between the emotion
> And the response
> Falls the Shadow
> (*CPP*, p. 85)

with any number of the short lyrics Auden was writing in the late 1920s and early 1930s:

> Between attention and attention
> The first and last decision
> Is mortal distraction
> Of earth and air
> ('XXXIV', *EA*, p. 52)

or:

> For what as easy
> For what though small
> For what is well
> Because between
> To you simply
> From me I mean.
> ('I', *EA*, p. 113)

It is in fact far more difficult to posit any direct influence in Auden from the more spectacular and 'luxuriant' *Waste Land*, unless one takes up Hynes's very general point that the complexity of this work is the inspiration behind Auden's *The Orators* (see above, p. 2). The more important point I wish to make, however, is that any interchange between Eliot and

Auden of a classic 'narrow strictness' was two-way. In bringing
out Auden's *Poems* with Faber in 1930, Eliot was, I suggest,
particularly absorbed by that formal, detached, rather prosy
voice that anticipates the diction and tone of the *Quartets*. Such
an anticipation is evident in the third section of 'It was
Easter. . .', for example:

> So, insecure, he loves and love
> Is insecure, gives less than he expects.
> He knows not if it be seed in time to display
> Luxuriantly in a wonderful fructification
> Or whether it be but a degenerate remnant
> Of something immense in the past but now
> Surviving only as the infectiousness of disease
> Or in the malicious caricature of drunkenness;
> Its end glossed over by the careless but known long
> To finer perception of the mad and ill.
>
> (*EA*, p. 39)

There is nothing quite like this in Eliot's early work, but its
deliberately rather pedestrian, exegetical character is an
important influence in Eliot's development.

Barbara Everett has recently called attention to Eliot's
expertise in mimicking an American colloquial idiom in 'Sweeney Agonistes', its two parts first published in the *Criterion* in
October 1926 and January 1927. As she points out, however, a
third fragment exists in the shape of a finale spoken by a Time/
Father Christmas figure, written in a totally different 'voice':
indeed she labels the passage 'a piece of lightweight, second-
rate, and . . . entirely derivative Audenesque prose' and
suggests it was written some time later than 1928, when Eliot
received Auden's play *Paid on Both Sides*, with its Father
Christmas figure, for publication by Faber.[3] Certainly what
Humphrey Jennings called the 'Audenesque trick' of the
knights' prose address to the audience in *Murder in the Cathedral*
might well derive from Father Christmas's initial entry in *Paid
on Both Sides* (see *EA*, p. 8).[4] My suggestion is that in the later
1920s, Eliot, with his increasing absorption into English contexts – royalism, Anglo-Catholicism – and his growing interest
in classic English, would have seen in the public-school and
Oxford-educated Auden an authentic English voice, from

which he could learn; and that this commitment to 'English' is all the more remarkable given his success in creating what Everett calls the 'Americanness' of 'Sweeney Agonistes'; and that in the three parts of this unfinished drama we witness Eliot committing himself to the transatlantic shift.

The major import to Eliot from Auden, however, was the abundant use of the definite article; indeed, this 1930s mannerism was favoured by many poets. There is, however, some confusion over who originated it; Bergonzi (pp. 42–3) and Hamilton (p. 4) both see Eliot himself, in 'Ash-Wednesday', as the inventor, and point to lines like 'The vanished power of the usual reign' and 'The infirm glory of the positive hour' from the first part of that poem. In the collection brought out by Spender in 1928, however, Auden already has lines displaying the characteristic impersonality and rhythmic self-containment we associate with such a usage, as in 'The heel upon the finishing blade of grass'. Although the poem this is taken from, 'Consider if you will how lovers stand' (EA, p. 438), was not reprinted in the 1930 Poems, poems Eliot presumably approved of like 'The crowing of the cock' are there reprinted from the earlier pamphlet, and include lines like 'The snowstorm on the marsh, / The champagne at the lip –', this poem being written in September 1927 according to Mendelson (EA, p. 24). Then there is Paid on Both Sides, where the 'mannerism' is already noticeable, as in 'The hopper's steady feed, the frothing leat' (EA, p. 12).

Auden's extreme reliance on the definite article for the purpose of constructing a readership has been discussed by David Trotter, who places the emphasis correctly on Eliot's manner of employing it during the 1930s deriving from Auden and not the other way round.[5] It remains with Eliot until well into Four Quartets as examples quoted below will show, and indeed in writing The Family Reunion Eliot was warned about the article's over-frequent use (see Browne, p. 109). The implications of the usage in Eliot and his contemporaries were ably discussed long ago by Rostrevor Hamilton in The Tell-Tale Article, though no commentator, to my knowledge, has addressed the relation of the line built round the article and the noun group to my present concern of 'classic design' in 1930s poetry. It would be best to quote other instances of the usage first:

145

The moment in the arbour where the rain beat;
The moment in the draughty church at smokefall;
The stumble and the wail of little pain;
the small disaster on the limitless plain;
The rigid promise fractured in the garden;
The failure in the putting-competition;
The pot of ivy trained across the window;
The enlarged portraits of the successful sons.[6]

I discussed the attempt to create the 'autonomous' art object in the 1930s above (pp. 71-2), and it is clear that the tendency of objects to confidently 'realize' themselves in the poetry of the period without any suggestion of a perceiving 'I' is very much abetted by this use of the definite article; the fact that the technique is interchangeable, so to speak, across the work of several poets emphasizes the fact that we are dealing with a world of common 'reality' and not personal viewpoint. In attacking the technique, Hamilton complained that by elevating the noun groups and by subduing 'the native energy of the verb', Eliot was not only damaging 'the structure of the English language' but emphasizing, again, an anti-humanist trend common to modern writers; the technique might suit Eliot's own 'agonised quietism' and religious passivity, but made no allowance for 'the active virtue and strength which even today survive in ordinary men' (pp. 54-9). He later relates Eliot's position back to Hulme's classicism, with its fondness for the rigid geometrical line, in keeping with Hulme's notion of man as 'an extraordinarily fixed and limited animal' (p. 79); the implication is that the use of the definite article in the manner discussed above is indicative of a belief that man is held in a web of impersonal classification, no longer a source of action himself in his 'verbless' state. Hamilton also anticipates Trotter in noting how this use of the direct article is a 'signal' to what he calls the 'elect reader', who is thus enabled to share with the author what Hamilton parodically calls

the superior wink of the shared secret.
(p. 40)

This type of line necessarily introduces (often around its midpoint) formulations like 'in the', 'of the', 'on the' and so on, plain, prosy, unstressed language that prevents the line taking on any heavy metrical beat and imparts a relaxed, confident, slightly 'dawdling' character to the whole. The fact that one of the examples above, from Auden's *The Orators*, as well as Hamilton's 'parody' itself are in prose not poetry confirms the rhythmical inconspicuousness, so to speak, of the technique. I noted above (p. 60) how concerned Eliot was in his dramatic writing of the 1930s to 'avoid any echo of Shakespeare', leading him to eschew the iambic pentameter and introduce light syllables into his lines to break up regular stress in the interests of a 'conversational' tone; the definite article deployment we are discussing was obviously useful here. Writers like Auden (and the classic example would be his poem 'Spain') deliberately use the technique in a similar rejection of 'poeticality', the preference of the flat over the ornamented voice, impassive and what we might now call 'laid back'.

Rhythmicality is not, however, abolished completely, and the fact that nearly all the examples quoted above (as well as Hamilton's parody) are endecasyllables is significant. What actually evolves in the 1930s is a kind of 'standardized' line, drawn upon by many poets for a variety of uses from social documentation to recording moments of spiritual illumination; in utilizing it himself, Eliot certainly seems to feel that he is working within the conventions of the desired 'common style'. If the quest for such a style ends successfully with 'Little Gidding', as suggested above (p. 40), then we shall not be surprised to find traces of this standardization there; I refer to the encounter with the ghost in part ii of the poem, written throughout in endecasyllables, and opening with the familiar definite articles:

> In the uncertain hour before the morning
>   Near the ending of interminable night
>   At the recurrent end of the unending . . .[7]

In fact what I am calling the standardized line might be seen as occupying in 1930s neo-classicism a place similar to that of the heroic couplet in the eighteenth century. Of course, the intervention of *vers libre* in the early twentieth century means that there can be no real possibility of a return to metrical consensus, and indeed the verse of the 1930s shows an extraordinarily wide range of forms and rhythms. Even so, the

device discussed above does provide some degree of col-
lectivization, a familiar rhythmic measure giving some kinship
to widely differing poems, a classic 'tendency'; a device that, in
favouring the endecasyllable, opts for a less regular music than
that provided by the 'usual' iambic pentameter. The line built
round the noun group does not of course need to be an
endecasyllable, and in Auden's 'Spain' its flexible, prosy character becomes even more attenuated: 'The construction of
railways in the colonial desert' and so on (EA, p. 210). In this
poem Auden takes 'standardized lines' and, as is characteristic
in 1930s poetry, binds them together into lengthy lists; or, to
use an architectural metaphor, assembles 'prefabricated' units
into three monolithic blocks labelled 'Yesterday', 'To-day' and
'To-morrow' which constitute the structural design of the
whole. In thus foregrounding the simplicity of its structure,
'Spain' can be seen as another prominent manifestation of the
neo-classic aesthetic, along with the Quartets.

This introduces us, however, to important distinctions to be
drawn between Auden and Eliot, however much they might be
linked in terms of diction and design. Their political and
religious differences in the 1930s are immediately apparent,
and it seems in fact that there are various satirical digs at Eliot
in Auden's work at the time. I am not thinking of the 'Dream-
ing of nuns' phrase in The Orators (EA, p. 105), as much as the
satire (also presumably directed at 'Ash-Wednesday' to some
extent) on man's 'favourite pool betwen the yew-hedge and the
roses' (and later on on 'medievalism' generally) in the chorus to
the final scene of The Dog Beneath the Skin.[8] Also in that scene we
find the hilarious sermon from the jingoistic vicar incorporat-
ing echoes from Eliot:

But mind, God first! To God the glory and let Him reward!
God is no summer tourist. We're more than scenery to
Him. He has a farmer's eye for ergot and tares. Oh delight
higher than Everest and deeper than the Challenger Gulf!
His commodores come into His council and His lieuten-
ants know His Love. Lord, I confess! I confess! I am all too
weak and utterly unworthy. There is no other want. All
actions and diversions of the people, their greyhound
races, their football competitions, their clumsy acts of
love, what are they but the pitiful, maimed expression of

that entire passion, the positive tropism of the soul to
God!

(p. 168; EA, p. 141)

One might spot in this excerpt a reference to the close of part iii
of 'Ash-Wednesday' ('Lord, I am not worthy / but speak the
word only') as well perhaps as a kind of satire on the type of
'flashing phrase' that Eliot admired in the writing of Lancelot
Andrewes (compare 'God is no summer tourist' with 'Christ is
no wild-cat', the latter quoted by Eliot in his Andrewes essay
(*SE*, p. 349)). In the vicar's dismissal of popular entertainments,
we might also see satire directed at the position of disgust Eliot
takes up in 'The function of criticism' towards those who 'ride
ten in a compartment to a football match at Swansea, listening
to the inner voice, which breathes the eternal message of
vanity, fear and lust' (*SE*, p. 27). If Auden does draw upon Eliot
in his portrayal of the vicar, it is interesting that he associates
the reactionary stance of the latter with the insular, backward-
looking English village whose appearance on stage suggests 'a
pre-war musical comedy' as the stage directions to I.i have it
(*The Dog Beneath the Skin*, p. 17). A year or so after the play was
first published, Auden was involved in negotiations with Faber
about the title of the third book of poems he published with
them, *Look, Stranger!* (1936). 'I might call it *Piddle-in-the-hole*', he
joked, 'on the analogy of *Burnt Norton*.' [9] The jest surely indicates
that he saw Eliot's newly published poem as confirmation of the
kind of evasive, rural England affiliation satirized in *The Dog*; 'So
this is rural England!', says one of the journalists in the play,
'just another lousy racket!' (p. 149). But for reasons given in the
previous chapter, it seems to me that Eliot's poem no more
endorses the rural myth than does Auden's and Isherwood's
play, which concentrates on the bogus nature of 'Pressan
Ambo' and those it attracts:

> Those who sang in the inns at evening have departed;
>   they saw their hope in another country. . .
> But their places are taken by another population,
>   with views about nature,
> Brought in charabanc and saloon along arterial roads;
> Tourists to whom the Tudor cafés
> Offer Bovril and buns upon Breton ware
> With leather work as a sideline: Filling stations

149

Supplying petrol from rustic pumps. . .

Man is changed by his living; but not fast enough.
His concern to-day is for that which yesterday did not
   occur.
In the hour of the Blue Bird and the Bristol Bomber,
   his thoughts are appropriate to the years of the
   Penny Farthing. . .

(pp. 12–13)

Auden's attack in this excerpt on an outmoded traditionalism
and nationalism in terms of design (later in the play (p. 127) he
will refer to the 'sham-Tudor villas' so popular in England in
the 1920s and 1930s) restates in a sense Eliot's resistance in his
later work to the Elizabethans, to a nationalistic Shakespeare
and to 'Shakespearian' landscape, discussed previously in this
book. In the inter-war years a veritable cult of the Tudor is
often remarked upon by contemporary commentators as the
middle-class Englishman's 'defence' against new movements in
design, the antithesis between the two harbouring synonyms
like English:foreign, individual:typical, freedom:repression and
so on. Thus the 'Tudor:modernist' debate is a feature of Evelyn
Waugh's *Decline and Fall* (1928) where Margot Beste-Chet-
wynde's replacement of King's Thursday, 'the finest piece of
domestic Tudor in England', by Herr Silenus's 'surprising
creation of ferro-concrete and aluminium' is scathingly treated
by Waugh.[10] In his support for Le Corbusier-type standardized
and centralized building programmes to improve working-class
housing conditions, Roger Hinks in the *Criterion* aptly sums up
the antitheses noted above:

> The new buildings will be called ugly, soul-destroying,
> bolshevistic, and so forth. . . . The devotees of crazy
> pavements and all the other delights of arterial Tudor
> semi-detachment will protest in the name of England,
> home and beauty.[11]

It is ironic that, looking back now, much 1930s suburbanism
seems to us the ultimate in conformity, though there were
indeed critics at the time who realized that the 'Tudorbethan'
was in danger of out-standardizing the standardization it was
fleeing from.[12]

The conclusion to Auden's early sonnet 'Sir, no man's enemy'

150

seems to equate the advent of modern design with hopes of social/political reform – 'look shining at / New styles of architecture, a change of heart' (EA, p. 36) – but by 'Letter to Lord Byron' (1936), Auden's fondness for the machine age is being illustrated by Victorian heavy engineering, with more recent styles themselves being castigated:

> Tramlines and slagheaps, pieces of machinery,
> That was, and still is, my ideal scenery.
>
> Hail to the New World! Hail to those who'll love
>   Its antiseptic objects, feel at home.
> Lovers will gaze at an electric stove,
>   Another poésie de départ come
>   Centred round bus-stops or the aerodrome.
> But give me still, to stir imagination
> The chiaroscuro of the railway station.
>
> Preserve me from the Shape of Things to Be;
>   The high-grade posters at the public meeting,
> The influence of Art on Industry,
>   The cinemas with perfect taste in seating;
>   Preserve me, above all, from central heating.
>
> (EA, pp. 175–6)

Indeed, Auden's fondness for 'chiaroscuro' might be seen as a measure of the distance between himself and any thoroughgoing adoption of the principles of modern design in his poetry. Ludovici in his support for 'Ruler-Art' and political absolutism (above, p. 21) had explained chiaroscuro as 'a blending of colours together, an elimination of all those sharp contrasts which the compromising spirit of a democratic age cannot abide'. It can only exist 'at the cost of the life of all definite lines' (Nietzsche and Art, p. 214). A fondness for definite lines and for absolute contrasts of light and shade is a prevalent feature of 1930s art, be it in architecture, abstract painting, the school of design known as 'Art Deco', or in landscape painting and poster art. An art of stark contrasts can be said to represent a decade of stark political choices, between the massed blocks of right and left; the liberal middle ground becomes increasingly difficult to occupy. In 'Burnt Norton', Eliot himself, following on from 'The hollow men', castigates the 'dim light' where absolutes become mixed into the 'chiaroscuro' of spiritual evasion:

> Here is a place of disaffection
> Time before and time after
> In a dim light: neither daylight
> Investing form with lucid stillness
> Turning shadow into transient beauty
> With slow rotation suggesting permanence
> Nor darkness to purify the soul
> Emptying the sensual with deprivation
> Cleansing affection from the temporal.
> Neither plenitude nor vacancy.
>
> (*CPP*, pp. 173–4)

'It is better, in a paradoxical way, to do evil than to do nothing: at least, we exist', Eliot observed in a famous statement from the Baudelaire essay (*SE*, p. 429), and the necessity to choose between good and evil, or between right and left, is paralleled in design terms by the contemporary prevalence of linearity and the simplification and definition of form. Chiaroscuro represents, not this honing down to essentials, but blending and plurality, and thus with Auden, as we shall see below.

Thus the 'classic' elements in Auden's work adumbrated thus far – the 'narrow strictness' of a spare, 'flat' diction, his partaking of a common measure of 'standardization', the foregrounding of a poem's 'architectural idea', and the impersonality of much of his early poetry – these features which make for a formalism akin to Eliot's are in fact offset by what one might call abundant local detail and 'ornamentation', these latter elements representing a resistance to the type of centrism displayed in the *Quartets*. In the final sonnet of 'In time of war', written in 1938, Auden outlines both the power and the inappropriateness of the classic option:

> Wandering lost upon the mountains of our choice,
> Again and again we sigh for an ancient South,
> For the warm nude ages of instinctive poise,
> For the taste of joy in the innocent mouth.
>
> Asleep in our huts, how we dream of a part
> In the glorious balls of the future; each intricate maze
> Has a plan, and the disciplined movements of the heart
> Can follow for ever and ever its harmless ways.

We envy streams and houses that are sure:
But we are articled to error; we
Were never nude and calm like a great door,

And never will be perfect like the fountains;
We live in freedom by necessity,
A mountain people dwelling among mountains.

(EA, p. 262)

Here the enticements of the classic ideal, its simplicity, monumentality, innocence, perfection and order, are impossibilities
to man, with his necessarily 'barbaric' nature, a mountain
creature who has exchanged prelapsarian joy for the freedom
of the will. Eliot's response to man's imperfection was to adopt,
following Hulme, a 'puritanical' classicism whose severity
emphasizes order, simplicity and monumentality, and in the
Quartets language is disciplined into formal order and 'purged' of
its richness and plurality as part of that monist definition of
England and English described in chapter 2. Auden's awareness
of the disjunction between life and the antique ideal does not,
however, lead him to this more uncompromising 'classicism';
rather, his work in the 1930s can be seen as a constant debate
between pro- and anti-classical positions. His awareness of
original sin – 'Men are not innocent as beasts and never can
be, / Man can improve himself but never will be perfect' [13] – has
a far more sympathetic, 'liberal' element than Eliot's; witness,
for example, the place the word 'crooked' often has in his work
in the period. From the picture of 'crooked Europe' in *The Dog
Beneath the Skin* (p. 111) to the famous lines 'You shall love your
crooked neighbour / With your crooked heart' in 'As I walked
out one evening' (EA, p. 228), Auden shows a marked acquiescence in imperfection, irregularity and eccentricity; as he puts it
in 'Letter to Lord Byron', 'I hate the modern trick to tell the
truth, / Of straightening out the kinks in the young mind' (EA,
p. 193). If classicism posits the establishing of what Babbitt calls
the 'normal type' as its controlling centre (see above, p. 46), or
in Bakhtin's phrase pursues 'verbal-ideological centralization'
(above, p. 74), then Auden's affiliations are certainly with the
periphery:

> Goddess of bossy underlings, Normality!
> What murders are committed in thy name!

Totalitarian is thy state Reality,
  Reeking of antiseptics and the shame
  Of faces that all look and feel the same. . .

From thy dread Empire not a soul's exempted.
        ('Letter to Lord Byron', *EA*, p. 193)

Antagonism to the 'norm' is also directed at the formalism that offers to straighten out the crooked, be it aesthetic or political;[14] thus in the poem ' "O who can ever gaze his fill" ', the following fatalistic voice pouring scorn on humanity's more positive visions is itself mocked as an echo of fears and lies:

The desires of the heart are as crooked as corkscrews
  Not to be born is the best for man
The second best is a formal order
  The dance's pattern, dance while you can.
Dance, dance, for the figure is easy
  The tune is catching and will not stop
Dance till the stars come down with the rafters
  Dance, dance, dance till you drop.

                      (*EA*, p. 206)

This was written in September 1936, and seems to me again to contain more than a hint of opposition to the recently published 'Burnt Norton', with its lament over the 'ridiculousness' of man's temporal existence, its 'formal order', and its celebration of the dance 'at the still point of the turning world'. I mentioned above Auden's fondness for chiaroscuro, and observed that the softening of stark formalism it brings has both aesthetic and political implications; there is much of an 'ethical chiaroscuro' in Auden too, and his elevation of the crooked over the straight also brings design and politics together. There is thus no need for Alan Robinson, in his meticulous study of *Poetry, Painting and Ideas*, to be surprised at 'Ruler-Art' theorists like Ludovici expressing horror at the picturesque (Robinson, pp. 98–9; see above, p. 83).

'Classic' beauty is seen in Auden as the preserve of the moneyed classes, set often in antithesis to the luckless have-nots on the periphery to whom, however, the future belongs. Thus he is constantly equating the 'public school' with the 'handsome profile' (p. 123), the privileged with the 'well-shaped' (p. 156), or deriding the

> splendid person, you who stand
> In spotless flannels or with hand
> Expert on trigger;
> Whose lovely hair and shapely limb
> Year after year are kept in trim
> Till buffers envy as you swim
> Your Grecian figure.
>
> (EA, p. 121)

That beauty is not truth, and the Grecian urn (or one's attraction to it) culpable is the implication of several poems of the period in which Auden explores the relation between private love and public responsibility:

> Let the florid music praise,
> The flute and the trumpet,
> Beauty's conquest of your face:
> In that land of flesh and bone,
> Where from citadels on high
> Her imperial standards fly,
> Let the hot sun
> Shine on, shine on.
>
> O but the unloved have had power,
> The weeping and striking,
> Always; time will bring their hour:
> Their secretive children walk
> Through your vigilance of breath
> To unpardonable death,
> And my vows break
> Before his look.
>
> (EA, pp. 158–9)

What seems then to emerge in Auden is a rejection of several key features of the classic aesthetic, discipline, order, 'imperial' beauty, on the grounds of their falsity or inadequacy; at bottom, however, it is the inevitable standardization of classicism that Auden abhors. One of the most conspicuous features of his work, to the point of mannerism, is his itemiza-

tion of eccentric, unlikely components that make up whatever
whole – social, geographical, or historical – he is surveying:

> For the virgin afraid of thunder; for the wife obeyed
> by her husband; for the spinster in love with Africa,
>   O Bear with the Ragged Staff, hear us.
>
> (*The Orators, EA*, p. 67)

> One has a unique collection of indigenous insects. One is
> promoted for his suggestions respecting overhead
> charges. One makes a fortune out of his locking device for
> lifts. One receives a grant from a fund for research; one is
> invited to give a course of lectures on a philosophical
> subject. One discovers a new variety of sneeze wort; it
> shall be called by his name.
>
> (ibid., p. 70)

> To-morrow the rediscovery of romantic love;
> The photographing of ravens; all the fun under
>   Liberty's masterful shadow;
> To-morrow the hour of the pageant-master and the
> musician.
>
> ('Spain', *EA*, p. 212)

And so on, *ad infinitum*. Hamilton noted with some exasperation
the strangeness of Auden's characteristic use of the definite
article when it enforces, not a kind of consensus view of reality
which we should expect it to bring, but an 'eccentric claim to
our recognition of the far-fetched' (p. 45); other critics like Paul
C. Ray have posited a surrealist influence on Auden's 'catalogue
of objects that have no rational connection with each other',
but are held together by a 'dream-logic'.[15] David Trotter has
criticized the vision of 'To-morrow' in the concluding section of
'Spain' for its inadequacy, its 'draining off' of optimism in the
'very arbitrariness' of its details, its 'sponsoring of
ostentatiously relative values' (p. 122), but such arbitrariness is
no more evident in 'Spain' than elsewhere in Auden's work. It
represents, I suggest, his argument with classicist monism and
centralization, his sympathy with the eccentric periphery, his
admittance of, and insistence on, plurality in his visions of
landscape and timescape. *The Orators* is subtitled *An English Study*,
as if its strange lists and infinite variegation represent a
resistance to centralization and commitment to an eccentricity

that is seen as peculiarly English; as if the difficulties of discovering any homogeneity or thematic unity in reading the work itself is precisely the point. It stands at the opposite pole to 'Little Gidding', where plurality is excised in the interests of a monist 'England' realized in solitary epiphanies:

> So, while the light fails
> On a winter's afternoon, in a secluded chapel
> History is now and England.
>
> (*CPP*, p. 197)

And yet one feels a certain unease in simply positing the Auden of the 1930s as a kind of liberal champion of differentiation and plurality. He does indeed turn classicism on its head by using what I have suggested is a common, quasi-standardized poetic diction for presenting the most uncommon, unstandardized things; an outrageous choice of details is presented in a seemingly 'straight', documentary, impersonal tone, heavily dependent on the definite article. Yet the implication of a detached, impregnable *knowingness* often follows from these devices; witness, say, the anatomy of the train party in *The Dog Beneath the Skin*:

> Picture the Pullman car with its deft attendants
> And the usual passengers: the spoilt child, the corridor addict,
> The lady who expects you to admire her ankles: the ostentatious peruser of important papers, etc. etc.
>
> (p. 80)

In order to survey plurality, the poet needs to be in a position of power; he needs that omniscience of viewpoint which stations like the aerial view offer, and from which he is not implicated in what he sees. Many of Auden's poems adopt this viewpoint, and thereby suggest that the inclusive, as well as exclusive, claim to speak for 'History' or for 'England' can have its authoritarianism too, a point I pursue in the concluding part below, where the plural nature of Auden's England is contrasted with Eliot's centrist one.

Auden's sonnet quoted above (pp. 152–3) shows his awareness

of the attractions of a whole range of classic iconography located in 'an ancient South', but then has him throwing in his lot with the dispossessed inhabitants of northern mountains. In the treatment of England in his writings of the 1930s, Auden is similarly concerned to explode any south-country epitomizing of the type we have looked at, and is constantly stressing the opposing force of regional variegation, often via the 'aerial view'. A unitary England is indeed often set up in his work, only to be subsequently challenged, as in 'O Love, the interest itself in thoughtless Heaven' (*EA*, pp. 118–19), which, as Hynes noted, begins with an evocation of John of Gaunt's 'this England' (above, p. 90); what Hynes omits to add is that we immediately move on into economically distressed regions of the island – Lancashire, Glamorgan, Dumbarton – that deliberately complicates and unsettles any narrowly 'projectible' nationhood such as that called for by Sir Stephen Tallents, as if his England is being countered by the untidier sprawl of Britain (above, p. 89). This poem is indeed one instance (the opening chorus of *The Dog Beneath the Skin* being another) where as Edward Mendelson has noted (*Early Auden*, p. 336) Auden is indebted for his geographical details to Anthony Collett's *The Changing Face of England* (1926). Collett's insistence on 'drawing attention to the contrasts of shire and shire' and the extensive travelogue round the island his book incorporates themselves contrast with the attempt of many writers of the period to 'find' England in some particular corner.[16] Such a work undoubtedly fed Auden's sense of the country as a complex and 'changing' entity, not easily susceptible to being 'fixed'.

The poem 'O Love, the interest itself' acted as the prologue to Auden's 1936 volume *Look, Stranger!*, and the setting-up/discomfiting strategy seems to be encapsulated in the relation between the title-poem of this collection and the book's contents.[17] 'Look, stranger, at this island now' is an exercise in presenting England as abstract chalk idyll, reminiscent of Connolly's or Forster's comments above (pp. 81, 90) or indeed of a Batsford book-jacket (Plate 10):

Look, stranger, at this island now
The leaping light for your delight discovers,
Stand stable here
And silent be,

That through the channels of the ear
May wander like a river
The swaying sound of the sea.

Here at the small field's ending pause
Where the chalk wall falls to the foam, and its tall ledges
Oppose the pluck
And knock of the tide,
And the shingle scrambles after the suck-
ing surf, and the gull lodges
A moment on its sheer side.

Far off like floating seeds the ships
Diverge on urgent voluntary errands;
And the full view
Indeed may enter
And move in memory as now these clouds do,
That pass the harbour mirror
And all the summer through the water saunter.

(*EA*, pp. 157–8)

The emphasis of *Look, Stranger!* is precisely to oppose such a
picture of 'this island', to go into the details that reveal a much
more composite national identity. Such a project is already at
the heart of *The Orators* (1932), the first book of which opens
with an imagined inspection of the nation by 'a picked body of
angels', sent out into 'rain-wet Scotland', the 'furnace-crowded
Midlands', Cornwall, the Severn, King's Lynn (a deliberately
eccentric choice) and so forth to report back to the capital with
the famous question 'What do you think about England, this
country of ours where nobody is well?' (*EA*, pp. 61–2). In an ode
from the final section of *The Orators* this plurality is recomposed
in the form of a boarding-school rugby fifteen, where team-
mates from conspicuously far-flung and contrasting regions –
Skye, the Wash, Aberdovey and Cornwall are highlighted – are
saluted in their cup-winning triumph (pp. 96–8). Whatever vein
of irony runs through this poem, there is no doubt that the
1930s Auden feels a deep attraction towards an England thus
reconstituted, *e pluribus unum*, and that his attacks on national
reductivism of the Pressan Ambo type, as in *The Dog*, are part of
a nationalist affiliation not subject, I believe, to the deep
qualifications about nationalism we find in Eliot.

Thus a sense of detail and difference is combined in Auden with an ideal of the composite whole, something of a federalist notion of England which embodies Eliot's insistence throughout *Notes Towards the Definition of Culture* on a nation's requisite 'variety in unity', though the *Quartets* themselves as we have seen emphasize the reverse of such a viewpoint. Certainly much of Auden's work is too close to the land it surveys to permit that comfortable view of a unitary England where distancing hides division and composes the island into wholeness – 'this precious stone set in the silver sea', and so forth. Many of Auden's poems are rather like an ordnance survey of individual localities, where every feature (and blemish) is seen, as in 'industrial slump' poems like 'Who stands, the crux left of the watershed' (*EA*, p. 22). At the same time the urge to find some panoramic viewpoint in which such details, while not being lost, will take their place in a national whole is marked, a 'hawk's-eye' viewpoint in which keen-sightedness is combined with aerial breadth. Auden wants both the whole and the part, and we can often find a bias in individual poems to either of these viewpoints. Thus in 'O Love, the interest itself' he seems as we saw to resist any Gaunt-like glossing of England by unearthing the intractable details of regions like Glamorgan that 'hid a life / Grim as a tidal rock-pool's in its glove-shaped valleys' (*EA*, p. 119). Another state-of-the-nation poem from *Look, Stranger!*, 'Here on the cropped grass of the narrow ridge I stand', has, however, a rather more cursory reference to regionality, with the meditation on 'England' afforded by the station of the Malvern Hills taking in its purview only a brief glimpse at Wales. Auden does in fact often use England as an umbrella term in his work, as in the 'English study' of *The Orators*, to encompass Wales, 'rain-wet Scotland', rugby players from the Isle of Skye and so on. 'Letter to Lord Byron' similarly shows England as a term preferred to Britain, in a land moreover where various poets are all presumably 'English' too:

> England, my England – you have been my tutrix –
>   The Mater, on occasions, of the free,
> Or, if you'd rather, Dura Virum Nutrix,
>   Whatever happens I am born of Thee;
>   And Englishmen, all foreigners agree,
> Taking them by and large, and as a nation,

All suffer from an Oedipus fixation.

With all thy faults, of course we love thee still;
  We'd better for we have to live with you,
From Rhondda Valley or from Bredon Hill,
  From Rotherhithe, or Regent Street, or Kew
  We look you up and down and whistle 'Phew!
Mother looks odd to-day dressed up in peers,
Slums, aspidistras, shooting-sticks, and queers.'

Cheer up! There're several singing birds that sing.
  There's six feet six of Spender for a start;
Eliot has really stretched his eagle's wing,
  And Yeats has helped himself to Parnell's heart;
  This book has samples of MacNeice's art;
There's Wyndham Lewis fuming out of sight,
That lonely old volcano of the Right.
                                        (EA, pp. 197–8)

Here, rather than representing a resistance to Tallents's 'national projection' Auden shares a complicity with it, like many of his contemporaries; we might note that Collett's *The Changing Face of England*, in spite of its title, includes a survey of Wales. That somewhat reductive emblematization of England we find in the title-poem of *Look, Stranger!* then might be seen to embody the pull towards centralization in Auden which is elsewhere resisted, the volume itself like *The Orators* showing a highly ambiguous relationship towards nationhood.

In his writing of the second half of the 1930s Auden's striving for panorama becomes more and more ambitious, not so much a 'hawk's-eye' view of a nation but a 'moon's-eye' view of an entire continent or the globe itself, a federation now world-wide. The European scale of Auden's surveying is a feature of *The Dog Beneath the Skin* (1935), with its concomitant attack on Little-England nationalism; here too a global perspective – 'Now through night's caressing grip / Earth and all her oceans slip' (p. 115) – anticipates Auden's most ambitious exercise in this kind, the sonnet sequence 'In time of war', with its verse commentary (1939). Here we have on a larger scale a combination of the broad expanse and the individual detail similar to that of Auden's English surveys:

Night falls on China; the great arc of travelling shadow

Moves over land and ocean, altering life:
Thibet already silent, the packed Indias cooling,
Inert in the paralysis of caste. And though in Africa
The vegetation still grows fiercely like the young,
And in the cities that receive the slanting radiations

The lucky are at work, and most still know they suffer,
The dark will touch them soon: night's tiny noises
Will echo vivid in the owl's developed ear,

Vague in the anxious sentry's; and the moon look down
On battlefields and dead men lying, heaped like treasure,
On lovers ruined in a brief embrace, on ships

Where exiles watch the sea. . .

(*EA*, p. 269)

As so often with Auden (with parts of *The Dog Beneath the Skin*, for example), the political and geographical stimulus for this passage comes from Dante, whose ideal of unifying the nations has just been referred to in the poem, and whose own 'global perspectives', in which daylight and darkness merge the nations, are a regular feature of the view back to earth the other world affords:

> Già era 'l sole a l'orizzonte giunto
>   lo cui meridian cerchio coverchia
>   Ierusalèm col suo più alto punto;
> e la notte, che opposita a lui cerchia,
>   uscia di Gange fuor con le Bilance.[18]

Auden's absorption of Dante's secular concerns contrasts markedly with Eliot's rather reductive reading of him (see above, p. 47). Eliot tends to exclude much in Dante – politics, humanism, 'voices' – as he himself works towards an exclusive construction of England, whereas the panoramic vein in Auden naturally foregrounds the Dantesque panorama.[19]

I discussed above Auden's desire for both whole and part in terms of an extraordinary dual allegiance in his work to both classic form and non-conformist detail, which, in cases like the historical panorama 'Spain', results at once in structural simplicity and thematic variegation as if Auden's History, like his England, is an ordered totality of eccentrics. It is therefore unsurprising that Auden's tastes in design seem to encompass both 'New styles of architecture' ('Sir, no man's enemy', *EA*, p. 36) and the Victorian 'chiaroscuro of the railway station' they offer to supplant ('Letter to Lord Byron', p. 175). When resisting notions of a centralized norm Auden not unreasonably, given the context we have been exploring, adopts a north versus south metaphor, as in the final sonnet of 'In time of war'. As Isherwood confirms, Auden's 'romantic travel-wish was always towards the North. He could never understand how anybody could long for the sun, the blue sky, the palm-trees of the South.' [20] Yet metaphorically speaking Auden is unwilling to surrender the South that easily, and is frequently alive, as in the sonnet, to its attractions, in particular to the ideals of clarity and planning that underlie classic art. The attempt indeed to synthesize the metaphorical and aesthetic associations of north and south, intricacy with planning, differences with wholeness, the region with the centre, the eccentric with the norm, pervades his writing, and in national terms, as I have suggested above, leads to some slippage between 'Britain' and 'England'. The epilogue to *Look Stranger!*, the poem beginning 'Certainly our city', surveys as his later poems will those sources of light dotted in all directions of the globe which might symbolize an embryonic world-federalism: 'There was Nansen in the north, in the hot south Schweitzer' (*EA*, p. 165). This is precisely the union of differences Eliot turns his back on in his poetry, whether in early work like 'Gerontion' or *The Waste Land*, where plurality of races and nations is synonymous with chaos, or in the *Quartets* where 'England' can be constructed only via a process of rigorous exclusion.

The foregoing observations may throw some light on what is Auden's most famous landscape poem, 'In praise of limestone', written in 1948. Such a poem presents a classic landscape indeed, one that is temperate, non-extremist, 'homocentric', 'a stone that responds' to any will to form humans exercise upon it. The poem carries on from the sonnet 'Wandering lost upon the mountains' in converting such a lost prelapsarian landscape into an image of the paradisal garden after time, of 'a faultless love / Or the life to come'. [21] Yet limestone synthesizes the idea of the classic norm with an element of abnormality, taking the form of hill-top temples and secret systems of 'caves and conduits', a stone both tractable and irregular, smooth and intricate, well-behaved yet mysterious, open yet 'underground', and supporting inhabitants confederate yet not totalitarianized:

> Watch, then, the band of rivals as they climb up and down
> Their steep stone gennels in twos and threes, at times
> Arm in arm, but never, thank God, in step.
>
> *(Selected Poems*, p. 185)

Limestone is of course related to chalk, but has none of that nationalism or authoritarianism with which chalk has been repeatedly inscribed, discussed in chapter 3; far from being a landscape of what we have called stripped classicism it metamorphoses itself in Auden's poem into features like 'Innocent athletes and gesticulating fountains'. It becomes indeed a (romantically infiltrated) landscape of the traditional antique ideal, precisely that place of empathy which the harsher neoclassicism considered in this book rejects. Its actual location is also crucially important: limestone is the landscape of the dales and moors of northern, not southern, England, not the fully 'romantic' mountain-landscape of the northern Lakes but a kind of *via media* between that and the chalk. Here qualities of north and south converge and are yet retained, the one not precluding the many.

Even if, in Auden's England of the 1930s, the representation of the many is foregrounded, one hesitates as I noted above (p. 157) to salute Auden as the voice of freedom and plurality in opposition to the monologic emphases of Eliot. In spite of the individualistic components of Auden's picture, there remains an ambitious urge towards totality that seeks out some detached, omnipotent prospect whence all of England, History, or the World is magisterially surveyed. Ultimately the all-inclusive England is but the reverse of the all-exclusive one; that which gives the work of these poets its immense power is in part precisely that which to this reader at least is intellectually and politically specious. Nationalism has in many ways suffered so much over the last fifty years (and anyone capable of understanding Eliot or Auden is unlikely to be impressed by its Thatcherite recurrence) that any wheeling forth on to the stage of a definitive 'England' can hardly be looked on without irony or scepticism. One's suspicions that some sort of establishment manipulation is about to be set on foot are instantly aroused; perhaps a writer like myself from a northern working-class background is likely to feel this more than most, given that 'England' still carries the southern legacy explored in these pages. Eliot's England is in many ways a critique of that legacy, though it is ironic that the *Quartets* have appealed, and still do appeal, to readers for whom the very mention of England – as in 'History is now and England' – is an immediate trigger for nostalgic reverie, which the England actually on offer in the *Quartets* – a spartan enough place in all honesty, with notice of eternity constantly dinning in its denizens' ears – does very little to fuel directly.[22] Such is, or was, the potency of the England myth: if during the Second World War itself the *Quartets* were read, not unreasonably, for their 'patriotism', it is testimony to that potency that such a reading is still frequently practised, and has gone largely unchallenged.[23] The last three quartets were, Eliot himself said, 'primarily patriotic poems' (quoted above, p. 26), but there is a patriotism that can be a challenge to nationalism and separatism, especially when one's true *patria* is in the hereafter. In an article written during the war itself Eliot asks his audience to consider that, especially for the Christian, 'patriotism is a loyalty which requires to be balanced by other loyalties' and that 'the place of patriotism in the Christian life' needs to be thought about.[24] Though earthbound, Eliot is straining in the *Quartets* after a kind of aerial view, but one not at all like Auden's; rather like Dante's in the *Paradiso*, who looked down on the insignificant 'aiuola' (threshing-floor) of this world (XXII.151).

In his article 'The myth of England', John Holloway argues that such a myth has 'just faded out' of recent consciousness because of a host of inner contradictions that have increasingly presented themselves to would-be mythographers.[25] All attempts to find some embodiment of archetypal England in historical figure or geographic location founder on an embarrassment of riches, which all constructions of England must conspicuously fail to encompass. By comparison with some other countries, there was 'just too much' English history: 'too much had happened, too many different and contrasting things had happened, too much could be made of it, too many ways' (p. 672). John Davidson's poem 'St George's Day', with its inexorable drift towards the elevation of England from a radical beginning that challenges this position on behalf of British difference, ends by 'smoothing all into one' in

Holloway's phrase, and the procedure closely parallels the tendencies noted in Auden (p. 672). Such writers overreach themselves in the face of the 'too much' that Holloway notes; 'when it's easy to say too much and get in a fix', he suggests, 'it's a good idea to say very little' (p. 671). And it's much easier to say very little when, as in Eliot, there is the aspiration to look on this England and all its history from the perspective of the timeless moment.

NOTES

The place of publication of books is London unless otherwise stated.

INTRODUCTION

1 R. H. Wilenski, *The Modern Movement in Art* (Faber, 1927), preface, p. ix.
2 Bernard Bergonzi, *Reading the Thirties: Texts and Contexts* (Macmillan, 1978). Bergonzi admits that there is 'nothing about the later writings of the major modernists' in his study (p. 8).
3 Julian Symons tends to polarize the 'wonderfully refreshing' qualities of Auden's early work against 'the dryness of Eliot and his imitators', and more generally to insist on a sharp 'break' in the poetry of the 1930s with that of the 1920s. See *The Thirties: a Dream Revolved* (Cresset Press, 1960), pp. 15, 12. I attempt to counter those claims above, pp. 145-8. I also feel there are important ways in which Angus Calder's reading of 'Burnt Norton' in 'deliberate dissociation from [historical] period' can be challenged, as will become clear. *T. S. Eliot*, Harvester New Readings (Brighton: Harvester, 1987), pp. 140-1.
4 Valentine Cunningham, *British Writers of the 1930s* (Oxford: Oxford University Press, 1988). Eliot is prominent, however, in Cunningham's essay 'Neutral?: 1930s writers and taking sides', in *Class, Culture and Social Change: a New View of the 1930s*, ed. Frank Gloversmith (Brighton: Harvester, 1980), pp. 45-69.
5 Samuel Hynes, *The Auden Generation: Literature and Politics in England in the 1930s* (Bodley Head, 1976), p. 89.
6 In the 1930s Eliot conducted 'a one-man retreat into a private world of abstractions'. See D. E. S. Maxwell, *Poets of the Thirties* (Routledge, 1969), pp. 31-3.
7 See Michael Roberts's preface to *New Signatures* (Hogarth Press, 1932), p. 18.
8 Syllabus of Eliot's second Oxford University extension lecture on modern French literature, reprinted in A. D. Moody, *Thomas Stearns Eliot: Poet* (Cambridge: Cambridge University Press, 1979), p. 44.

9 'To criticize the critic', *TCTC*, p. 23.

10 See Ronald Schuchard, 'Eliot and Hulme in 1916: toward a revaluation of Eliot's critical and spiritual development', *PMLA* 88 (1973), 1083–94.

11 D. E. S. Maxwell, 'The new classicism', in *The Poetry of T. S. Eliot* (Routledge, 1952), pp. 36–47.

12 D. J. De Laura, 'The place of the classics in T. S. Eliot's Christian humanism', in *Hereditas: Seven Essays on the Modern Experience of the Classical*, ed. and introd. Frederic Will (Austin, Tex.: University of Texas Press, 1964), p. 186.

13 'Religion without humanism', in *Humanism and America: Essays on the Outlook of Modern Civilisation*, ed. Norman Foerster (New York: Farrar & Rinehart, 1930), pp. 105–12.

14 J. Middleton Murry, 'The "classical" revival', *Adelphi* 3 (1926), 585–95 and 648–53.

15 Edward Lobb, *T. S. Eliot and the Romantic Critical Tradition* (Routledge, 1981), p. 93.

16 Steve Ellis, *Dante and English Poetry: Shelley to T. S. Eliot* (Cambridge: Cambridge University Press, 1983), pp. 210–46.

17 C. K. Stead, *The New Poetic: Yeats to Eliot* (Hutchinson, 1964), p. 140.

18 'Ulysses, order, and myth', *Dial* (November 1923), rpt. in *Selected Prose of T. S. Eliot*, ed. and introd. Frank Kermode (Faber, 1975), pp. 176–7.

19 'Baudelaire', *SE*, p. 424.

20 Stead's animus against the *Quartets* is evident not only in *The New Poetic* but also in his chapter on Eliot in *Pound, Yeats, Eliot and the Modernist Movement* (Macmillan, 1986), pp. 194–235.

21 In 'What is a classic?' he attempts to 'remove' his approach to classicism 'from the area of the antithesis between "classic" and "romantic" ', *OPAP*, p. 53.

22 See chapter iv of his *English Culture and the Decline of the Industrial Spirit, 1850–1980* (Cambridge: Cambridge University Press, 1981). As well as other writers discussed later, see Simon Featherstone, 'The nation as pastoral in British literature of the Second World War', *Journal of European Studies* 16 (1986), 155–68.

23 The formulation '1930s' is often preferred in this book to the more cumbersome '1930s and early 1940s', even though the dates of publication of the *Quartets* spread over the two decades. Most of the texts I relate the *Quartets* to date from the 1930s. A practice of making 1939 a strict cut-off date no doubt accounts for the tendency for Eliot to be underplayed in critical accounts of the decade referred to above.

1 CLASSIC DESIGN

1 In T. E. Hulme, *Speculations: Essays on Humanism and the Philosophy of Art*, ed. Herbert Read, 2nd edn (Routledge, 1936), p. 96.

2 A comparison of the two passages is included in my *Dante and English*

Poetry: Shelley to T. S. Eliot (Cambridge: Cambridge University Press, 1983), pp. 241–3.

3 Orwell's *Poetry London* review of the first three *Quartets* is reprinted in Bernard Bergonzi (ed.), *T. S. Eliot: Four Quartets: a Casebook* (Macmillan, 1969), pp. 81–7.

4 'Mystic and politician as poet: Vaughan, Traherne, Marvell, Milton', *Listener*, 2 April 1930, p. 591.

5 'John Dryden – I. The poet who gave the English speech', *Listener*, 15 April 1931, p. 622.

6 See 'The classics in France – and in England', *Criterion* 2 (1923–4), 104–5.

7 Eliot's statement is from an unpublished lecture of 1933 quoted in F. O. Matthiessen, *The Achievement of T. S. Eliot*, 3rd edn (New York: Oxford University Press, 1958), p. 90.

8 Adolf Loos, 'The luxury vehicle', in *Spoken into the Void: Collected Essays 1897–1900*, trans. Jane O. Newman and John H. Smith, introd. Aldo Rossi (Cambridge, Mass.: MIT Press, 1982), p. 40.

9 Walter Gropius, *The New Architecture and the Bauhaus*, trans. P. Morton Shand, introd. Frank Pick (Faber, 1965 edn), pp. 23–4.

10 Le Corbusier, *Towards a New Architecture*, trans. and introd. Frederick Etchells, 2nd edn (Rodker, 1931), pp. 158–9. The original was published in 1923 and based on a series of articles appearing between 1919 and 1922.

11 That Eliot may have seen such buildings as harshly mechanistic is suggested by his publication of John Gould Fletcher's poem 'Elegy on an empty skyscraper' in *Criterion* 11 (1931–2), with its *Waste Land*-inspired antagonism directed at 'stone blocks bound in glittering steel', p. 439.

12 For the use of these terms see, for example, David Watkin, *A History of Western Architecture* (Barrie & Jenkins, 1986), pp. 507–61 *passim*, and Lars Olof Larsson, 'Classicism in the architecture of the XXth century', in *Albert Speer: Architecture 1932–1942*, ed. Leon Krier (Brussels: Archives d'Architecture Moderne, 1985), pp. 233–45 *passim*.

13 By 1930 in most European countries 'classicism in its simplified, to some extent "objectively" or "abstractly" determined mode of expression, was a well-established part of the spectrum of moderate Modernism', Larsson, p. 238.

14 *Unit One: the Modern Movement in English Architecture, Painting and Sculpture*, ed. Herbert Read (Cassell, 1934), p. 89.

15 *Criterion* 13 (1933–4), 632.

16 On Le Corbusier's 'Platonic idea that certain fundamental ratios underlie cosmic order', see Charles Jencks, *Le Corbusier and the Tragic View of Architecture*, revised edn (Harmondsworth: Penguin, 1987), pp. 44–5, 66.

17 Paul Valéry, *Eupalinos: or the Architect*, trans. William McCausland Stewart (Oxford: Oxford University Press, 1932), p. 40.

18 Barbara Everett, 'Eliot's *Four Quartets* and French symbolism', *English* 29 (1980), 9.

19 *Criterion* 17 (1937-8), 88.

20 See, for example, C. K. Stead's recent assertions about the demise of Eliot's poetic powers in his later work in *Pound, Yeats, Eliot and the Modernist Movement* (Macmillan, 1986), pp. 194-235.

21 T. E. Hulme, 'Humanism and the religious attitude', in *Speculations*, p. 47.

22 Michael Roberts, *T. E. Hulme*, introd. Anthony Quinton (1938; rpt. Manchester: Carcanet, 1982), p. 59.

23 Wilhelm Worringer, *Abstraction and Empathy: a Contribution to the Psychology of Style*, trans. Michael Bullock (Routledge, 1953), p. 102.

24 Wilhelm Worringer, *Form in Gothic*, ed. and introd. Herbert Read (G. P. Putnam's Sons, 1927), p. 37.

25 Adolf Loos, 'Glass and clay', in *Spoken into the Void*, p. 36. Reyner Banham has pointed out how in 1899 the French architectural historian Auguste Choisy can be found praising the Doric order's 'abstract purity of undecorated form'; as Banham wryly notes, 'triglyph and metope were not decoration to him'. See *Theory and Design in the First Machine Age* (Architectural Press, 1960), p. 33.

26 On this preference see ibid., pp. 86-96, and Benedetto Gravagnuolo, *Adolf Loos: Theory and Works*, trans. C. H. Evans, pref. Aldo Rossi (Milan: Idea Books, 1982), p. 37. The ascendancy of Rome over Greece in Eliot's classicism is touched on by Frank Kermode, *The Classic* (Faber, 1975), pp. 19-20.

27 Anthony Ludovici, *Nietzsche and Art* (Constable, 1911), pp. 207-11.

28 See *Theory and Design*, p. 76, where Banham quotes at length from what he calls Muthesius's 'key-note' speech to the Werkbund Congress of 1911.

29 George Orwell, *Nineteen Eighty-Four* (1949; rpt. Harmondsworth: Penguin, 1954), p. 7.

30 I quote from a typical example of Hellenistic fervour by T. G. Tucker, *Life in Ancient Athens* (Macmillan, 1907), p. 186.

31 Paul Jacobstal, 'Views and valuations of ancient art since Winckelmann', *Criterion* 4 (1926), 146-7.

32 See J. M. Richards, 'The condition of architecture and the principle of anonymity', in *Circle: International Survey of Constructive Art*, ed. J. L. Martin *et al.* (Faber, 1937), pp. 185-6.

33 David Mellor, 'British art in the 1930s: some economic, political and cultural structures', in Frank Gloversmith (ed.), *Class, Culture and Social Change* (Brighton: Harvester, 1980), pp. 186-7.

34 See Henry-Russell Hitchcock and Philip Johnson, *The International Style: Architecture Since 1922* (1932), rpt. as *The International Style* (New York: Norton, 1966).

35 Myfanwy Evans, 'Order, order!', *Axis* 6 (Summer 1936), 5.

36 See the review signed 'R. M.' in the *New Statesman*, 31 July 1937, pp. 189-90; also that in the *Studio* 114 (1937), 277.

37 Eliot's quotation is taken from Demant's *God, Man and Society* (Student Christian Movement Press, 1933), p. 146; see the *Criterion* 13 (1933-4), 277. Eliot supports Demant's observation at about the same time in *After Strange Gods: a Primer of Modern Heresy* (Faber,

1934), p. 20, where he insists that 'the concept of a nation is by no means fixed and invariable'. I return to the importance of Demant's work for Eliot in chapter 3, pp. 122ff.

38 Given Eliot's rather complex approach to patriotism, it is interesting to note that this statement, from the first draft of his essay 'The three voices of poetry', was later cancelled by him. See A. D. Moody, *Thomas Stearns Eliot, Poet* (Cambridge: Cambridge University Press, 1979), p. 203.

39 'Commentary', *Criterion* 17 (1937–8), 82.

40 'American literature and the American language', *TCTC*, p. 56.

41 See Helen Gardner, *The Composition of 'Four Quartets'* (Faber, 1978), pp. 26–7.

42 *De vulgari eloquentia* I.xix.1, in *Le opere di Dante*, ed. M. Barbi *et al.*, 2nd edn (Florence: Società Dantesca Italiana, 1960), p. 312.

43 The indebtedness of Eliot's classic English to Dante's theory of the *volgare illustre* is ably discussed by Kermode in *The Classic*, pp. 36–8, though he overlooks the fact that by the time of the *Commedia* itself Dante had incorporated a far less 'purified' vernacular into his work, a development Eliot takes no cognizance of; on this 'more varied and vigorous' language, compared with that of the *De vulgari*, see, for example, Cecil Grayson, 'Dante and the Renaissance', in *Italian Studies Presented to E. R. Vincent*, ed. C. P. Brand *et al.* (Cambridge: Heffer, 1962), pp. 70–1.

44 Graham Greene, *England Made Me* (1935; rpt. Harmondsworth: Penguin, 1973), pp. 34–5, 77, 82, 120.

45 Rpt. in *The Collected Essays, Journalism and Letters of George Orwell*, ed. Sonia Orwell and Ian Angus, Vol. I, *An Age Like This 1920–1940* (Secker, 1968), p. 134.

46 In Stephen Spender, *Collected Poems 1928–1985* (Faber, 1985), pp. 39–40.

2 ELIOT'S ENGLISH

1 I have discussed this already in *Dante and English Poetry, Shelley to T. S. Eliot* (Cambridge: Cambridge University Press, 1983), pp. 229–33.

2 The parallels between Eliot's play and *Hamlet* were already being pointed out in 1939 by Desmond Hawkins, 'Hamlet and T. S. Eliot', *New English Weekly*, 20 July 1939, pp. 221–2.

3 *Antony and Cleopatra* V.ii.340–2, in William Shakespeare, *The Complete Works*, ed. Stanley Wells *et al.* (Oxford: Clarendon, 1986), p. 1166.

4 *The Tempest* I.ii.400–6, in ibid., p. 1322.

5 See his remark to Ford Madox Ford quoted in *The Waste Land: a Facsimile and Transcript of the Original Drafts Including the Annotations of Ezra Pound*, ed. Valerie Eliot (Faber, 1971), p. 129.

6 'John Dryden – III. Dryden the critic, defender of sanity', *Listener*, 29 April 1931, pp. 724–5.

7 *The Waste Land: a Facsimile*, pp. 10–11.

8 See his discussion of Donne's line in 'The metaphysical poets', *SE*, p. 283.

9 'John Dryden – II. Dryden the dramatist', *Listener*, 24 April 1931, p. 681.

10 For Shelley's lines see *The Cenci* V.iv.48–50, in *Poetical Works*, ed. Thomas Hutchinson, corr. G. M. Matthews, 2nd edn. (Oxford: Oxford University Press, 1970), p. 331.

11 One might also compare the rather mundanely portrayed 'tosses up our losses' episode of 'The Dry Salvages' with the 'masterly but artificial' portrayal of a similar subject in Tourneur's *The Atheist's Tragedy*, which Eliot comments on in *SE*, pp. 187–8. See also his discussion of the 'pathology' of Elizabethan rhetoric in 'Imperfect critics', in *The Sacred Wood: Essays on Poetry and Criticism*, 7th edn (Methuen, 1950), pp. 30–1.

12 Loos's equation between 'ornament' and 'crime' is spelled out in his famous essay of 1908, 'Ornament und verbrechen', rpt. in Ludwig Münz and Gustav Künstler, *Adolf Loos: Pioneer of Modern Architecture*, trans. Harold Meek, introd. Nikolaus Pevsner (Thames & Hudson, 1966), pp. 226–31. See also Reyner Banham, 'Ornament and crime: the decisive contribution of Adolf Loos', *Architectural Review* 121 (1957), 88.

13 'Four Elizabethan dramatists', *Criterion* 2 (1923–4), 122–3.

14 'American literature and the American language', *TCTC*, p. 53.

15 See Read's review of Hopkins's published letters in the *Criterion* 14 (1934–5), 478, and Day Lewis, *A Hope for Poetry* (Oxford: Blackwell, 1934), p. 71.

16 F. R. Leavis, *New Bearings in English Poetry: a Study of the Contemporary Situation* (1932; rpt. Harmondsworth: Penguin, 1972), pp. 125–7. See Hopkins's letter to Robert Bridges of 26 November 1882, in which he explains that he is 'learning Anglosaxon and it is a vastly superior thing to what we have now'; *The Letters of Gerard Manley Hopkins to Robert Bridges*, ed. and introd. Claude Colleer Abbott (Oxford: Oxford University Press, 1935), p. 163. 'It was', says Tom Paulin, 'from various regional and working-class vernaculars that Hopkins drew his essential melodic inspiration', a fact that would also place him beyond the pale of Eliot's classic English. See 'On the rampage', *Times Literary Supplement*, 14 August 1987, p. 863.

17 Alexander Pope, 'An essay on criticism', in *Poetical Works*, ed. Herbert Davis (Oxford: Oxford University Press, 1966), l.152, p. 68.

18 Eliot refers to the unpublished lectures in the preface to *OPAP*, pp. 11–12.

19 Eliot himself insisted that there was no essential incompatibility between the two Milton articles. See, for example, his letter to the *Sunday Times*, 16 November 1947, p. 6, responding to Desmond MacCarthy's charge of inconsistency in an article from the previous week: 'I had two purposes in mind [in the second Milton lecture]. The first was to correct certain affirmations of my own

and to give a wider context for the views which I continued to hold. I hoped that I had defined the limits of my change of mind.'

20 John Middleton Murry, 'More about romanticism', *Adelphi* 1 (1923), 557–69.

21 John Middleton Murry, *Shakespeare* (Cape, 1936), pp. 14–19. Eliot reviewed the book in the *Criterion* 15 (1935-6), 708–10.

22 Herbert Read (ed. and introd.), *Surrealism* (Faber, 1936), pp. 31, 46. Read's position here had already been projected in Huxley's *Brave New World* (1932), where the Savage is armed so to speak with Shakespeare's works in his battle against the society of Our Ford.

23 G. Wilson Knight, *This Sceptred Isle: Shakespeare's Message for England at War* (Oxford: Blackwell, 1940), p. 35. On Wilson Knight's wartime Shakespeare, see Graham Holderness, 'Agincourt 1944: readings in the Shakespeare myth', in *Popular Fictions: Essays in Literature and History*, ed. Peter Humm *et al.* (Methuen, 1986), pp. 173–95.

24 Sherard Vines, *The Course of English Classicism: From the Tudor to the Victorian Age* (1930; rpt. New York: Phaeton Press, 1968), p. 153.

25 See Grant Webster, *The Republic of Letters: a History of Postwar American Literary Opinion* (Baltimore, Md: Johns Hopkins University Press, 1979), p. 87.

26 Irving Babbitt, *Rousseau and Romanticism* (Boston, Mass.: Houghton Mifflin, 1919), pp. 208–9.

27 In a letter to the *New English Weekly* replying to Maurice B. Reckitt's review of *ICS*, Eliot explains how his idea of the two 'ends' for humanity is taken from Thomas Aquinas, but also suggests how the natural end, as something 'merely natural' from the Christian viewpoint, is utterly subordinated and cannot itself 'create a Christian society'. See *ICS*, pp. 112–13.

28 Kenelm Foster, 'The two Dantes', in *The Two Dantes and Other Studies* (Darton, Longman & Todd, 1977), pp. 156–253.

29 Norman Foerster, *American Criticism: a Study in Literary Theory from Poe to the Present* (Boston, Mass.: Houghton Mifflin, 1928), p. 244.

30 Derek Traversi, *T. S. Eliot: the Longer Poems* (Bodley Head, 1976), p. 90, and G. Rostrevor Hamilton, *The Tell-Tale Article: a Critical Approach to Modern Poetry* (Heinemann, 1949), p. 37.

31 See Eliot's interview with John Lehmann for the *New York Times Book Review* (29 November 1953) rpt. in Bernard Bergonzi (ed.), *T. S. Eliot: Four Quartets: a Casebook* (Macmillan, 1969), p. 23.

32 Compare the Christian philosopher E. I. Watkin's *A Philosophy of Form* (Sheed & Ward, 1935), pp. 118–19, where he talks of God as a 'motionless energy', an absolute reconciliation of fullness of activity with ordering form. The creature, however, is characterized by a 'restless' motion, until, in moving closer to God, its energy is 'informed by a more adequate and more comprehensive form' whereupon 'its motion becomes so harmonious and so concentrated that it seems to be at rest, as when a wheel revolves at a sufficient speed its motion becomes invisible'.

33 Ronald Bush discusses at some length, though in somewhat different terms from mine, the 'radical differences' between 'Burnt

Norton' and the later quartets in *T. S. Eliot: a Study in Character and Style* (Oxford: Oxford University Press, 1984), pp. 211–20.

34 'The music of poetry' (1942), in *OPAP*, p. 37.

35 Mikhail Bakhtin, *Rabelais and his World*, trans. Helen Iswolsky (Bloomington, Ind.: Indiana University Press, 1984), p. 109.

36 Mikhail Bakhtin, *Problems of Dostoevsky's Poetics*, ed. and trans. Caryl Emerson, introd. Wayne C. Booth (Manchester: Manchester University Press, 1984), p. 200.

37 Introd. to Paul Valéry, *Le Serpent*, trans. Mark Wardle (Criterion, 1924), p. 9.

38 'Hulme and classicism', Commentary, *Criterion* 2 (1923–4), 232.

39 T. G. Tucker, *Life in Ancient Athens* (Macmillan, 1907), p. 196, quoting von Schelling, *The Philosophy of Art: an Oration on the Relation Between the Plastic Arts and Nature*, trans. A. Johnson (1845), p. 11.

40 Loos, 'Ornament and crime', in Münz and Künstler, p. 229; on the *Chicago Tribune* competition see ibid., p. 191.

41 Jules Lubbock, 'Politics of the portico', *New Statesman*, 1 May 1987, p. 21.

42 P. C. Mondrian, 'Plastic art and pure plastic art (figurative art and non-figurative art)', in *Circle: International Survey of Constructive Art*, ed. J. L. Martin *et al.* (Faber, 1937), p. 48.

43 Naum Gabo, 'Sculpture: carving and construction in space', in ibid., p. 108.

44 The dominance of 'formal pattern' in the play is referred to by E. Martin Browne, *The Making of T. S. Eliot's Plays* (Cambridge: Cambridge University Press, 1969), p. 42.

45 Quoted in ibid., p. 167.

46 See my *Dante and English Poetry*, pp. 242–3.

47 Bakhtin, *Problems of Dostoevsky's Poetics*, pp. 26–7, 30. Bakhtin tends to discount the ethical categorization of voices in the *Divine Comedy* and regards them all as possessing equal validity, attending to their dramatic impact on the ear of Dante *personaggio*, so to speak, rather than to their hierarchical organization by Dante *poeta*.

48 'Religion without humanism', in *Humanism and America: Essays on the Outlook of Modern Civilisation*, ed. Norman Foerster (New York: Farrar & Rinehart, 1930), p. 110.

49 Bakhtin, *Rabelais and his World*, p. 25.

50 'Quotations', in *Circle*, p. 75.

51 *Criterion* 17 (1937–8), 88, 93.

52 Herbert Read, *Art Now: an Introduction to the Theory of Modern Painting and Sculpture* (Faber, 1933), pp. 115–16.

53 Silbury Hill, Avebury appears opposite a Miró painting in *Axis* 8 (1937), 8–9, and Stonehenge in *Circle*, p. 117.

54 *William Wordsworth*, 'Oxford Authors' series, ed. Stephen Gill (Oxford: Oxford University Press, 1986), pp. 576–7.

55 Mikhail Bakhtin, 'From the prehistory of novelistic discourse', *The Dialogic Imagination: Four Essays*, ed. Michael Holquist, trans. Caryl Emerson and Michael Holquist (Austin, Tex.: University of Texas Press, 1981), p. 68.

56 Ibid., p. 62.
57 Bakhtin, 'Discourse in the novel', in ibid., p. 272.
58 'Catholicism and international order', *Christendom* 3 (1933), 178–9.
59 'The music of poetry', p. 31, and 'The social function of poetry', p. 23, both *OPAP*.
60 Eliot had actually attacked the centralizing programme of fascist governments in 'The literature of fascism', *Criterion* 8 (1928–9), 289.
61 Alan Robinson, *Poetry, Painting and Ideas, 1885–1914* (Macmillan, 1985), p. 96.

3 ELIOT'S ENGLAND

1 In *Eliot in His Time: Essays on the Occasion of the Fiftieth Anniversary of 'The Waste Land'*, ed. A. Walton Litz (Princeton, NJ: Princeton University Press, 1973), pp. 181–96.
2 Martin J. Wiener, *English Culture and the Decline of the Industrial Spirit* (Cambridge: Cambridge University Press, 1981). See chapter iv, esp. pp. 66ff.
3 'Public problems and private experience in British art and literature', in the exhibition catalogue to *Landscape in Britain: 1850–1950* (Arts Council, 1983), p. 29.
4 'The influence of landscape upon the poet', *Daedalus* 89 (1960), 422.
5 Commentaries in *Criterion* 17 (1937–8), 483 and 18 (1938–9), 60. See also *After Strange Gods: a Primer of Modern Heresy* (Faber, 1934), p. 17.
6 'The English tradition', *Christendom* 10 (1940), 226–7.
7 *Criterion* 14 (1934–5), 88.
8 Cyril Connolly, 'The new Medici', *Architectural Review* 76 (1934), 4.
9 Thomas Sharp, *Town and Countryside: Some Aspects of Urban and Rural Development* (Oxford: Oxford University Press, 1932), pp. 27–30.
10 Edward Thomas, *The Heart of England*, ed. Eric Fitch Daglish (1906; rpt. Dent, 1932), p. 184.
11 Paul Nash, 'The pictorial subject', *Listener*, 17 February 1932, p. 227.
12 W. A. Eden, 'The English tradition in the countryside: I. Making of the tradition', *Architectural Review* 77 (1935), 90–1.
13 'The English tradition in the countryside: II. The world of make-believe', ibid., 144–9.
14 Virginia Woolf, *Between the Acts* (1941; rpt. Grafton, 1978), p. 42.
15 Rex Warner, *The Aerodrome: a Love Story*, introd. Anthony Burgess (1941; rpt. Oxford: Oxford University Press, 1982), pp. 302, 298, 300.
16 C. Henry Warren, *England is a Village* (Eyre & Spottiswoode, 1940).
17 Patricia Craig and Mary Cadogan, *The Lady Investigates: Women Detectives and Spies in Fiction* (Gollancz, 1981), p. 164.
18 Agatha Christie, *The Murder at the Vicarage* (1930; rpt. Fontana, 1961), p. 108.
19 See Colin Watson, *Snobbery with Violence: English Crime Stories and their Audience*, revised edn (Eyre Methuen, 1979), pp. 169–70, and *Crime Writers* (London: 1978), p. 61, the latter quoted in Ken Worpole,

NOTES

Dockers and Detectives: Popular Readings: Popular Writing (Verso, 1983), p. 34.

20 Worpole, p. 33.
21 Beverley Nichols, *A Village in a Valley* (Cape, 1934), p. 11.
22 Stephen Tallents, *The Projection of England* (Faber, 1932), p. [5].
23 E. M. Forster, *Howards End*, ed. Oliver Stallybrass (1910; rpt. Harmondsworth, Penguin, 1975), p. 170.
24 Evelyn Waugh, *Vile Bodies* (1930; rpt. Harmondsworth: Penguin, 1938), pp. 199–200.
25 In Glen Cavaliero, *The Rural Tradition in the English Novel, 1900–1939* (Macmillan, 1977).
26 See his review of recently published poetry in the *Criterion* 13 (1933–4), 509.
27 J. C. Squire, Introduction to Edmund Blunden, *The Face of England. . .* (Longman, 1932), p. vii.
28 Edmund Blunden, *English Villages*, 2nd edn (Collins, 1942), p. 21.
29 John Moore, *Brensham Village* (1946) in *The Brensham Trilogy*, introd. Asa Briggs (rpt. Oxford: Oxford University Press, 1985), pp. 302, 226.
30 That the English village could be seen as both standardized microcosm (as discussed in the previous section) and as locus of abundant individuality/freedom, might help to explain its featuring extensively in the work of writers from both right and left, a duality fruitfully puzzled over by Cunningham, *British Writers of the Thirties* (Oxford: Oxford University Press, 1988), pp. 230–8.
31 One recalls Hulme's assertion in 'Romanticism and classicism' that 'no romantic would ever have written' the lines from Shakespeare's *Cymbeline* (IV.ii.263–4), 'Golden lads and girls all must, / Like chimney sweepers come to dust' (*Speculations: Essays on Humanism and the Philosophy of Art*, ed. Herbert Read, 2nd edn (Routledge, 1936) p. 121). Of course, Eliot's protagonists have never been 'golden' to start with.
32 George Bornstein, *Transformations of Romanticism in Yeats, Eliot and Stevens* (Chicago: University of Chicago Press, 1976), p. 162.
33 F. R. Leavis, *The Living Principle: 'English' as a Discipline of Thought* (Chatto, 1975), pp. 196–7.
34 C. K. Stead, *The New Poetic: Yeats to Eliot* (Hutchinson, 1964), p. 180.
35 A recent restatement of the Stead–Bornstein line comes from Angus Calder, who sees 'East Coker' i as a 'near-Georgian' evocation of England directly comparable with the ruralism of works like Blunden's *Cricket Country*, and not, as I am arguing, to be radically dissociated from such works (on theological grounds too: see my following section). It is hardly surprising that Calder is unable to make much sense of 'East Coker' thereafter, holding that the 'affirmation' of part i is oddly denied by what follows, in particular by part iv. He thus concludes that 'East Coker as a whole is *not* a whole', and the door is thereby opened to the usual complaints about Eliot's ineptitudes and inconsistencies and so forth. See

Angus Calder, *T. S. Eliot*, Harvester New Readings (Brighton: Harvester, 1987), pp. 142–50.

36 Leavis observes that it was such 'yokels' who 'created the English language . . . and made possible in due course Shakespeare, Dickens and the poet of *Four Quartets*. A language is a cultural life, a living creative continuity' (pp. 196–7); he thus points up nicely Eliot's demotion of the spoken word in the *Quartets*, as discussed above, pp. 63–4.

37 P. H. Butter, '*Four Quartets*: some yes-buts to Dr Leavis', *Critical Quarterly* 18, 1 (1976), pp. 34–5.

38 J. M. Reibetanz, '*Four Quartets* as poetry of place', *Dalhousie Review* 56 (1976), 527. The article is reprinted with minor alterations as the epilogue to her *A Reading of Eliot's 'Four Quartets'* (Ann Arbor, Mich.: UMI Research Press, 1983), pp. 189–200.

39 Wordsworth, 'Lines written a few miles above Tintern Abbey. . .', in *William Wordsworth*, 'Oxford Authors' series, ed. Stephen Gill (Oxford: Oxford University Press, 1986), p. 135. That Eliot is *not* doing precisely what Reibetanz and others claim he is seems confirmed by his statement that 'Modern English verse . . . has a tendency always to decline into an ecstatic contemplation of peaceful landscape . . . which I cannot share'. In the same lecture (which has only recently been published) Eliot admitted that 'possibly I do not fully appreciate any English poetry subsequent to Samuel Johnson'. 'Tradition and the practice of poetry', *Southern Review* 21 (1985), 882, rpt. in *T. S. Eliot: Essays from the Southern Review*, ed. James Olney (Oxford: Clarendon, 1988), pp. 17–18.

40 N. D. Hargrove, *Landscape as Symbol in the Poetry of T. S. Eliot* (Jackson, Miss.: University of Mississippi Press, 1978), p. 138.

41 See Helen Gardner, *The Art of T. S. Eliot* (1949; rpt. Faber, 1968), p. 159.

42 Ford Madox Ford, *The Heart of the Country* (1906), quoted in Wiener, p. 51.

43 G. Reeves, *T. S. Eliot: a Virgilian Poet* (Macmillan, 1989), chapter iv, 'Empire and agrarian ideal', pp. 96–116.

44 John Holloway, 'The myth of England', *Listener*, 15 May 1969, p. 672. The quotation given here is taken from William Watson's description of the poetry of Alfred Austin, referred to by Holloway. Eliot discusses the connection between imperialism and rusticality himself in his essay on Kipling, *OPAP*, p. 245.

45 See the final lines of C. Day Lewis's translation of *The Georgics of Virgil* (Cape, 1940), p. 95. Eliot recommended Lewis's translation in 'Virgil and the Christian world', *OPAP*, p. 125.

46 'Commentary, Britain and M. Siegfried', *Criterion* 7 (1928), 194.

47 Eliot's insistence on the work-ethic of the *Georgics* is traced by Reeves (pp. 111–16) back in part to his reading of Theodor Haecker's *Virgil, Father of the West* (Sheed & Ward, 1934).

48 Two years after *The Heart of England* appeared Thomas published a set of essays on *The South Country*, ably discussed in connection with the construction of (southern and Tudor) England by Alun

NOTES

Howkins, 'The discovery of rural England', in Robert Colls and
Philip Dodd (eds), *Englishness: Politics and Culture 1880–1920* (Croom
Helm, 1986), pp. 62–88.

49 'The face of Britain', *Architectural Review* 77 (1935), 84.

50 On the Batsford book-jackets, see Brian Cook Batsford, *The Britain
of Brian Cook*, foreword Sir Hugh Casson, pref. Ian Logan (Batsford,
1987).

51 See, for instance, the catalogue to the Arts Council exhibition
Landscape in Britain: 1850–1950 (1983), and Ian Jeffrey, *The British
Landscape: 1920–1950* (Thames & Hudson, 1984).

52 See, for example, A. L. Maycock, *Nicholas Ferrar of Little Gidding*
(SPCK, 1938), p. 189; 'Every feature of life at Little Gidding bore
the stamp of his [Ferrar's] personality. . . . To describe Little
Gidding is to describe the mind and ideals of Nicholas Ferrar.'
Reviewing this book in the *Criterion*, Bernard Blackstone offered
thanks that 'the trappings of romance' that had invested the
community of Little Gidding since Shorthouse's *John Inglesant* had
now been discarded (*Criterion* 18 (1938–9), 156). Eliot's poem
certainly takes us much further down the same road.

53 John Keats, 'Ode on a Grecian urn', *Poetical Works*, ed. H. W. Garrod
(Oxford: Oxford University Press, 1956), p. 210.

54 R. Williams, *The Country and the City* (Chatto, 1973), p. 211.

55 See Freda Constable, *The England of Eric Ravilious* (Scolar Press,
1982), p. 29.

56 Ibid., p. 30.

57 H. J. Massingham, *English Downland*, 2nd edn (Batsford, 1942–3), p.
85.

58 H. Belloc, *The Old Road*, new edn (Constable, 1910), p. 179.

59 W. H. Hudson, *A Shepherd's Life: Impressions of the South Wiltshire Downs*,
17th edn (Methuen, 1944), pp. 14, 27.

60 A full discussion of Massingham can be found in W. J. Keith, *The
Rural Tradition* (Brighton: Harvester, 1975), pp. 233–52.

61 F. J. Harvey Darton, *English Fabric: a Study of Village Life* (Newnes
[1935]), preface, p. 5.

62 Compare this position with that discussed by Christopher
Chippendale of certain modern ideas of a 'Mycenaean' Stonehenge,
or more generally Wessex, 'sending out law and order, and justice,
and the Pax Britannica, diffusing culture in all directions'. *Stonehenge
Complete* (Thames & Hudson, 1983), pp. 198–211.

63 G. K. Chesterton, *The Ballad of the White Horse*, 9th edn (Methuen,
1927), prefatory note, p. viii.

64 That misplaced critical ingenuity which is seen in the line from
Eliot's 'The Journey of the Magi' – 'And an old white horse galloped
away in the meadow' – a direct reference to Chesterton's poem,
would, even had it been right, been right for the wrong reasons;
the fading of the white horse in the final section of the *Ballad* does
not represent 'the death of paganism under the onslaught of
Christianity' but the threat of precisely the reverse; and had Eliot
wished to put Chesterton's horse to rout in his poem he would

178

have done so for the somewhat more complex reasons given above. See Robert B. Kaplan and Richard J. Wall, 'Eliot's "Journey of the Magi" ', *Explicator* 19, 2 (November 1960), item 8.

65 'A commentary', *New English Weekly*, 5 October 1939, pp. 331–2. Eliot acknowledges Demant's importance to him in the prefaces to both *ICS* and *NDC*. See also above, p. 26.

66 Ibid., p. 331.

67 T. E. Hulme, 'Humanism and the religious attitude', in *Speculations: Essays on Humanism and the Philosophy of Art*, ed. Herbert Read, 2nd edn (Routledge, 1936), p. 8.

68 Eliot's friend George Every had found part iv of 'East Coker' Jansenist; Eliot admitted that it was 'very un-English'. See Helen Gardner, *The Composition of 'Four Quartets'* (Faber, 1978), p. 109.

69 See Philip S. Richards, 'Plato, Aristotle and the Christian Church', *Criterion* 17 (1937–8), 673.

70 C. Day Lewis, 'The magnetic mountain' (1933) in *Collected Poems* (Cape, 1954), pp. 120–1; John Lehmann, 'Some revolutionary trends in English poetry: 1930–1935', *International Literature* 4 (April 1936), p. 75.

71 'God's grandeur', *Gerard Manley Hopkins*, ed. Catherine Phillips, 'Oxford Authors' series (Oxford: Oxford University Press, 1986), p. 128.

72 J. Maritain, *True Humanism*, trans. M. R. Adamson (Geoffrey Bles, 1938), pp. 65–6.

73 Eliot's undervaluing of the Shakespearian hero and his lack of sympathy with Renaissance humanism is discussed and disapproved of by C. B. Watson, 'T. S. Eliot and the interpretation of Shakespearean tragedy in our time', *Etudes Anglaises* 17 (1964), 502–21.

74 Ian Glenn, 'Karl Barth and T. S. Eliot', *Standpunte* 35 (1982), 35–42.

75 *The Epistle to the Romans*, trans. Edwyn C. Hoskyns (Oxford: Oxford University Press, 1933), pp. 110, 149–52, 497–9.

76 Karl Barth, 'II', in *Revelation*, ed. John Baillie and Hugh Martin (Faber, 1937), p. 51.

77 Robert H. Canary, *T. S. Eliot: The Poet and His Critics* (Chicago: American Library Association, 1982), pp. 227–8.

78 Ibid., p. 228. See Nathan A. Scott, Jr, *The Poetry of Civic Virtue: Eliot, Malraux, Auden* (Philadelphia, Pa: Fortress Press, 1976), p. 38.

79 'Catholicism and international order', *Christendom* 3 (1933), 179.

80 R. Kojecký, *T. S. Eliot's Social Criticism* (Faber, 1971), p. 69. Eliot announces his sympathy for decentralization in England in 'The literature of fascism', *Criterion* 8 (1928–9), 289.

81 See David Mellor, 'The body and the land: neo-Romantic art and culture', in the exhibition catalogue for *A Paradise Lost: the neo-Romantic Imagination in Britain 1935–1955*, ed. Mellor, Barbican Gallery, 1987, pp. 24, 67.

82 C. M. Grieve ('Hugh McDiarmid'), *Criterion* 10 (1930–1), 599.

83 Interestingly, McDiarmid averts in his article to 'that most romantic of all movements, the search for a new classicism to-day', which

179

is for him 'not a quest for any mere neo-classical formalism' but an attempt to get back beyond the international academicism of the Renaissance to the nationalist culture of the Greeks, and the inspiration it provides for the revival of national cultures, like the Scots, in the present (p. 612).

84 See, for example, 'Modern English furnishing', *Architectural Review* 67 (1930), 44; rpt. in *Room and Book* (Soncino Press, 1932), p. 6.

85 A. Causey, *Paul Nash* (Oxford: Clarendon, 1980), p. 271.

4 ELIOT AND AUDEN

1 Geoffrey Grigson, preface to the anthology drawn from *New Verse* (Faber, 1939), pp. 19–20.

2 See the original opening to 'The fire sermon' in *The Waste Land: a Facsimile and Transcript of the Original Drafts Including the Annotations of Ezra Pound* ed. Valerie Eliot (Faber, 1971), pp. 22–3, and J. S. Cunningham, 'Pope, Eliot and "The mind of Europe" ', in *'The Waste Land' in Different Voices*, ed. A. D. Moody (Edward Arnold, 1974), pp. 67–85.

3 Barbara Everett, 'The new style of *Sweeney Agonistes*', in *Poets in Their Time: Essays on English Poetry from Donne to Larkin* (Faber, 1986), pp. 195, 189. The extra passage is printed in Carol H. Smith, *T. S. Eliot's Dramatic Theory and Practice: from 'Sweeney Agonistes' to 'The Elder Statesman'* (1963; rpt. New York, Gordian Press, 1977), pp. 62–3.

4 Humphrey Jennings, 'Eliot and Auden and Shakespeare', *New Verse* 18 (December 1935), p. 6. That what dramatic cross-fertilization there is between the two writers runs from Auden to Eliot and not the other way round is a fact that tends to scupper Morton Seif's essay, 'The impact of T. S. Eliot on Auden and Spender', *South Atlantic Quarterly* 53 (1954), 61–9.

5 David Trotter, *The Making of the Reader: Language and Subjectivity in Modern American, English and Irish Poetry* (Macmillan, 1984), pp. 113–24. Helen Gardner's suggestion that passages from *The Waste Land* like 'A rat crept softly through the vegetation / Dragging its slimy belly on the bank' / are the origin of this 'tiresome trick' with the article in the 1930s is surely untenable. See 'The landscapes of Eliot's poetry', *Critical Quarterly* 10 (1968), 322.

6 The quotations are from Eliot, 'Burnt Norton' (examples one and two) and *The Family Reunion, CPP*, p. 329; Auden, 'The orators' and 'XXII', *EA*, pp. 70, 153; Auden and Isherwood, *The Ascent of F6* (1936; rpt. with *On the Frontier*, Faber, 1958), p. 28; and Louis MacNeice, 'Eclogue from Iceland' and 'The Hebrides', in *Collected Poems*, ed. E. R. Dodds (Faber, 1966), pp. 42, 64.

7 Several more lines of this type were present in the first draft of this section of 'Little Gidding', but were later cut, presumably because of John Hayward's objection to the frequency of the definite article. See Helen Gardner, *The Composition of Four Quartets* (Faber, 1978), p. 228.

8 *The Dog Beneath the Skin: or Where is Francis?* (1935; rpt. Faber, 1968), p. 155. The stanza on the 'Dare-devil mystic' in 'Brothers, who when the sirens roar' might well have been provoked by 'Ash-Wednesday' too. See *EA*, p. 122.

9 See Edward Mendelson, *Early Auden* (Faber, 1981), p. 340.

10 Evelyn Waugh, *Decline and Fall* (1928; rpt. Harmondsworth: Penguin, 1937), pp. 115–20. Herr Silenus is probably based on Peter Behrens, whose house 'New Ways', built in Northampton in 1926, was according to F. R. S. Yorke 'probably the first manifestation in England of the new manner': *The Modern House in England*, 3rd edn (Architectural Press, 1948), p. 10.

11 Roger Hinks, 'Art Chronicle', *Criterion* 12 (1932–3), 481.

12 See F. R. Leavis and Denys Thompson, *Culture and Environment: the Training of Critical Awareness* (Chatto, 1933), pp. 1, 32, and Graham Greene's caustic comments on the gimcrack nature of newly built 'Shakespeare Avenue' in *A Gun for Sale* (1936; rpt. Harmondsworth: Penguin, 1974), p. 44.

13 'Commentary' to 'In time of war', *EA*, p. 268.

14 Compare Eliot's praise of Dryden as the man who 'put the English language straight again' after Milton, quoted above, p. 11.

15 Paul C. Ray, *The Surrealist Movement in England* (Ithaca, NY: Cornell University Press, 1971), p. 273.

16 Anthony Collett, *The Changing Face of England* (1926; rpt. Cape, 1932), p. 7.

17 Although Auden was unhappy with *Look, Stranger!* as a title for the collection, the title he preferred for the American edition, *On This Island*, plainly retains the same title-poem. See Mendelson, *Early Auden*, p. 340.

18 *La Divina Commedia*, ed. Giorgio Petrocchi, Vol. II, *Purgatorio* II.1–5 (Verona: Mondadori, 1967), p. 19.

19 There is nothing in Eliot remotely resembling Auden's *Inferno*-based survey of an economically depressed England in the unfinished poem 'In the year of my youth', published by Lucy S. McDiarmid, *RES* 29 (1978), 267–312. On the Auden–Dante relationship see also Monroe K. Spears, 'The divine comedy of W. H. Auden', in *Dante Among the Moderns*, ed. Stuart Y. McDougal (Chapel Hill, NC: University of North Carolina Press, 1985), pp. 82–101.

20 Christopher Isherwood, 'Some notes on Auden's early poetry', Auden Double Number of *New Verse* 26–7 (November 1937), 8. Further examples of the oppositional use of 'The North' in the 1930s are given by Cunningham, *British Writers of the Thirties* (Oxford: Oxford University Press, 1988), pp. 166–7, and Orwell discusses the 'cult of Northernness' in *The Road to Wigan Pier* (1937; rpt. Harmondsworth: Penguin, 1962), pp. 98–102.

21 'In praise of limestone', *Selected Poems*, ed. Edward Mendelson (Faber, 1979), pp. 184–7.

22 Thus 'History is now and England' is the very last line in the very last piece chosen by Kenneth Baker for his anthology *The Faber Book of English History in Verse* (Faber, 1988), p. 432, as if Eliot upholds the

entire patriotic tradition. One wishes that critics who voice dis-
satisfaction at the privileging of a 'Little-England' outlook in the
Quartets (see Angus Calder, *T. S. Eliot*, Harvester New Readings
(Brighton: Harvester, 1987), p. 160) had rather traced their dis-
satisfaction to Eliot's readers.

23 Eliot himself questioned the assumption that 'the unity of wartime
should be preserved in time of peace' in *NDC*, p. 51.

24 'Christian and natural virtues', *Christian News-Letter*, 3 September
1941, rpt. in *The Idea of a Christian Society and Other Writings*, pp. 125–6.

25 *Listener*, 15 May 1969, p. 670.

INDEX

Lehmann, John 128
Listener 112
Lobb, Edward 4–5, 104
Loos, Adolf 13, 15, 21, 37, 57
Lowell, J. R. 109
Lubbock, Jules 58
Ludovici, Anthony 21, 82–3, 151, 154

McDiarmid, Hugh 138
MacNeice, Louis, 141, 146
Maiden Castle 113, 119, 139
Maritain, Jacques 130–1
Mary Queen of Scots 71
Massingham, H. J. 116–20, 138, 140
Maurras, Charles 103, 136
Maxwell, D. E. S. 2, 3
Mellor, David 137
Mendelson, Edward 2, 145, 158
Milton, John 10, 11, 12, 40, 62–3
Miró, Joan 113
Mondrian, Piet 58
Moody, A. D. 102, 129
Moore, Henry 137
Moore, John 95–6
Murry, John Middleton, 4, 41–3
Muthesius, Hermann 21

Nash, Paul 24, 83–4, 111, 112, 138–40
New English Weekly 122
New Signatures 2, 141
Nichols, Beverley 88
Nicholson, Ben 16, 71–2
Nietzsche, F. W. 75–6

Orwell, George 9, 22, 29, 34

Parmenides 18
Parthenon 13, 16, 19, 21, 23
Pascal, Blaise 46, 126–7
Pevsner, Nikolaus 14, 72
Pick, Frank 72
picturesque landscape 83–4, 93–4, 111, 116, 154
Piper, John 137
Pope, Alexander 10, 11, 38, 42, 44, 141

Pound, Ezra 5
Priestley, J. B. 92, 93

Rabelais, François 54, 66, 96, 113
Ravilious, Eric 84, 111, 112, 113, 114–15, 120, 138
Ray, Paul C. 156
Read, Herbert 20, 38, 41–2, 58, 72, 95, 138
Reeves, Gareth 108
Reibetanz, J. M. 104–6, 134
Roberts, Michael 2, 19, 93, 141
Robinson, Alan 75–6, 83, 154
Rotha, Paul 111
Rousseau, Jean-Jacques 46, 48
Ruskin, John 5, 6, 82, 83, 85, 111
Rymer, Thomas 42

Schelling, F. W. J. von 57
Scott, Nathan A., Jr 134–5
Shakespeare, William 24, 29, 31–43, 44, 60, 90, 94–6, 114, 120, 131, 142, 147, 150, 158
Sharp, Thomas 82, 111
Shell posters 81, 111, 113, 119
Shelley, P. B. 35
Speer, Albert 15
Spender, Stephen 2, 29, 145
Squire, J. C. 93
Stead, C. K. 5–6, 101–2
Stonehenge 72–3, 113, 114, 115, 137
stripped classicism 14–15, 22, 24, 84, 122, 139, 164
surrealism 41–2, 156
Sutherland, Graham 111, 137
Symons, Julian 167 n.3

Tallents, Stephen 89, 158, 161
Tennyson, Alfred, Lord 14, 36, 83, 106
Thomas Dylan 138
Thomas, Edward 83, 92, 95, 109–10
Traversi, Derek 49
Trevelyan, G. M. 26
Trotter, David 145–6, 156